In the Grip
of Desire

In the Grip of Desire

A Therapist at Work with Sexual Secrets

GALE HOLTZ GOLDEN

Routledge
Taylor & Francis Group
New York   London

Routledge
Taylor & Francis Group
270 Madison Avenue
New York, NY 10016

Routledge
Taylor & Francis Group
2 Park Square
Milton Park, Abingdon
Oxon OX14 4RN

© 2009 by Taylor & Francis Group, LLC
Routledge is an imprint of Taylor & Francis Group, an Informa business

Printed in the United States of America on acid-free paper
10 9 8 7 6 5 4 3 2 1

International Standard Book Number-13: 978-0-415-99157-5 (Hardcover)

Library of Congress Cataloging-in-Publication Data

Golden, Gale Holtz.
    In the grip of desire : a therapist at work with sexual secrets / by Gale Holtz Golden.
        p. cm.
    Includes bibliographical references and index.
    ISBN 978-0-415-99157-5 (hardback : alk. paper)
    1. Sex. 2. Psychosexual disorders--Case studies. I. Title.

HQ23.G65 2009
616.85'8306--dc22
2008043463

Visit the Taylor & Francis Web site at
http://www.taylorandfrancis.com

and the Routledge Web site at
http://www.routledge.com

For Gabe

"This is my beloved; this is my friend"

Song of Songs

In gratitude for all the people who for the past 45 years let me in their lives and from whom I have learned so much.

Contents

Acknowledgments

While there were times when I felt I was a solitary writer slugging away in a bare room, in truth, the making of this book involved many people. I am warmed and humbled when I take stock of those who have sustained me during this project. All the clients who put their trust in me over the years have played a role in creating this book. They also patiently put up with my taking time off on several occasions to accomplish this task. Thank you all.

In more concrete, immediate, and practical ways, there literally would be no book if Gabe had not provided everything I needed to maintain life beyond writing. He was the number-one chief, cook, and bottle washer around here for a few years, as well as "in-residence" computer techie. With Gabe and Karen Martell backing up my domestic life, I was able to maintain my focus on writing. Gabe was the first and last reader of the several versions of each chapter. He put up with my mental absence, my moods and madness. And then there are our children and grandchildren (collectively the "Harto'golds"), who often did without the attention they deserved. And what about my friends who have tolerated me through yet another lifetime event? How could we survive life without family and friends?

Suki and Al Rubin were notably involved. Suki not only read some of the work but was always there encouraging a balanced life, sending funny cards and insisting I stop, take a walk, eat ice cream. Alan always stopped by the library to offer cheer, give a pat on the back, compare socks, and chat a bit.

As I sat writing, cocooned in my private world, life marched on. Al Cooper, who inspired and supported this project, died suddenly and is sorely missed as a colleague and friend. Heather Zavod, Amy Johnston, and Bill Gotwald, published and experienced

a reliance on sexual activity as a major defense against anxiety and other dysphoric feelings; sometimes used as an equivalent to compulsive sexuality or hypersexuality."

So what then do we call sexual behaviors that people find excessive, exaggerated, disruptive, or out of control? My personal philosophy has been not to label the sexual behaviors of my clients. I sometimes use the phrase "compelling sexual behaviors" or "sex in the too-much category." Most often I follow the lead of my clients and settle on whatever attribution they give to these behaviors and what feels right to them. Sharon Nathan, Ph.D., M.Ph. (1995), a master clinician in the field of sexology, observes that clients "usually have a commitment to one term or the other, and I tend to use the term they prefer." For example, one of her clients who had other addictions preferred the label "sex addiction" because "it condenses a lot of assumption about the nature of the problem (a disease), its resolution (abstinence, sobriety, recovery), means of treatment (12-step groups, rehabs), and prognosis (difficult, but possible with everlasting vigilance) into one word." She also observes that "patients who use the term 'sexual compulsivity' tend to think of overcoming the problem in a more traditionally psychodynamic way."

In 1989, before HMOs and the intrusion of the insurance industry into the psychotherapeutic process, Irvin Yalom, a well known psychiatrist and author wrote his opinion of labels, to which I also subscribe: "Even the most liberal system of psychiatric nomenclature does violence to the being of another. If we relate to people believing that we can categorize them, we will neither identify nor nurture the parts, the vital parts, of the other that transcend category." Most diagnostic terms do not adequately describe each person's unique experience, and inaccurate labels or classifications can be destructive. Unfortunately, such labels have become facile codes for insurance companies and health professionals. But even accurate labels can distort reality and trivialize human experience. One size does not fit all!

There has been an evolution in the use of diagnostic terms over the past 50 years. Sexual behaviors have been pathologized and then depathologized. As scientific and public attitudes about sexual behavior have evolved, so too has the American Psychiatric Association's Diagnostic and Statistical Manual (DSM), which since 1952 has attempted to catalogue and describe emotional states and mental illnesses. Fortunately, over the years the manual has depathologized many sexual behaviors, including masturbation and homosexuality (Zucker & Spitzer, 2005). In 1976, Harold Lief, a psychiatrist and pioneer in the field of sex education for the medical professions, observed, "Although psychiatrists must always retain a concern for compulsive, stereotyped sexual behavior that limits the freedom and flexibility of the patient, yesterday's perversion, so far as society is concerned, is today's deviation, and tomorrow's variation." This view is still relevant. While the DSM has moved in the direction of depathologizing many sexual behaviors, "sexual behavior that limits the freedom and flexibility of the patient" is nevertheless problematic and, for many people, lies at the center of the taxonomy debate. The taxonomy of sexual behaviors is being studied and debated for the DSM-V which will likely be published in 2012. Hopefully this will result in a clearer more accurate lexicon for these behaviors.

Drs. Charles Moser and Peggy Kleinplatz delivered a paper at the American Psychiatric Association in 2003 that speaks to the significance of getting the correct words to describe a psychiatric condition (or any health condition). It also highlights the influence of the DSM.

> [The DSM] serves as a resource for mental health professionals. Although its primary influence is in the United States, its impact is global. A psychiatric diagnosis is more than shorthand to facilitate communication among professionals or to standardize research parameters. Psychiatric diagnoses affect child custody decisions, self-esteem, whether individuals are hired or fired, receive security clearances, or have other rights and privileges curtailed. The equating of unusual sexual interests with psychiatric diagnoses has been used to justify the oppression of sexual minorities and to serve political agendas. (Moser & Kleinplatz, 2003)

It is well to be thoughtful about how you label an "excess of sex," which may not be illegal at all but a behavior that some find abhorrent for reasons best known only to them. For example, a man was fired from his job for chatting in an adult consensual sexual chat room while at work. At the same time, his co-worker was discovered constructing his own web site for his own profit and was not dismissed. While using the computer for personal reasons during work may be against company rules, the sexual content—in this instance consenting adult sexual behavior—was treated differently. None of us can predict what a sexual thought or behavior may evoke in anyone else.

Some legal sexual acts may be seen as abhorrent and criminal. J. Paul Federoff, M.D., (2003) an expert in illegal sexual behaviors, has cautioned us to consider that sexual interest in or sexual fantasy about nonconsensual sexual material is not necessarily criminal, and people who have these interests may not act on them. Many people are quick to believe that "if you think it, you'll do it." There are certainly contextual nuances and subtleties to sexual behavior that we must be attentive to. However, fantasies are not behaviors. Our imaginations are infinite, and most of us may think about things from time to time that we would never do. Having fantasies does not necessarily mean that we want to live out our fantasies or are even capable of fulfilling them.

Martin Kafka, M.D., (2000) has done a good deal of research on these sexual behaviors. He prefers to label legal but "exaggerated expressions" of human sexual behavior as "hypersexual" behaviors and "paraphilia-related disorders (PRD)." He points out that there are many similarities between sexual behaviors that are legal and consensual and those that are illegal and nonconsensual. The often thin line between legal and illegal sexual behaviors, as well as the many similarities in their manifestations, can contribute to the hysteria about some of the legal sexual behaviors explored in this book. Both legal and illegal sexual behaviors may be compelling, repetitive, out of control regardless of negative consequences, preclude a connected and intimate sexual relationship with one's spouse or partner, be inconsistent with the person's perceived value system, interfere with a satisfying lifestyle, and coexist with a variety of other mental health conditions (Reid & Wooley, 2006). Sex in both categories may become ritualistic and objectified. As Drs. Moser and Kleinplatz pointed out in their 2003 paper, both legal and illegal sexual behaviors can entail severe consequences.

There are many sides to this debate. Psychoanalyst Aviel Goodman, M.D. (1998) makes a case for the accuracy of the label *sex addiction*. Patrick Carnes (1991), a proponent and pioneer of the 12-step approach for sex addiction, as well as others who subscribe to the label sex addiction, refer to partners or spouses of sex addicts as coaddicts.

While in reality repetitive and compelling sexual behaviors (CSB) are far more complex and varied than addictions to alcohol and other substances, there are some useful analogies and treatment methodologies that can be borrowed from the field of alcohol and substance addiction. Sexual behaviors of any kind have different reinforcers and consequences, both psychologically and physiologically, than do alcohol and drugs. Simply put, erotic feelings are pleasant, and orgasms are even more so. Hangovers are not. Muench et al. (2007) write, "Like eating, sex is a part of the human condition and healthy functioning. Unlike excessive eating or substance abuse, it is entirely possible to engage in excessive amounts of sexual behavior without experiencing physical harm." Muench prefers the term compulsive sexual behaviors also referred to as CSB.

Many people who suffer from alcohol or substance abuse may also have some form of sexual compulsivity, a term used by Eli Coleman, Ph.D, (1986). John Bancroft, M.D., emeritus director of the Kinsey Institute, and his colleague Zoran Vukadinovic (2004) also weigh in on the taxonomy debate in this way: "We prefer the general descriptive term *out of control* to describe sexual behavior that is unregulated for a variety of possible reasons." At the same time, they are also quick to point out that while much research has been done on issues of definitions, less has been done on explanations about the *causes* of these sexual behaviors. John Wincze (2000) uses the nomenclature "atypical sexual behavior."

Most recently, Rory Reid (2007) offered the following comprehensive list for these behaviors: "sexual impulsivity, sexual compulsivity, sexual addiction, sexual dependence, unrestrained sexual desire, sexual disinhibition, hypersexuality, sexual torridity, sexual sensation seeking, sexual desire disorders, excessive sexual desire, hyperlibido, hyperactive sexual behavior, uninhibited sexual desire, paraphilia related sexual disorders,, non-paraphilic sexual disorders, Don Juanism, erotomania, nymphomania and, satyriasis." The common denominator of these sexual behaviors, no matter what the label, is that a person will "engage in some form of sexual behavior in a pattern that is characterized by two key features: recurrent failure to control the behavior and continuation of the behavior despite significant harmful consequences" (Goodman, 1998).

At the end of the day, the label debate may not tell you much more than there are many of us who are struggling to understand these types of behaviors. More importantly, this debate can also be seen as avoidance to come to grips with what sexuality means to the individual, and neglects the primary importance of self-attribution. It is comforting to know that people are thinking about this issue and trying to solve it. It is my experience that people like to know what they "have" or what the diagnosis is. If you are a "purple duck," it is nice to know that there are other purple ducks out there.

WHO ARE PURPLE DUCKS AND WHAT DO THEY DO?

What do people who have compelling sexual behaviors actually do? The more common types of sexual behavior in this category are repetitive and compulsive masturbation, chatting on or searching the Internet for sexually explicit scenes or sexual encounters, telephone sex, frequent predatory or anonymous casual adult couplings, or persistent attempts at sexual contact with a spouse or partner (once a day to several times a day) that may be incompatible with the partner's conception of a satisfying relationship (Cooper, Golden, & Marshall, 2006; Kafka, 2007). Although these behaviors are legal, a client's family, friends or an employer who may discover them often feel as if a loathsome crime has been committed.

Typically my clients have other mental and emotional conditions that coexist with these sexual behaviors. These co-existing conditions include depression, anxiety, hyperactivity, poor impulse control, alcohol or drug abuse, attention deficit disorder, bipolar disorder, post traumatic stress disorder, marital and family dysfunction, brain injuries, Tourette's syndrome, and Asperger's syndrome. The early research of Patrick Carnes (1991) found that in his cohort of "sex addicts" and "sexual coaddicts" there was virtually the same percentage of subjects with a history of sexual abuse (81%), physical abuse (72%), and emotional abuse (97%). All of these conditions deserve attention and treatment. They often mask the sexual dilemmas the person is living with and are often treated without any clue that a sexual problem exists. The opposite could be true as well. The sexual problems may be so overwhelming that the coexisting conditions can be ignored. It may be easier for some to admit, for example, that they have depression or marital difficulties than to deal with the sexual behaviors that coexist with these problems. Sometimes it is easier for the therapist to ignore sexual behaviors, as well. "Don't ask, don't tell" is not good practice. Clients should be asked about their sexual behaviors and preferences and given a chance to have them heard nonjudgmentally, even when something is difficult to listen to.

The majority of my clients are men. Prevalence studies reveal that men account for the majority of people with compelling sexual habits (Goodman, 1998; Kafka, 2007). Nevertheless, in this book I also address the unique issues that women have, not only with secret sexual habits but also as partners of men who have compelling sexual behaviors. In addition, there is a chapter on the issues families face when a member is found to have sexual behaviors that have been secret. In spite of a paucity of research on gay, lesbian, and bisexual populations with compelling sexual behaviors, some of the unique issues that these groups experience are also included in this discussion.

Many of my clients have sought me out because they feel out of control with an excess of sexual thoughts or behaviors. Or perhaps a spouse or partner has betrayed them with their sexual secrets. I am often the first person with whom they share their sexual habits. Many have lived with these secrets eating away at their life for years. It is humbling for me to listen to the secrets people bring to me and difficult to hear the pain that accompanies these secrets.

For the most part, people with secrets connected to sexual behavior keep these issues hidden until someone blows the whistle. This does not mean that anyone wants these behaviors to continue or began doing them purposely. Many lead double lives for a long time. Kay Jamison, Ph.D, (2000), a psychologist at Johns Hopkins University, has manic depressive illness, or what is now called bipolar disorder, and has written some helpful books about her experience and struggles with this sometimes lethal illness. In sharing the battles she has had with her illness, she seems to have gained some jurisdiction over it. Hopefully, this may help others do the same. This description of her hidden thoughts may well be the experience of people with sexual secrets:

> Because the privacy of my nightmare had been of my own designing, no one close to me had any real idea of the psychological company I had been keeping. The gap between private experience and its public expression was absolute; my persuasiveness to others was unimaginably frightening. (Jamison, 2000)

Daunting though these sexual issues may seem, they are highly treatable. Many clients can, at the very least, get to a better place than "out of control." The following chapters discuss the many and varied treatment options available for those with compelling sexual habits. It is encouraging to note that as word gets around that treatment is possible, more people are seeking treatment for compelling sexual issues voluntarily. Treatment can often be effective particularly when meted out by an empathic, experienced clinician who understands the possibilities and treatment options and is flexible and creative as well.

WHAT IS THIS THING CALLED THERAPY?

I set about writing this book because I wanted to convey the clinical context within which treatments for legal and compelling sexual habits take place. I invite the reader into my consulting room and write about what I think during the sessions and how my clients respond. Many books have tried to capture the essence of therapy: for example, Avodah Offit's *Night Thoughts* (1981), Illona Rabinowitz's *Inside Therapy* (1998), or Irvin Yalom's *Love's Executioner* (1989). In the past few years, therapy has become a popular fascination in the media as well: *Analyze This* (1999), *The Sopranos* (1999), and *In Treatment* (2008). I cringe when my clients tell me that they learned about therapy from the media. It evokes an expectation of the one-hour fix and always makes me wonder how I measure up to Hollywood's standards! I don't believe that it is really possible to describe what it is like to do therapy or to be in therapy. Each person and situation is unique. Yet here I am joining the ranks of thousands before me who have attempted the task.

What I have come to realize is that therapy is generally best understood in hindsight. Looking back over sessions, assessing where we were at the beginning of the work, and then looking at what has been accomplished, reveals a subtle but clear and seemingly seamless process. Therapy reminds me of what it was like when I was a child watching the ants at the beach crawl over the sand. I knew that there was logic to what seemed their endless backtracking and crisscrossing. It would eventually lead to the building of a highly complex city in which ants lived and thrived, but it was always a work in progress.

Therapy is centered on the relationship between the client and the therapist. I invite the reader to view the process in which the client and I establish a relationship as therapy unfolds. I share mistakes and triumphs. If this book were to more truly mirror the experience of therapy, it would not be divided into chapters and would have no ending. Nevertheless, I have laid the chapters out in somewhat the classical order: initial meetings, assessment, treatment, Internet sex, unique issues of women who have or live with a spouse who has compelling sexual behaviors, the fine line between legal and illegal behaviors, family systems, and relapse prevention.

To establish the therapeutic relationship as an egalitarian process and because I dislike labels, I call the people I work with clients, which conveys a position of empowerment. I am guided by the perspective that I am being "hired" by a client as an informed consultant. The people you will read about are not my "patients," as the medical model would insist. I do not think of them as being sick or pathological, although they already may have labeled themselves that way. I do not want to distance myself with the words I use. Irvin Yalom (1989) puts it this way: "We cannot say to them you and your problems. Instead, we must speak of us and our problems, because our life, our existence, will always be riveted to death, love to loss, freedom to fear, and growth to separation. We are, all of us, in this together."

Each chapter has case material that aims at highlighting a particular aspect or stage of therapy. We all need some structure, and just as the time between sessions is as important as the sessions themselves, the division of the therapeutic process into chapters gives us pause to digest the material and provides a road map that can be followed if needed. It is my habit to use analogies and metaphors as a way to connect with people and help them understand and be comfortable with some concepts of treatment. While I have based a great deal of the book on the rich and far-reaching academic literature in the field, I also strive to express the universality and depth of the affect involved in this endeavor.

CONFIDENTIALITY

There are many common threads and recurring themes that people who have sex in the "too-much" category share. Some may read something that sounds familiar and think I may be writing about them. However, I fiercely protect my clients' privacy and fulfill the promise of confidentiality. I will not write about any particular person, although their gifts of trust and their lives inform my writing. The stories in this book are a composite view of many people, fragments put together to give a whole picture. They are fictional-ized accounts of plausible events.

I work and live in a small, but densely populated, urban com-munity surrounded by a large rural area. The anonymity provided by large urban areas does not exist here. This is significant if, for example, one may be seen entering my office, attending a self-help group for sex addicts, or attending an Alcoholics Anonymous meeting. Sometimes a client tells me that he or she has run into an acquaintance, coworker, or perhaps a child's teacher at these meetings. Some people can make it work, others cannot. I often see my clients when I am out and about—at a restaurant or theater, perhaps taking a walk or at a dinner party, at the synagogue, or shopping. We generally anticipate these possibilities, and we talk about what each client would feel comfortable with when these chance meetings might occur. I have to be vigilant not to treat people in the same family, friends, or employer and employee. I manage anonymity and confidentiality as best I can. On occasion my vigilance in these matters does not succeed, and we have to negotiate a solution.

ON A PERSONAL NOTE

I have often wondered why I wandered into the field of sexual-ity and have spent most of my life exploring its landscape. My parents hoped I would become a schoolteacher. One of my many flaws as a compliant daughter was that I evaded the conventional. I became a clinical social worker, psychotherapist, and eventually a clinical sexologist. When I began my professional life in the early sixties, research into sexual behavior was in its infancy. There was not much to know about the field of sexology. I became caught up in the events swirling around the emerging "sexual revolution." Reproductive technology provided the oral contraceptive, effec-tively separating sex for pleasure from sex for reproduction. Flower children promoted free love. Women's rights and reproductive prerogatives were being widely debated. It was an exciting time. "Make love not war" was the mantra of the '60s. It's still not a bad idea today!

In this context, people came to my office wanting greater satis-faction from sexual relationships. They wanted more frequent sex, more and better orgasms, longer and stronger erections. Bigger, better, more are the hallmarks of the last half of the twentieth century and the beginning of the 21st century. Today the concerns people bring to me are more often about an excess of sex. We have surpassed the sexual revolution, which was fueled by reproductive technologies, and now are enveloped and driven by the computer chip revolution, with all its attendant possibilities and pitfalls.

It is not my aim to offer any powerful new paradigms or recipes for treatment for compelling sexual behaviors. Treatment strategies are growing and developing as research evolves in this field. At this writing there are many treatment models and techniques that seem to work well for these highly treatable behaviors. The clients I write about are ordinary people who work and live in the community. While from time to time a sensational event involving sexual secrets hits the headlines—e.g., President Clinton or Governor Spitzer—the average client quietly indulges in behaviors that are neither illegal nor even particularly sensational or salacious. Nevertheless he or she may enter treatment because their sexual habits interfere with a satisfying life style or productivity at work. Perhaps some feel out of control and come to treatment voluntarily. Or perhaps someone discovers their habits and gives them an ultimatum to seek treatment.

The slowing-down or stopping of compelling sexual behaviors is not necessarily an end-point in therapy, and in this book I discuss the concepts of coping strategies for the long haul. Without sounding pessimistic, I believe it is important to be realistic about the long-range outlook for people who have had many years of acting out sexual secrets. It has been my experience that some people never leave their secret sexual habits completely behind although the behaviors diminish to a tolerable level—whatever that may be for them. When therapy is tapered down and a mutually agreed-upon termination occurs, the client may feel the habits they had are truly ended forever. To be honest, I will never know about "forever." There are no data to allow such a prediction. However, I do believe that forever might be a possibility.

This book aims to speak to a spectrum of clinicians with a variety of skills, training, and orientations, including addiction and master's level counselors, social workers, master's level and Ph.D. psychologists, psychiatric nurses, psychiatrists, marriage and family therapists, clergy, and sex therapists or clinical sexologists. However, it is important to note that "A background in treating other addictive or psychological disorders does not insure an ability to meet the specific needs of sexually compulsive clients" (Herring, 2001). There are emerging training programs and certification standards that a clinician can participate in to develop skills specific to this population.

Almost every day there is new information and research available, allowing us to continue to learn about these challenging behaviors and deal with the situations they create. Even experienced clinicians might neglect to assess for compelling and repetitive sexual behaviors and their sequellae which might result in insufficient treatment. In a survey of 218 counselors, members of the American Mental Health Counselors Association and International Association for Addiction and Offender Counselors, 25% felt that sex addiction was often undiagnosed or misdiagnosed, and 45% indicated that this was because counselors failed to deal with these issues because of unresolved difficulties with their own histories with sex abuse or sex addiction. In addition, 35% of these counselors attributed this to inadequate preparation of counselors in training programs (Swisher, 1995). This data was collected almost 15 years ago, but anecdotally I find this still to be true. Compelling sexual habits have proliferated with the computer chip revolution, and professionals have barely begun to come to grips with it. But rest assured we are working on it.

Clinicians, too, can have personal issues with sexual dilemmas. Working with the sexual problems in our cultural milieu and particular time in history "is by no means a province for the unskilled or faint of heart" (Leiblum & Rosen, 2000). It is easy to overpathologize the sexual habits therapists unearth in the sessions. I would advise fellow therapists and counselors who choose this work to have a clear understanding of their own limitations and attitudes about sexual issues. As Eli Colman, Ph.D., (1995) has observed, "It is important for professionals to recognize and be comfortable with a wide range of normal sexual behavior." However, there are times to say, "I don't know about this; let's find someone who can help." Most of my colleagues are happy to consult or supervise. Information is readily available, even if all the answers are not definitive.

Although it may be appropriate to make a referral, it is important that the therapist not send the message that clients are being referred out because their sexual concerns or behaviors are "bad, dirty, and/or shameful" and even their therapist does not want to hear about them! Irving Binik, Ph.D., and Marta Meana, Ph.D.,

(2007) gave a paper at the 31st annual meeting of the Society for Sex Therapy and Research in Atlanta, Georgia, in which they observed that referring clients out when sexual issues are raised is "the professional equivalent of 'Why don't you go ask your mother about that?'" The message from the therapist may be a negative one and the client may feel shamed when it is more likely an issue for the therapist. When the problem really the therapists' problem. This stance marginalizes sex and compartmentalizes it from the rest of life, something therapists should not be promoting. Armed with more information and insight into these complex therapeutic challenges, a therapist might then be able to assess if they can (or want to) handle the situation, get consultation, or make an informed and supportive decision that someone else might be of more help to the client. The therapist must ensure the referral is done in a respectful, thoughtful manner so the client will not feel abandoned, admonished, and "sent away."

Among several motivations for writing this book was to fill in some of the blanks and basics for many clinicians and demystify the therapeutic process for those seeking help. I will be pleased if professionals find this book helpful. But I will be truly fulfilled if this book validates the experience some people have with sex, informs them that they are not alone in their struggle with sexual secrets, and nudges them to seek help. For those who have a friend, spouse, lover, or family member who wrestles with these problems, I hope to encourage a thoughtful consideration of sexual behavior that inspires compassion rather than condemnation. My wish is that therapists and clients alike will find in these pages some sustenance to make the journey from secrecy to honesty and from revelation to freedom from the burden of their sexual secrets.

I am also writing from a perspective of what it is like not to have great numbers of referral resources for groups, clinics, or professionals who are knowledgeable and willing to administer medications to this unique population. I am envious of colleagues in big urban areas where the resources and collegiality may be more abundant, or where the university has a thriving sexual medicine program. For colleagues who live and practice in rural areas, I hope to offer some creative solutions to the lack of resources.

Another motivation for writing this book was to further my work as an advocate for healthy sexual attitudes. If we expect clients to come out of denial about their personal sexual issues, our society must also understand the realities of these behaviors. "Don't ask, don't tell" is unacceptable. Zero tolerance may be necessary in some instances but like "just say no," it is naïve and insufficient. I like to believe that both the sexual revolution and the computer chip revolution have promoted a climate in which subjects that used to be banned from public debate can now be openly discussed and examined.

I have often felt that in many important ways the political and social climate of this century is not much different than it was when Kinsey began his work in the 1940s. I hope we can protect our freedom to continue the debate, because public policy and research *can* lead to treatments and solutions—a "joining with" rather than a "distancing from." In spite of the paranoia into which the 21st century has been born, I believe we can view sexual behavior through a lens that is salutogenic—health-affirming. While it may be foolish optimism, I stubbornly cling to the idea that I might help engender a public attitude that has perspective, is balanced, and is less hysterical about things sexual.

Gale Holtz Golden
Burlington, Vermont

Chapter 1

Becoming transparent

We are all, in a sense, experts on secrecy. From earliest child-hood we feel its mystery and attraction. We know both the power it confers and the burden it imposes. We learn how it can delight, give breathing-space, and protect. But we come to understand its dangers, too: how it is used to oppress and exclude; what can befall those who come too close to secrets they were not meant to share; and the price of betrayal.

Sissela Bok

Desperation is not a good starting place for any relationship. But desperation is often what drives clients to my door. The decision to seek therapy for secret sexual behaviors is more likely the result of an ultimatum than a self-motivated choice. Often, a spouse, part-ner, or employer discovers a sexual secret and "blows the whistle," threatening grim consequences if the person doesn't get help. The first meeting with a client marks the beginning of a relationship between two not-so-perfect strangers. What a leap of faith for both of us to begin a journey together not knowing where it will end!

THE EMPEROR'S NEW CLOTHES

When David called for an appointment, he said he was in crisis and asked to be seen as soon as possible. I gave him an appointment as soon as I could, giving up some time I had earmarked for myself. I was feeling cranky, overbooked, and slightly martyred, with no one to blame but myself. When I asked who referred him, he said he had heard my name "around," and had "Googled" me. *Googled?*

Having been born before the advent of television, I was still not quite comfortable with the Internet and its wonders. I felt exposed and not a little paranoid, which nudged me into a deeper empathy for the acute sense of exposure that many have when they come to see me. What was on the Internet about me? It was not entirely altruism on my part that I gave David an appointment right away, although when someone says they are "in crisis" I generally try to find time for at least a consult.

David brought ambivalence and fear into the room as we sized each other up. I had imagined David to be a self-confident, savvy, take-charge sort of person who would stride confidently into my office. After all, he researched people on the Internet, so he would be prepared and knowledgeable before putting his life in some therapist's hands. Instead, I greeted a small, thin young man in my waiting room. He was slightly hunched over and looked as if he had spent most of his 28 years apologizing for himself. The gloomy, rainy day was prescient of David's mood when he entered my office, making apologies for being three minutes late and for having wet shoes. His fragility and tentativeness quickly dispensed with my feelings of paranoia about being exposed on the Internet. They were replaced with my maternal feelings that are chronically in need of watching. I did not want to protect David from himself. Or did I? From his defensive posture, hunched over and apologetic, I began to understand why David needed to find out more about me before he made the appointment. We all deserve to keep ourselves safe. It is important for the therapist to understand that whether a client seeks help by choice or by chance, "psychotherapy takes time and produces emotional turmoil for the [client]" (Cooper & Marcus, 2003).

David's opening words were, "I feel transparent, psychically naked." David's fiancée, Anne, discovered that David had been soliciting sexual encounters on the telephone and the Internet for the past few years. Her anger resulted in the ultimatum that David must seek help. What she did not know was that he was constantly preoccupied with sexual fantasies even when he was not on the phone or the Internet. He had been exposed, accused, and left blinking in the light for all to see. He enjoyed telephone sex and surfing the net for images of naked women and, while he kept it secret, he rationalized that it wasn't harming anyone to do this. After all, his father read *Playboy Magazine* and hid it under the mattress! David could not understand why Anne was so upset and angry when she found out about it, but he was willing to talk with me. This moment, the first visit with me, may carry the illusion that change is welcome, but in truth it belies a need to hold desire tight, to keep near the comfort it serves. David's ambivalence and resistance to alter his habits were normal reactions under these circumstances. At this moment of transparency, I needed to see the emperor's new clothes.

Revelations are a lot to take in all at once. When someone comes to my office on the verge of revealing sexual secrets, I must be the midwife to honesty, guiding the birth of secrets so that it is done with clarity and with the strength of insight and understanding. This opportunity is rare because, for the most part, sexual revelations burst on a family or a partner like a bomb. The revelations are unwanted, and everyone scatters.

THE CLIENT'S QUESTIONS

The first visit is typically taken up with questions. Mistrust is the subtext. Most of the people with compelling sexual behaviors do not trust anyone, especially themselves, so why should they trust me? The questions I have ready are not as urgent as the ones that pour out of my clients. Forced into therapy by an angry spouse, partner or family, my clients raise many questions that are often an attempt to convince me that they do not really have to be in therapy. Fair enough. Defensiveness and denial are familiar companions for this uncertain moment. Questions spill out from David: "Will you tell anyone else? Are these habits legal or illegal? Who gets these sexual habits? Why me? Am I a pervert? Do I really need help if I can just stop? How can Anne be so upset about a fantasy? Will she leave me? Who is hurt by what goes on in someone's mind? It's just sex; it's *her* I love! What else does Anne need to know about this? Does it really matter how many times I masturbate? Am I really being unfaithful to Anne if my sexual encounters are consensual, impersonal, anonymous, or a one-night-stand? I love Anne; why is she so upset? Whose problem is this anyway?" Whose indeed?

For David and many of my clients, becoming transparent is a kind of death, a great and permanent loss. For the first time in their lives, their secret garden has been revealed. Their inner sense of control has been swept away, even though it was a fragile illusion to begin with. When I offered David empathy about being exposed, he described what it had been like when he went to his secret place:

> It was like planning to rob a bank. I fantasized about the money I would have and how I would spend it. The fantasy was very pleasant. After I robbed the bank I ran from the police. When I succeeded at eluding them, I went to a secret place where it felt safe. I caught my breath and had the pleasure of counting my money. I dreamt about spending it. Quickly, I realized I had to leave and pretend nothing had happened. I have been constantly looking over my shoulder. I realize now that what seemed to be a safe refuge was merely a place that separated me from the rest of the world. I am ambivalent about my behavior, filled with shame and guilt. I never really feel safe, only secretive.

I listened to David's analogy, powerful and rich with its allusions—stealing, police, fear of exposure, and his fantasy of finding safety. I also heard his need to have some answers from me about what was happening or could happen. He was fragile and very frightened. My job was to be "in it" with David, to accept him the way he was at that moment, to be supportive and nonjudgmental, to promote an egalitarian relationship (Rogers, 1957) and a safe environment, holding his secrets and hearing his fears. Most people who seek me out for help have felt inadequate and insecure about themselves for many years. It is common for hypersexual people to have intimacy and relationship problems, as well as attachment disorders (Coleman, 1995; Cooper & Marcus, 2003). As I pointed out in the Prologue, many have been neglected in childhood, as well as sexually, emotionally, and physically abused (Carnes, 1991). The therapeutic relationship can mitigate these difficulties with relationships. My clients are very lonely people, even when surrounded by those who love them. Their sexual secrets, closely held companions in life, may have been acted upon for almost a lifetime, a balm for life's exigencies. What will fill the void if secrets must be relinquished?

DIFFERENT CHALLENGES

Assessing and treating sexual behaviors provides different challenges than do other mental health issues. As clinicians we must always keep in mind that the intrinsic nature of sex is unique, and its impact both on us and our clients is profound, powerful, and intensely private. Martin Kafka, M.D., a leading expert, researcher and clinician who has worked with these sexual issues for many years, observes that "sexuality disorders are arguably the most shame- and guilt-inducing contemporary psychiatric conditions" (Kafka, 2007).

Therapists may find it counterintuitive to consider that some people need their sexual behaviors contained when many of us have spent years helping people expand upon their sexual repertoires for greater pleasure (Nathan, 1995). John Bancroft, M.D. (2003), observes the paradox that some people have trouble inhibiting sexual expression and some people inhibit their sexual feelings too much. He points out that for most people, depression or anxiety diminishes interest in sexual activity, while for others a depressed and/or an anxious mood may be a precursor to disinhibition of sexual urges. Unlike problems with alcohol, substance abuse or perhaps other mental health issues such as depression, those with compelling and repetitive sexual habits are less likely to see the need for change. They rationalize that no one knows so it cannot hurt anyone. It is legal and consensual, so why fix it? But for many, the preoccupation with sex precludes all connection to loved ones, to employment, and to a reasonably happy life.

The erotic charge is heightened by risk and secrecy for some people. They live on the edge of being discovered but still cannot resist acting on their impulses. A client once told me that for him sex was not a rational act. Hypersexual or compelling sexual behaviors are not absolute in terms of severity; rather there are degrees from moderate acting out to severely risky behaviors. There has been research that demonstrates that people who have higher scores on the Kalichman and Rompa (1995) Sexual Compulsivity Scale are more likely to have a greater number of sexual partners and take greater risks than people who score low rates on the scale (Reid, 2007).

In part, we can account for this difference by understanding that sexual desire is intrinsically pleasurable and thus very difficult to give up no matter what the consequences. A client once described his feelings of powerlessness when he was in the pursuit of an erotic experience:

It's like I am standing on train tracks, paralyzed in the headlights of an oncoming train. I have nowhere to go. The danger arouses me and rivets me to the spot. I am in its grip. Nothing will distract me from the pulsing eroticism I feel, not even the steady approach of the train.

It is possible to hide compelling sexual habits for a lifetime, and such secret behavior can have far-reaching and overwhelming emotional consequences for all involved. A woman called me for help after her husband died suddenly of a heart attack at 62. While cleaning out his tool shed in the garage, she came upon a secret door cleverly disguised as shelves for odds and ends. Inside this small hidden room was a collection of expensive gowns, wigs, and shoes. There also was a dressing table filled with cosmetics and perfumes, a large three-way mirror, a couch, stereo, and mini-bar. It had been her husband's hidden "pleasure palace" for many years. She had no idea he was a cross-dresser and had a secret life.

Dire physical consequences of these behaviors are less common but when they occur, the impact can be profound and destabilizing. For some it may be lethal. Physical consequences most likely take the form of sexually transmitted infections, such as Chlamydia or AIDS, or self induced auto-asphyxiation (more commonly called "snuffing"), blackmail threats, or bodily harm or death from an encounter with a sexual predator for whom death or disfigurement is part of their ritual. The horror of having been exposed to AIDS or other sexually transmitted infections evokes a panic-filled vulnerability in a spouse or partner who finds that she may have been exposed to a terminal illness.

The discovery of sexual secrets within a relationship is most assuredly a devastating event. While there was no proof that her husband's cross dressing was truly an erotic experience for him or even connected to any sexual act, it was nevertheless overwhelming and demoralizing to deal with the posthumous revelation about her husband's secret habits. Her reality was that her husband not only had "another woman" but that he *was* the other woman. She had been deceived. It was a nightmare to think she had been married to a man for 40 years and had not known him at all. In spite of all her feelings she was determined to hide his lifetime secret, particularly from their three adult children. In her resolve to make her husband's secret her secret also, she paid a great emotional price. Betrayal can take many forms, but when it involves a perceived sexual infidelity it has an entirely unique emotional impact. The ripples have the potential to affect family, friends, co-workers and even the community, especially if the behavior happens to hit the headlines.

BUILDING THE THERAPEUTIC RELATIONSHIP

The therapeutic process is not magic, although sometimes it seems as if it is. There have been volumes written about the first interview and the process of therapy in an effort to convey its essence. Some years ago I was reading about how Zingara, the fortune teller in Robertson Davies' book, *The World of Wonders*, sized up customers who were looking for some clues about their future. I have never read a better description of how a therapist engages with, and sizes up, a new client:

> You have to learn to look at people. Hardly anybody does that. They stare into people's faces, but you have to look at the whole person. And you have to let them see that you're looking. Most people aren't used to being looked at. Feel around, and give them a chance to talk, you know as soon as you touch the sore spot. Tell them you have to feel around because you're trying to find the way into their lives, but they're not ordinary and so it takes time. It's part kindness and part making them feel they're perfectly safe with you. No saying, you're safe with me or anything like that. You have to give it out, and they have to take it in, without a lot of direct talk. You got to look at them as if it was a long time since you met an equal. But don't push, don't shove it. You got to be wide open to them, or else they won't be wide open to you. (Davies, 1975)

Both palmistry and therapy may appear cloaked in mystery, but for the therapist and palmist it involves a deliberate and well-studied process designed to achieve specific goals.

If there is to be a significant change for the client with compelling sexual behaviors, therapists from the first meeting, must pay attention to building a relationship with the client that includes warmth, support, trust, honesty, as well as clear boundaries and expectations. Educating a client about therapy and making a treatment plan is one thing, but motivating a client to make necessary changes is another. Moyers and Rollnick's (2002) work on motivational interviewing emphasizes that building a therapeutic alliance maximizes behavior change and prevents premature termination and relies on the actions of the therapist and *not* on stopping client behavior. The following steps will more likely pave the way for change than dogma or judgments would.

1. **Express Empathy** by using reflective listening to convey understanding of the client's message.
2. **Develop Discrepancy** between the client's most deeply held values and current behavior.
3. **Roll with Resistance** by meeting it with reflection rather than confrontation.
4. **Support Self–efficacy** by building confidence that change is possible.

Psychoanalyst Donald Winnicott (1969) talks about providing the client with "a safe holding environment." I like the image of a space that will hold the client safely, a place to exhale. The psychotherapeutic relationship and process is unique. People come to the office, we sit across from each other, the room is quiet and private, and we talk about intimate things. The topics of conversation are personal and private and may never have been revealed, even to the most intimate friend or to a spouse. Clients and clinicians are both vulnerable to basic human feelings and attractions. If clinicians are honest, they ask themselves: Can I work with this person? Do I like this person? Do I like this person too much? What about hypersexual people who masturbate frequently or men and women who are trolling daily for sexual encounters? Will I be aroused by sexual material, repelled by it, perhaps both?

Many people who work with clients who have sexual dilemmas are not trained in or subscribe to the concept of transference and do not explore it in supervision. Whether the therapist agrees with these concepts or not, I believe it is an essential and ethical mandate that the therapist be self-aware and pay close attention to personal reactions to the clients. I will explore the issues of transference, countertransference, and boundaries in more detail as we move on, but suffice it to say for the moment that I am of a mind "that not only does the client project onto the therapist feelings that are based on earlier relationships (transference), but that the therapist's own emotions and experiences inevitably color his or her feelings about the client (countertransference)" (Corley & Schneider, 2002).

Sex stirs up positive and negative feelings in all of us. I don't know anybody who is neutral on the subject. Therapists are no exception, and they must be vigilant about what is being stirred up. Therapists also have sexual issues in their past of one kind or another and hopefully understand when these issues interfere with their work. It is a mistake to ignore them. If not examined and understood, the feelings unleashed in the clinician may result in many premature terminations.

I have had occasion to supervise some therapists who have experienced sexual traumas such as rape and abuse. Some believed that by reliving their own trauma while working with a client who has been abused or raped, they might help themselves. This may or may not be true, but it warrants a full examination with a supervisor or colleague because it has the potential to be destructive to both client and therapist. Ethical boundaries around self-disclosure from a clinician to a client have been discussed in many scholarly papers, including Johnson (2000), Herring (2001), and Corley & Schneider (2002). Having an eating disorder, for example, does not necessarily qualify a clinician to treat others with the same malady. It has the potential for the clinician to over-identify with the client and thus suspend some clinical judgment or recommend treatment models that do not fit with client's needs. For example, "this worked for me, it will work for you" risks early termination or inadequate treatment altogether.

There is always some sexual energy in the room when people meet and talk about sexual topics. These feelings need monitoring. It is never appropriate for a clinician to act on sexual feelings and breach the fiduciary responsibility of the therapeutic relationship. "Establishing trust is one of the first challenges when building a relationship. The earliest seed of trust is planted by explicitly establishing a solid therapy frame that includes 'rules,' such as frequency of sessions, the fee, and cancellation policies" (Cooper & Marcus, 2003). The clinician must establish boundaries and be clear about the limits of the therapeutic contract. These should be spelled out at the very beginning of therapy and modeled throughout by the therapist's demeanor and actions. Much has been written about professional boundaries in the mental health field (Peterson, 1992; Plaut, 2003, 2008). The key question for all professionals who have a relationship founded in confidence and trust with a client, patient, student, or congregant is: "Whose needs are ultimately being met? Appropriate boundaries are always the result of a constant search for a golden mean. We can also be too distant by not providing the closeness and caring that makes for a supportive, trusting clinical or mentoring relationship" (Plaut, 2008). Above all do no harm.

The initial visit with a person with sexual secrets brings with it a sense of urgency. While the family or employer may want to crack down on the recently discovered sexual behavior, it is essential not to join with those outside the door. "This masturbation must stop and now!" may be what everyone else wants, but what does the client want? Being judgmental or moving too fast may be the reason the client never returns. Stopping or containing the behavior may have to wait; it is the client's work, not anyone else's. Of course, there are instances when high-risk behaviors may have to be dealt with more quickly, a situation we will examine more closely in Chapter 2.

Typically people seek out psychotherapeutic intervention because they want to make some change in their behavior. However, when treatment is mandated by someone other than the client, it changes how the client views the therapy and the therapist. Consciously or unconsciously, change may not be the desired goal. It is more likely that the goal of the client is to pacify the people who have "outed" him or her and still find a way to maintain a secret erotic life. It would not be unusual for the client to initially experience the therapist as the judge and jury; the balance in the relationship is off kilter even before it starts. The client is likely to perceive the therapist in the same way he or she views those who have discovered the behaviors: Will I try to take away his or her sex life? Rip him out of denial? Strip away defenses? And perhaps even report him to the law?

The task of creating a therapeutic alliance with people who have compelling sexual habits can be difficult and frustrating. Many of my clients have limited capacity for trust, and this will play itself out in our relationship. They are often like frightened birds trapped in a cage. They are always looking for a way out and therefore become difficult to "capture" and engage. While I attempt to build a trusting relationship from the first visit, to remain supportive and be nonjudgmental from the outset, there are times when someone bolts from the office and never returns or stays for only a few visits and terminates without any notice or discussion. They make an appointment and do not show up. Did I go too fast? Did I consciously or unconsciously project judgment? Was I too empathic or not empathic enough? What did I miss? It haunts my dreams.

David's dilemmas and David's questions

The questions David threw at me are not easy ones, but their themes are common to most of my clients. I hear the deep insecurities and the need for acceptance that are the subtext to most of the questions. Sexual behaviors are often used to "medicate" bad feelings. The therapist needs to follow those feelings right down the yellow brick road. "Why me? Do I really need treatment? Can I be helped?" David asked these questions, hoping I might join with him in his denial. If I said to him, "Yeah, it's no big deal; telephone sex, it's legal, doesn't harm anyone; you don't even have to be with the person; it's just a fantasy; masturbate and hang up!" it might comfort David's fears. He might want to take the answer I gave him home to Anne: "See, my therapist thinks it's okay!" But, of course, this is another fantasy. I don't give permission for David's behaviors, but I can offer empathy for his trapped, exposed feelings. Empathy is more likely to get us on the yellow brick road.

As we continued to talk, David told me about his struggle with his values and his religion, which had taught him to contain his sexual urges and desires. This was a different message from the one his dad had unknowingly given him. David found his dad's hidden stash of *Playboy* magazines and assumed his dad used it for fantasy material while he masturbated. For most of his life, David felt chronic guilt and shame after he masturbated. Anne compounded David's shame and distress about having sexual feelings because she was invested in being a virgin until they married. David rationalized that he was helping both of them meet their religious goals. But in reality David had struggled with this "discrepancy between his most deeply held values and current behavior" (Moyers & Rollnick, 2002) long before he met Anne. Even during his inner dialogue with his conscience and fleeting resolve to relinquish his sexual habits, David had not considered the impact his telephone encounters would have on his relationship with Anne, or on his bank account. The discrepancy between David's goals and behavior would be helpful benchmarks further into the therapy.

David wanted desperately to have sex with Anne and could not reconcile it with his guilt. They were very affectionate, kissing, hugging and holding each other tight in bed. David was conscious of the boundaries Anne had set and yet he always hoped she would "cave." David laid out his struggle with the competing ideologies of his own conscience, Anne's beliefs, and his anguish over his own body's need. Many clients struggle with the dissonance between their own values, their sense of themselves and the magnetism of erotic needs. It seemed like an unending tug of war for David.

> A certain ill-defined disgrace hung over his efforts, a sense of failure and waste and, of course, loneliness. And pleasure was really an incidental benefit. The goal was release—from urgent, thought-confining desire for what could not be immediately had. How extraordinary it was, that a self-made spoonful, leaping clear of his body, should instantly free his mind. (McEwan, 2007)

All my clients ask many questions during the first visit, and David was no exception. I told him some could be answered now, some would have to wait, and some answers would be discovered as we proceeded with the therapy. I gave him some information about the process of treatment and the *Reader's Digest* version of what is known about his sexual habits to offer a measure of hope and reassurance. As the session continued, David seemed less anxious and depressed. He looked me in the eye when he talked and seemed more engaged.

Answering the questions

There are a lot of theories about how sexual habits or preferences begin and develop throughout life. Clinically, it is easy to observe that sexual habits, whatever form they may take in adult life, are germinated during childhood (Barlow & Durand, 1998; Wincze, 2000). Ariel Goodman (1998) also points out that many of these habits are likely to fade by the time a person is 25 to 30 years old. My clients often tell me about the hidden stash of sexually explicit movies, videos, and magazines found in a garage, a basement, under the parent's bed or deep in a closet. Perhaps clients often watched their mother change her clothes or were frequently bathed with a sibling until puberty. Perhaps they were sexually abused. Money and Lamacz (1989) hypothesized that "love maps" are formed in the child's brain at an early age when they are exposed to some form of sexual or erotic experience and become "etched indelibly" throughout life. They believed that these love maps are a result of the psychosocial environment and a biological predisposition.

Gene Abel, M.D., a researcher and clinical sexologist, in a personal communication with John Wincze, Ph.D. (2000), postulated that when children are exposed to sexually explicit material or events, there are four possible ways they may react. Wincze speculates that this explains why some people who have early sexualized experiences become attached to them while others do not.

1. A child is exposed to an erotic experience either directly or indirectly. For example, the child may have been stimulated when bathed, perhaps overheard or observed a sexual event, or may have been actually sexually abused.
2. The child will then mull it over and rehearse the event in his or her mind and imagine the consequences, which could be positive or negative, or the child may feel both pleasure and anxiety about the event and its consequences.
3. The child then may actually try out the behavior and directly experience the positive and/or negative feelings and consequences.
4. Lastly, the behavior may be repeated and thus reinforced depending on the consequences; if the consequences are very negative, the behavior may not be repeated. For example, a child may be discovered masturbating and is humiliated and punished severely by a spanking or beating.

Bob was severely punished by his father when he was discovered masturbating using his father's magazines. It did not stop him from masturbating, but he no longer used magazines for images. From then on, he only masturbated using images of women he knew (his cousins or his teachers) or other women he saw when he was out and about. He masturbated in places where no one would be likely to see him and fantasized that people did see him. He was very ashamed of these fantasies and his desire to masturbate. He tried to distract himself, but eventually the need for release took over and he had an orgasm. He was puzzled that the need for release seemed greater than the pleasure of the orgasm. In spite of the shame and humiliation that came with it, he continued in this vein until he married. After he married in his late twenties, his "hidden" exhibitionism faded. He seldom masturbated at all, and when he did it was in a locked bathroom and the images were only of his wife. However, in his 40s, with stress from his job and family demands, he began to use images he found on the Internet and expanded his masturbatory preferences to women in a variety of situations.

This speaks to still another theory about the plasticity of the brain and how early sexual preferences can morph and change throughout life. Bob's changing erotic preferences, as well as those of many other clients, highlights "that the human libido is not a hardwired, invariable biological urge but can be curiously fickle, easily altered by our psychology and the history of our sexual encounters. And our libido can be finicky" (Doidge, 2007).

Some theorize that a mix of neuropsychogenic, biological, and environmental influences predisposes some people to these sexual problems (Coleman, 1995; Fedoroff, 2003; Goodman, 1998). "Sexual addiction is presented as a manifestation of altered neuro-chemistry brought about by behavioral excess. Sexual addiction, although more complex than drug addiction, is not fundamentally different" (Sunderwirt, Milkman, & Jenks, 1996). Behavioral or process addictions depend on chemicals produced by the brain (Schneider, 1994). There are no sociocultural or economic predictors. They can happen to anyone, in any culture, educated or not, rich or poor, from presidents to peddlers.

People do not wake up one day and decide to be obsessed with masturbating or some other sexual habit. It more likely starts with an isolated event that is highly erotic and escalates out of control. The pleasure of orgasm, accessing that unique bundle of nerve endings, reinforces the behavior. Clients often tell me it is the *pursuit* of arousal, the *feelings* of desire and pleasure, that become the goal, rather than the orgasm itself. More often than not it is a balm for some emotional dilemma: lack of trust, anxiety or depression, loneliness and boredom. Who of us has not experienced a highly erotic moment or extreme desire in our lifetimes? How we have pursued it, on the other hand, is another story. Feelings of desire are part of the life force. Yet those feelings of desire have the power to propel us beyond our most valued boundaries.

While the question "Why me?" still leaves us unsatisfied, we do know that the anticipation of pleasurable release and/or the orgasm itself can reinforce the desire to repeat the activity. Sam is an example. He was in his 50s and had worked hard and long at containing his desire for orgasms. When I met him, he had cultivated a technique of keeping himself in a state of anticipatory pleasure for hours while he cruised the Internet for particular combinations of men and women having group sex. He would alternate between the erotic site on the screen and the weather report, thus delaying his orgasm for a long time. After a prolonged period of arousal, he would allow himself to ejaculate. He got lost in this activity until he was fired from his job for lack of productivity. He was doing this all night and slept very little. He had a fairly good outcome from treatment, and I hadn't seen him for a few years when he called saying he needed a "booster shot." When he came to the office he said he had been able to pull back from temptation to go online again by this thought: "I began to think about how many orgasms I had managed in my lifetime, and it was overwhelming to even think about it. So then I thought, 'What's one more orgasm going to do for me?'" It was his way of keeping his habit in check, and it worked most of the time. Nevertheless, he wanted some reassurance that he was on the right track and was not going back to his old ways.

The question "Am I crazy?" requires exploration, reassurance, and warrants discussion. Clients often believe they are crazy and perverted because sexual behavior, even if private and consensual, is connected to so many condemnations, taboos, and myths. When I mention that medication might also be helpful, this question seems even more urgent and provocative. People may have had a parent, sibling, or relative who struggled with a serious mental illness and the client worries that they will be the same way. It is essential for clinicians to assess for co-existing mental health issues, socioeconomic pressures and relationship dysfunctions. For example, it would not be unusual for those with compulsive sexual habits to have multiple marriages (sometimes at the same time, sometimes serially) and divorces, multiple short-term relationships, one-night-stands, or be on the brink of bankruptcy because they are paying a great deal to prostitutes. All of these complexities are facets of hypersexuality and will become part of the treatment issues. If they are overlooked and the sexual act is isolated as the only issue, the treatment will not be effective.

Co-existing psychiatric conditions are found in a preponderance of people with compelling sexual behaviors. Studies on both men and women with compelling sexual issues have found that Axis I diagnoses are prevalent in this population (Kafka & Prentky, 1994, 1998; Kafka & Hennen, 2002). Axis I diagnoses are characterized as "co-existing clinical disorders or conditions that may be a focus of clinical attention" (DSM-IV-TR, 1994). These psychiatric conditions include "multiple lifetime comorbid mood, anxiety, psychoactive substance abuse, and/or other impulse disorder diagnoses" (Kafka, 2007).

Clients ask anxiously, "Does therapy work? What can you do?," hoping I will have the answers they want to hear. The truth is that there are effective treatments for compelling sexual behaviors. But clients and families, and perhaps employers, are often looking for a "cure." J. Paul Fedoroff, M.D. (2003) cautions, "Do not tell someone you just met that he or she is incurable. What you *can* say is that these habits are highly treatable and that people can get to a place that feels a great deal better than when they began treatment."

Truth be told, there really aren't a lot of answers to the questions David and most clients pose. Because these sexual habits are hidden, it is hard to obtain prevalent data and treatment outcome statistics (Goodman, 1998). We know that both men and women can have secret and repetitive sexual behaviors. Kafka's research reveals that the ratio is more or less five men for every one woman. The more common hypersexual habits of men are compelling and repetitive masturbation, protracted promiscuity, dependence on sexually explicit images, telephone sex dependence, passive or active sexual activity on the Internet, severe sexual incompatibility, or dependence on having a relationship (often referred to as "love addiction").

Kafka (2007) also points out that women tend to be involved more in "compulsive masturbation, protracted promiscuity (including prostitution), severe sexual desire incompatibility, and the paraphilia sexual masochism." In addition, women also tend to have acute attachment issues resulting in dependency on relationships with men, commonly called "love addiction" and also have "obsessional fixations" and "crushes" (Hollender & Callahan, 1975; Carnes, 1991; Coleman, 1992; Goldstein & Laskin, 2002). Researchers continue to dissect these behaviors and try to find answers. This has resulted in a growing body of information to guide clinicians.

It is helpful to clients just to know that there are others with their problems and that researchers are working on them. It speaks to the isolation that people experience when they have secret lives. Many of my clients are very surprised to find that others have the same issues. Sissela Bok (1983) made these observations about secrecy: "how it is used to oppress and exclude; what can befall those who come too close to secrets they were not meant to share; and the price of betrayal." I'm not sure I believe in hell, but I often think that it must be something like what we experience when we yearn for answers when there are none: Why did I get cancer? Why doesn't my husband love me? Why can't I stop cheating on my wife? "Hell is made up of yearnings. They don't roast on a bed of nails; they sit on comfortable chairs and are tortured by yearnings" (Singer, 1979). To get back to David, he was sure that no one, particularly Anne or I, could possibly understand what he was going through. He tried to describe what it was like when he was in the grip of his erotic desire. He wanted me to understand that his secrets have been a constant source of both great anxiety and great pleasure, and also, in a strange way, that they served as protection from many things. He asked: "Can you really understand how *compelling* this is for me?" I had to acquiesce that David was correct. The reality is that there is only so far each of us can go in truly understanding the other's experience. Because I've never had a broken leg, for instance, or prostate cancer, it is not be possible for me to really understand what it feels like. As a female, I cannot really experience what it is like to be a male and vice versa. When a husband or wife hurls the charge "you don't understand me!" at their spouse, they often are correct. However, it should not prevent us from listening, *trying* to understand, and regarding it as an opportunity to do what we can: be supportive, bring a cup of tea, or get a footstool for the broken leg.

Kay Jamison, Ph.D., describes what it is to have a life apart— one filled with thoughts, feelings, and images that uncontrollably flood her head— and to know others do not have any sense of what it is like. This description mirrors the experience of people who have secret sexual lives.

> Understanding at an abstract level does not necessarily translate into an understanding at a day-to-day level. I have become fundamentally and deeply skeptical that anyone who does not have this illness can truly understand it. And, ultimately, it is probably unreasonable to expect the kind of acceptance of it that one so desperately desires. It is not an illness that lends itself to empathy. (Jamison, 1996)

I told David, as I do all my clients, that what I *can* offer with confidence is the perspective of many years of working with clients who have had these dilemmas. It helps to share this perspective. I know that people can survive therapy and learn to manage their sexuality in ways that serve them better and help them lead more contented lives. I acknowledge that treatment is difficult at times, but people find the struggle worth it. I asked David who he most wanted to understand him. He answered quickly and with certainty: his father first, Anne second. Later we would explore just how much his father misunderstood him. We discovered why it was easy for him to expect that no one would take the time to try to understand him. He was grateful to know that others have shared their secrets and survived. It sure keeps me coming back to the office!

THE THERAPIST ASKS QUESTIONS

But what about the questions I wanted to ask? I am a firm believer that I have to earn the right to ask personal questions. It probably began when my parents tried to impress upon me that I should *never* ask personal questions. I obviously had to get over that dictum in order to become a therapist, but some of it still floats around. Being a therapist requires that we ask personal questions that are relevant and germane to our work. Contextualizing the questions that I may ask David or any of my clients is important. Asking questions (or not asking the right ones) can evoke or repeat traumas or result in harmful experiences for many clients. So it is important to give the person a reason why I might want to ask certain kinds of questions about intimate sexual matters and private behaviors.

The obvious reason, of course, is that I want to make sure I have all the information I need to make the right plan for treatment (Kafka, 2007). But you never know what emotional landmine you might step on even when you think you are on safe territory. Before I launch into a formal assessment, I also talk about the issues of boundaries and privacy, and about how difficult it may be to answer my questions about intimate thoughts, feelings, and behaviors. It would not be unusual that my client has had her or his boundaries violated at some time in their lives, so I acknowledge how embarrassing and perhaps frightening it may be to talk to me about such issues. After all, I am virtually a stranger at this point. It is also likely that the person has never had a nonjudgmental and frank conversation about sexual matters. For instance, I might want to know about my client's relationship with a spouse, lover or partner; sexual performance or preferences; masturbatory habits; or fears and anxieties that have never seen the light of day. By taking the time to discuss the context and rationale for questions, I can provide a safer environment.

A bridge of trust is more easily built when the questions the therapist asks seem relevant and appropriate. It is also better to explore the specifics of sexual behaviors within the context of the person's life story rather than isolate them. Sex does not exist in a vacuum. As we begin to contextualize these sexual behaviors, construct some meaning for them, and get some perspective on them, I can see something shift, although it is almost imperceptible at first. My clients begin to see their sexual behavior as something they do but not necessarily as something that *defines* them. This is a good moment for both of us. I generally point out that sex intrinsically is not a moral issue. If it works well, it fits into life like everything else: work, play, eating, etc. But if sex does not work right, it takes up a lot of space in your head and becomes all you can think of. One of our goals in therapy is to depathologize sex intrapersonally—to disconnect it from shame and disgust—and then integrate sex into clients' lives as a safe and joyful behavior.

ANOTHER WORD ABOUT LABELS

Janis Abrahms Spring, Ph.D., author of *After the Affair: Healing the Pain and Rebuilding Trust When a Partner Has Been Unfaithful* (1996), and I share the same sensibility about labels. Spring takes care to not "categorize partners as *betrayed* or *betrayer* because these words convey a certain moral righteousness or condemnation, and put the burden of responsibility on one partner alone, which is almost never the case." I also don't like the label survivor because it is used in another context that I do not want to trivialize and has a personal valence for me. The labels *coaddict* and *codependency*, used in addiction literature, are not satisfactory either. They resonate with illness and blame and are not accurate in many situations. So I use wife, husband, partner, lover, and Spring's personal favorites: hurt and unfaithful. My strongest personal bias is the label of victim. I always cringe inside when I hear clients call themselves victims. The term conveys a passive and powerless acceptance of a particular self-image that I believe is destructive. Nevertheless, it is important for the therapist to explore what the label means to the client, learn about the roots of this self-attribution, and understand its meaning. The client is always the expert on his or her own feelings.

HONESTY IS THE BEST POLICY, BUT ...

Clients generally enter therapy wanting to be honest and effect changes. Nevertheless, ambivalence reigns, and the move toward honesty is slow and cautious. My therapist once said to me: "Honesty is the best policy; it's just not always a good idea." I have always believed this and have seen its wisdom in my own life, as well as in the lives of those who have come to my office. It is always appropriate (if not downright virtuous) to consider how and why we use honesty and attempt to predict its consequences.

Honesty is not an absolute. Some of the time, honesty is not appropriate, like expressing that you don't like someone's new haircut, which they think is wonderful. It can also be dangerous at times. In the therapeutic relationship, we move inexorably and mindfully toward honesty and accountability. But first we have to fully understand what honesty means and how we use it. This particularly becomes an issue when there is a spouse who has been deceived and feels betrayed. Mark Lasser, Ph.D. (1996) observes that while everyone's goal is openness and honesty, the problematic partner often believes: "'The person I'm most afraid of losing will be the person I'm the least likely to tell the truth to about myself.' A coaddict of any nature conversely often believes: 'If my partner loved me, he or she would tell me the truth.' These two beliefs work against each other to convince both partners in a relationship that they don't really love each other. Dishonesty and blaming are the typical results."

In Chapter 9, I will expand on how to handle the asking and answering of questions when there has been a deception in the relationship. Clients often ask how or if they should answer these seemingly never-ending questions. A spouse may believe they have a right to know every detail and yet the details may be even more damaging to the situation depending on the the context of the behaviors and the relationship. It is a Catch-22 for everyone and a damned if you do, damned if you don't situation. Eventually it can be worked out, but it is rare that everyone is satisfied with the resolution. Even years later, longed-for details and the need for answers can still churn and agitate. In every relationship, even a very good one, some things are better left unsaid. Maybe that is why the relationship is good. "You wonder about a conversation with nothing concealed—its real name is hell, I believe" (Yalom, 1993).

It is a difficult time in a person's life when something important feels as if it is being taken away rather than changed, especially sexuality. I attempt to reassure my clients: "You will still have a sex life. You can still have sexual feelings, but they will not be fraught with fear and anxiety." The look on their faces often prompts me to say, "I know this is one of those 'easy-for-*you*-to-say' moments." We are trying to trust one another. This first experience with transparency is a time to keep things simple, not to overwhelm. I point out that managing transparency and its attendant discomfort is like learning a new skill. You find a teacher, show up for class, do your homework, pay tuition, and you will end up with a new competency. Together we will try to understand what it will be like, on a day-to-day basis, to deal with the secrets, what it's like to show up, work the program, get honest, and become accountable to yourself and others. This is very tough stuff.

"You really made me think," David said with his hand on the doorknob. The session had ended, and he was actually smiling at me. I would learn that this was a rare gift from David. He would struggle, but eventually he left his secret garden behind. Anne stayed with him for the journey.

Chapter 2

Denial

The silent dialogue

Don't surrender your loneliness
So quickly.
Let it cut more deep.

Let it ferment and season you
As few human
Or even divine ingredients can.

Hafiz

The initial giving up of secrets, and the sense of relief it can bring, can quickly become an illusion. It reminds me of the wisps of mist on a lake in early morning, ghosts caught late at their nocturnal revels. I am held by this glimpse, but it quickly disappears with the light. Transparency is an illusion. If transparency is as far as we can get, then the person, family, community, and even the therapist can be fooled into thinking it is all that is needed. But it is just the beginning.

WORKING THE DEFENSES

When a crisis precipitates a visit to my office, the client and I begin by attempting to contain the resulting chaos. This generally leaves people feeling better for the moment. The secrets, at least some of them, are on the table. The families, and perhaps the community, are happy that "something is being done about this." Maybe it doesn't happen with the flash and the flair it does in Hollywood representations of the therapeutic process, with the attendant and ubiquitous promise of a peaceful and permanent resolution, but the impression given is that help is definitely on its way. However, the individual with sexual secrets may not be at all happy. Most likely he or she will be holding back some of the secrets and promise to stop the behaviors that have been revealed. Most people's defenses are too well ingrained for them to be true to their promises or be completely honest. The road to hell is paved with good intentions. There will be a mighty struggle between intentions and reality, between the transparent and opaque.

The psyche reflexively defends itself when it feels under attack. Most people instinctively run for cover when they feel emotionally exposed. The inclination to stay behind the garden wall is powerful. The sexual behavior is *in itself* a defense against well-entrenched emotional pain that accompanies feelings of self-loathing, worthlessness, inadequacy, loneliness, and rejection; the list is long and varied. Hopefully, the trajectory of therapy will help people "become conscious of their methods of bolstering falsehoods, and they [will] delude themselves less. Denial thrives in the darkness, and we wanted all the light we could get" (Weinberg, 1998). For many of my clients, sex has become a "method of bolstering the falsehoods." Denial is the mother of resistance.

Therapists and clients alike find that talking about sex is not an easy task. Our mutual inclination to deny sexual feelings appears early in our lives. While boys have erections beginning in utero and when girls discover their genitals it feels good, but the average parent provides a "don't ask, don't tell" model during childhood. So we grow up keeping the secret of how sexual and pleasurable our body can feel to us. When parents convey this neutral or negative message, sexual feelings and emotions become cut off from the self and thus are experienced during childhood as repressed, dirty, denied, and shameful (Winnicott, 1975; Kohut, 1997).

Most parents do not let on what happens behind their bedroom door or engage in displays of affection in front of the children. They may limit kisses to a peck on the cheek. In early childhood, the average parent transmits a sex-negative message without even being aware of it. If you ask clients about how they received the message that sex was not a topic for conversation, they are likely to answer with a shrug: "I don't know how I knew not to talk about sex; I just *knew* it!" Parents, well-intentioned though they may be, believe they have to protect their children from things sexual and to some degree this is not a bad thing. It is good to promote privacy and boundaries around the body and not have an overly sexualized atmosphere in the house. Too much information too soon can be overwhelming for children, as we will see further on.

On the other hand, it can be confusing when a child's body has pleasurable feelings that are denied and not talked about. The confusion is compounded when we are told, "Don't feel it now, wait until you are grown up!" In the same vein, it doesn't help when parents are seen arguing and saying hurtful, angry things to one another and the child who feels anger is forbidden to express it. When sex is forbidden, its erotic valence is often enhanced. This joining of sex and secrecy, of the forbidden and hidden, can be carried into adult life and has the potential to develop into compelling and secret sexual behaviors. And the mixed messages about expressing affection and mood can lead to a lifetime of relational difficulties. These days children's lives are also filled with confusing and over-sexualized messages from the media and computers. "Mommy, what's the matter with Janet Jackson's breast?"

Thus, therapists as well as clients must overcome sex-negative childhood experiences, models, or judgments. Therapists may have difficulty listening respectfully and nonjudgmentally to their clients describe a highly sexualized life acted out in distressing ways. Therapists must be aware of what they have incorporated from their own early childhood experiences, sexual biases, cultural attitudes, and judgments. For our clients with exaggerated expressions of sexual behaviors, it is not a matter of just ending the behavior but unraveling and healing a well-ingrained, confused, and negative sense of the self in relation to sexuality—tantamount to unraveling a Gordian knot.

Defenses take many forms, not all necessarily bad. The defenses our clients use are complex and informative. They serve many purposes, including keeping a person safe from feelings that are too painful. Some examples of defense mechanisms are denial, displacement, projection, sublimation, rationalization, fantasy, repression/suppression, intellectualization, withdrawal, and reaction formation. This is not an exhaustive list, but it is important to be on the lookout for them because defenses point the way to the pain. Anna Freud (1966) talked about "denial in the service of the ego," a psychic mechanism that serves to protect the self from many painful states. For example, denial may help us move through life while experiencing a serious illness or knowing that eventually we will die. Most of us are not paralyzed by the thought that we will die, we simply live with it. Perhaps this kind of denial protects the self from chronic and deep despair.

Charley's defenses

Charley had chronic and painful anxiety about women. His mother abandoned him when he was three years old. He had been raised by his father. He could not figure out how to talk with women and believed they would invariably reject and abandon him. He used telephone sex as a substitute for actually being with women. On the phone, he could fantasize about their loving and wanting him. The pain would go away, at least for a short time. He carefully guarded himself against the pain of rejection in all his encounters and was unwilling to take any social risks. One goal of therapy with Charley was to help him make the connection between the feelings behind his urge for sexual release and the resulting sexual behavior. Simply put, defense mechanisms are called into service to keep a person emotionally safe by burying affect. "Don't trust, therefore don't get hurt" or "Don't get mad, they won't like you, they'll reject you." Therapy is an attempt to confront and understand the meaning of the defenses used to protect a person from fears, urges, and needs—to help the client take charge of them rather than be controlled by them.

> Painful affects are not only painful; they are also meaningful, and their painful aspects are arrows that direct our attention toward their meanings. Getting rid of an important signal because our experience of it is uncomfortable is like shutting off the fire alarm because it makes an ugly sound. We do better in the long run to find the fire, address the fire directly, determine how the fire started, and then take steps to decrease the likelihood of another fire. (Goodman, 1998)

Denial begets resistance. When sexual secrets are uncovered, there is a scramble to cover up, make excuses, blame others, find fault, and deny accusations. Resistance to change is acted out in many ways. In the face of condemnation and dire consequences, people sometimes turn their feelings outward and blame circumstances and/or other people for their trouble. This is resistance against looking inside for answers to self-made dilemmas. An example of the resistance to therapy is when a client gets sidetracked blaming others. They sound something like this: "She won't have sex with me as much as I need to have it. My lover doesn't satisfy my needs even if I ask him. My boss pressures me too much. An affair will save my marriage because I will stop pressuring my husband for sex. My wife is pregnant and I need sex all the time; she won't give it to me. My sister abused me. It's just sex; I love my husband! It doesn't hurt any one if I fool around with people on line." "Just looking at pictures once in a while is not being unfaithful." "*She* seduced me; why do *I* get the blame?" "Men need sex more than women." "I am under so much stress; orgasms relieve the pressure. I can't help myself when women/men come on to me." There is some truth to many of these beliefs. Stress, boredom, and just plain being aroused and wanting sex may indeed be feelings that accompany many sexual encounters. However, not every man who has a pregnant wife will seek multiple anonymous sexual encounters. Perhaps someone may be reenacting a trauma of childhood rape or sexual abuse as a child when they engage in repeated and risky anonymous sex. What I hear from these distortions of reason, or what we call rationalizations, is the fear that I might try to take away the client's sex life, leaving him or her without an antidote for a troubled life. Where would they hide? How would they keep themselves safe?

Although my clients have lived in fear of being discovered, most people like to believe that their secrets are well hidden and no one knows about them. It is possible to have sexual secrets over a lifetime without anyone discovering them. Remember the cross-dresser whose wife discovered his habit when he died? More likely, family members will tell me that they have either known specifically what the client was doing or had a good idea about it for a long time.

I also know that children resonate with what is going on in the household even if cognitively they are not old enough to understand exactly what is happening. We often do not give children credit for their observational skills. Think about holding an infant who begins to cry when you become frightened or anxious about something. Children seldom miss anything going on around them (Cottle, 1980). They may not have fully understood the sexual behavior they might have experienced or observed or the sexual material they found. Nevertheless, in hindsight they may remember that they had experiences as children that did not serve them well and were harmful. Their bodies registered something for better or worse, or perhaps both. "There can be no secrets in a house where there are children" (Setterfield, 2006).

THE SILENT DIALOGUE

Listening to the message behind the message is at the heart of therapy. Both verbal and nonverbal communications are equally important.

Sometimes a person's behavior tells me a great deal more about what they are feeling than what is actually said. Actions really do speak louder than words. Ashley and I had worked together for about a month. She was an attractive, intelligent young woman of 29 and wanted to have a relationship, to get married, and to have children. For the first few weeks of our relationship I watched Ashley as she moved around the couch restlessly during sessions. It was very difficult for her to put words to her feelings. No one had ever asked her how she felt and the vocabulary of affect was foreign to her. We struggled with this until one day I asked her to tell me how she felt every time she had an impulse to move on the couch. She was taken aback that I noticed she was "squirming." I said, "How could I help but notice such restlessness? What do you suppose it means?" Ashley was surprised that anyone noticed what she did and equally amazed that I cared enough to ask. She began to put words to her discomfort and became less anxious.

During these first few weeks, Ashley was also often late for her appointments. I asked her how she felt about being late each time. What did it mean? She told me that although I had not yet judged her behavior, she was still really anxious about what I thought about her. She also said she was ambivalent about therapy. She couldn't understand why I did *not* become upset and critical and did not know how to handle it.

Ashley had an abusive, alcoholic father who would unpredictably fly into a rage about inconsequential things, which left her living life on the defensive, expecting criticism from most adults. My lack of criticism or anger was foreign, discomfiting, and anxiety producing. She was surprised when she realized that she had been bracing for abuse and criticism for many years. Sadly, Ashley told me, "I am so rotten that it doesn't matter what I do; people are always angry with me." She eventually was able to understand how her feelings about herself, which had originated with her father, had been projected or experienced as coming not only from me but from others as well.

Ashley had many sex partners, but when any of them wanted a relationship, she was gone. She expected rejection and believed that no one really wanted her, so she rejected others before she could be abandoned. She also felt she was very bad, a "slut" who had sex with anyone who asked her. Eventually, she was able to make sense of her feelings and understand the meaning of her actions. She stayed the course and remained in treatment long enough to learn how to trust herself and others. Unconsciously, she had been trying to keep herself safe from rejection. It did not get her where she needed to go. I told her it reminded me of Groucho Marx saying, "What kind of a club is this that wants *me* for a member?" She was too young to know about Groucho, but she identified with the sentiment. We discovered the meaning of her defensive tactics and the silent conversation she was having with me and everyone else in her life. In the end, Ashley tuned in and turned off the old tapes—well, most of the time.

DOES THERAPY WORK?

Clients, as well as their families, often ask: "Does therapy work? How does it work? How long will therapy take?" It's another way of saying: "I am anxious to get this over with," and "When will I feel better?" There aren't many answers to these questions, but we talk about their meaning and validate the anxiety behind the question. As we move along, I often check in with my client: "How are we doing? How does therapy feel to you? Is it getting you where you want to go?" We often take time to look back and see what has happened, to take note of how things have changed (or not changed) since we began this work. It is good when we can see that we have come closer to the goal. There's no telling how far we can go in the future. Yet the ambivalence about being in therapy always surfaces. There is always a tug of war between the "forces that are striving toward recovery and the opposing ones" (Freud, 1912).

During the beginning stage of therapy, while slipping back and forth between secrets and openness, we need to accomplish many tasks. "Resistance is inevitable in all therapy" (Cooper & Marcus, 2003), and it gets acted out with the therapist in much the same way a client has acted out in other relationships. At this tender time, I am figuring out how to join with this person, how to engage us in the work. I am listening not only to what is said but also to what is not being said. At the same time, I am attempting to foster openness and honesty, to leave denial behind. What is the meaning of this behavior? What is it telling us? The client is getting accustomed to being "in treatment," trying to get used to me and the very idea that life as they knew it has changed. It is no small task for people to develop a relationship with me when they have avoided closeness and intimacy all their lives. It is very difficult to learn to be open and honest, to identify and share feelings. But it is the essence of the work, the key to real growth and change. We must learn to dance together, in and out of denial and its attendant resistance, until we finally get the steps in synch.

Silent dialogues, like Ashley's restlessness or lateness for appointments, point the way to feelings. They "direct our attention to their meaning" (Goodman, 1998). Janice's husband could not understand why she never wanted him to hold her hand and frequently shook off his touch. She had been brutally raped when she was a teenager and always needed to be in control of anything that seemed potentially constraining or intimate. Her husband was finally able to understand this and stopped criticizing her for it. Equally important, he was also able to understand that it was not a rejection of him. Janice was keeping herself safe. Aware of the message, he was able to heed the silent request and be supportive and protective. They were able to use this nonverbal conversation as a springboard to negotiate a better verbal one. We can learn a great deal by connecting the dots between behaviors and feelings. Feelings are facts, verbally or nonverbally expressed. They are not to be debated or doubted, just heard and acknowledged.

We instinctively protect our secrets. It serves the psyche in many ways to remain hidden. Mostly it serves to protect ourselves from being hurt. The therapist may see eyes well up with tears while the person keeps talking. I will interrupt and ask about the tears. Even if the person is not ready to talk about the tears, at least I have not trivialized them by ignoring them. These tears are pointing the way to the pain. The therapist needs to take into account the details of the therapeutic hour—tears, lateness, squirming in the chair, playing the entertaining client rather than the working client. These are the details of resistance, ambivalence, and pain. "Details are wonderful. They are informative, they are calming, and they penetrate the anxiety of isolation: the patient feels that, once you have the details, you have entered into his life" (Yalom, 1989).

I often find myself asking questions that have never been asked before. Sometimes the answers have never been considered or explored. Quite often clients express great relief when we enter that lonely, isolated place of forbidden behavior, giving it light and recognition and not judging it. "How did you know that about me? Do you know others who do that, too?" At these moments, I feel that I have indeed entered a life. At the very least, I respectfully accept what I hear, and perhaps it will pave the way for my client to accept that part of themselves, as well. We will move together from judging, humiliation, shame, and guilt to a different place. On those days when I feel I have "penetrated the isolation" and connected with my client, I feel glad I have chosen to be a therapist.

Resistance comes in many guises: Lloyd and Mary Jane

When someone calls for an appointment, presumably for an evaluation, and perhaps treatment, I typically ask, "How can I be helpful?" I hope to get some clues about what I will be signing up for. The answers are many and varied. Some may tell me that their marriage is not working, that they have "fallen out of love" with their spouses or partners. Or, perhaps they tell me that they don't want to have sex with their spouse any more. Maybe they are depressed because they have lost their job, cannot have orgasms, ejaculate too soon, or are anxious all the time and cannot sleep. I have observed that many of these problems coexist with sex in the "too-much" category.

Depression and anxiety are ubiquitously combined with compelling sexual issues and are often believed to be the only "cause" of the sexual behaviors. Just fix the depression and all will be well. On the other hand, I also see people who want me to pay attention solely to the sexual issues and nothing else in their lives. I really wish it were that simple. Sexual issues are more complex than that and do not exist in isolation. In 1900, Havelock Ellis observed that "Sex lies at the root of life and we can never learn to reverence life until we know how to understand sex."

There is no denying that sex is central to our lives. Being opaque may offer a fragile and ephemeral comfort, but the secrets resonate around the edges of our conversations, and I begin to get glimpses of them even on the telephone. Take Lloyd, for example. He called me to request marital counseling. When I returned Lloyd's telephone call, both Lloyd and his wife, Mary Jane, got on the telephone. He explained that he had been depressed for a long time and had been treated for the past year by both a psychiatrist for medication and a psychotherapist for the issues involving his depression. He was not getting any better. Mary Jane confirmed this, although she said almost nothing during the phone call. The plan we agreed on was that I would see each of them in an individual session, then the three of us would meet for feedback and to develop a treatment plan. Lloyd was quite insistent that he come in first, which for me was a clue that maybe there was more to this than merely help with depression.

Lloyd appeared on time for his appointment. He was a tall thin man in jeans, a flannel shirt, and heavy work boots. His pale, drawn face was long and narrow, with sad dark eyes. His hair was long and scraggly. He was a little scary looking and had an air of great intensity about him. I felt somewhat anxious about his intensity: Where would it lead us? When I asked him to tell me about his depression and the choice for couple work, he told me he was very angry because his wife had insisted they begin marriage counseling. He did not like being controlled by his wife, but he feared a divorce even more. His twin boys were eight years old, and he did not want to be separated from them. Lloyd was emphatic that he did not want or need marriage counseling. He loved his wife very much, but she did not understand his struggle with depression. I definitely got the message that he did not want to be here.

When I asked him to tell me something about the development of his depression, he suddenly spilled out his sexual secrets as if they were hot rocks—burning, distasteful, and painful. Self-loathing and anger was heavy in the room. Defensively, he described the event that brought him to my door. He had a "fling" with a woman, just one night, and his wife found out. When I asked how his wife found out about it, he said she questioned where he had been after work and caught him in a lie. He "blurted out" where he had really been. He did not mean to tell her; it just came out. Hmmm!

It is usually helpful and interesting to learn how a spouse or partner finds out about extra-relational sex. It is a good question to pursue. I can get a sense of how badly a client wants to be dis-covered, at least unconsciously but perhaps consciously. In this case Lloyd was on the edge, and I believe he wanted Mary Jane to know about his activities. He knew he was out of control, and per-haps thought her threat of divorce would help him stop his sexual behaviors. It may also be that while he *said* he did not want a divorce, he really wanted his wife to throw him out, start divorce proceedings, and give him his freedom to have sex without guilt—to be rejected rather than having to do the rejecting. This agenda is not uncommon.

Lloyd was wrestling with an interesting paradox: He was angry with his wife for controlling him, but at the same time he was very frightened that he was out of control. He rationalized to her that if he had an occasional "fling," it might save their marriage because they argued about sex all the time. He wanted it frequently, and she did not. "How frequently?" I asked. He looked away with an expression of disgust on his face. After a moment, he said, angrily, "Every day or every other day." Without a pause, he then told me that he masturbated two or three times a day to fantasies of exhibiting himself. The women in his fantasy were very sexy and seemed to beckon him. While he said he had never actually acted upon this fantasy, it was highly erotic and tempting. He had recently begun to put nude pictures of himself on the Internet in various "sexually suggestive" positions.

I became the first person with whom he had ever shared his secrets. He had never discussed his sexual thoughts or any information about his sex life with either his previous therapist or with his psychiatrist. He did not want anyone to know what his sexual issues were and, most of all, he wanted Mary Jane to believe he was depressed.

Lloyd was certainly depressed and very anxious. My antennae were receiving danger signals. Why had he so readily spilled out his secrets to me in the first session but not to his individual therapist or his psychiatrist? It was not surprising that he was not getting much relief from his problems. After all, the focus of his treatment had been tailored for depression, and his sexual issues had not been revealed or discussed. On top of the vulnerability I was feeling from this "dark" and intense man, I became nervous about how fast and furious the secrets were given to me, although by this time Mary Jane knew some of his secrets and maybe he felt he had nothing more to lose. Maybe he was throwing himself at the mercy of the court? Maybe it was a "Hail Mary" pass? Perhaps a last ditch effort to save what he could of the marriage? Nevertheless, I wondered how he had managed his individual therapy so that his secrets remained hidden. Was he lying to his therapist? Had she not asked him about his sexual issues? Would I be able to reach him when no one else had been able to?

I listened attentively and nonjudgmentally. My sense of vulnerability faded and I felt more open to him. He "steam rolled" the conversation by telling me how he would not see the woman ever again; he had stopped going online for about a month. He met Shannon in a chat room and then at a hotel. It was clear to me that he was feeling trapped. He was frightened and needed to relieve himself of his burden, but I am not sure he wanted to go any further than unburdening himself. He needed to convince himself that he would never do these things again. It is wise to remember that the template for relationships with others is likely to be the template for the client's relationship with the therapist as well. I wondered how Mary Jane felt about him. What was Lloyd's agenda really? Did he hope I would reject him if he told me all? If so, he would not have to see me anymore. It could be an easy way out for him.

When he paused and looked at me, I acknowledged that he did indeed have a difficult dilemma and that the depression compounded it. He shrugged his shoulders and did not reply. I sat quietly for a while, giving us both a breather from the intensity. After a moment, I asked Lloyd what he hoped for in his relationship with Mary Jane. He said again he clearly did not want counseling because he did not want Mary Jane to know about his Internet activity. It was just about the end of the session. I said, "It must have been a burden to live with all those secrets and now to feel so exposed." I suggested that perhaps it would be better if he and I talked some more about what he wanted for himself before we signed up for marriage counseling. I offered him another appointment later in the week. He was silent.

Finally, Lloyd looked up at me with tears in his eyes and said, "Mary Jane's father is a minister. She grew up with moral imperatives that fill up all my breathing space. I am suffocating." I acknowledged how difficult this was and how sad he must feel. Lloyd looked away and talked as if he was alone in the room. I felt as though I was behind a screen or invisible to him. I resonated with his religious image. It brought to mind the screen in the confessional booth. But in the confessional booth both the listener and the confessant are unknown to each other. In a confessional the listener could give absolution. It occurred to me that he did not want help; he wanted absolution. He did not make another appointment. Mary Jane did not keep her appointment either, and they did not call. It was all too frightening and they took cover. Transparent 1; Opaque 2.

After each meeting, I reflect on the session, write notes to myself, and try to figure out what happened. Lloyd's self-loathing was so great. How could he let me get close if he disliked himself so much? His father-in-law was too powerful and present in their lives. Lloyd needed me (and his wife and her parents) behind the screen. He would only confess what he wanted us to know. I reviewed his behaviors: He was masturbating two to three times a day, he had escalated to sending nude pictures of himself to Internet chat rooms, and he had never told anyone, not even his therapist. I could empathize with how desperate and cornered he felt. I also wondered whether he was exhibiting himself, even obliquely, to others off-line. Did he leave the bathroom door unlocked, or partially opened? Is it true that no one had ever seen him?

I also wished I could have met Mary Jane and heard her experience of the marriage. The family dynamics, in this instance with her father, seemed to be an important piece of the problem. I speculated that perhaps Mary Jane might have been colluding in the situation in some way. I also wondered about the impact of growing up in a house where there were so many "moral imperatives." Spouses may find ways to collude in the sexual behavior just to keep the peace. Lloyd was not ready to leave his secret garden. He was used to the role of depression; it was a good cover. Now that he had entered the world of the Internet, I wondered if he might be "kicked out" of his secret places if Mary Jane discovered what he was doing. Or, if he was doing something illegal on the Internet, perhaps the computer police would find out. There are no secret places on the Internet. Anonymity is an illusion. I hoped they would return someday before it was too late.

What happened with Lloyd is not unusual. In spite of his many attempts to control his own behavior, his ambivalence and fears were too overwhelming. During the establishment of a good working alliance with each client, ambivalence, anxiety, fear, and denial prevail, sometimes even mine. They have a power and rationale all their own. Exposed and vulnerable, many will act out these feelings by being late, by not showing up for appointments, forgetting their checkbook or by chronically canceling and disappearing for a while. It is part of what you sign up for when you choose this work. Patience can be its own reward.

Rose and Larry

A colleague of mine had suggested to Rose that she might benefit from individual therapy. She had been in recovery from alcohol for many years. She and her husband Larry had been doing some half-hearted couple therapy for a few months but Larry was very resistant. He claimed he could honor his promise never to be unfaithful again, so why have therapy? He did not want to be involved.

Rose, however, thought that if she could get some therapy, Larry might eventually be willing to attend some sessions. She felt that therapy would be helpful, not necessarily because Larry had been unfaithful, but rather to improve their sexual relationship and emotional intimacy. He had difficulty being open with her about his thoughts, and he resented her frequent attempts to have dialogues about their relationship. Rose felt that she should improve her sexual response so she could "keep Larry at home." They had been married for four years. It was her second marriage and his fifth. There were no children. Shortly after marrying Rose, Larry began to look for sexual partners on the Internet and was caught when she discovered a note on the computer to him from one of the women. He wanted no part of therapy; he had promised to be faithful forever more; he "had things under control." Rose believed Larry was now faithful to her.

Rose was an attractive, intelligent, and well-educated 58-year-old woman. Through her eyes I saw a 60-year-old man who liked to flirt, who enjoyed socializing and drinking, and who was a free spirit. He was also a hard-core narcissist. He liked to meet his buddies after work at a local pub and would dance with whomever happened to come his way. Rose and Larry had a deal that he would not drink and drive. He already had one DWI, and if he had another he would lose his driver's license. He depended upon friends or taxis to bring him home. Rose was shy and rather straight-laced, and did not particularly like to socialize. She had a Ph.D. in research sociology, but to fill her time while Larry was away consulting she had a part-time job with the state police. Rose liked the structure of an easy part-time job that did not demand much from her. Always the sociologist, she observed the world from her desk.

Larry was obsessively perfectionistic, demanding, and controlling, which drove her to distraction. It was constant work for her to not react to some of his obsessive demands, to see them as *his* problem, and not get enmeshed with him at those times. Years in an AA program had tutored her in this strategy, and she did it fairly well. She told me several times that she would never tolerate another infidelity. Each time she mentioned it, I felt she was trying to bolster her own resolve. She was ambivalent about the marriage. Nevertheless, at this age she no longer enjoyed being alone, and married Larry shortly after they met. She was happy to have a partner in life after 14 years of being single. On the other hand, she sometimes felt it might be a relief to live without his obsessive and narcissistic personality to say nothing of her anxiety about his fidelity!

It was while Rose was describing Larry's lifetime behavior of predatory sex that I made what turned out to be a tactical error. Larry had called his habit a "sexual compulsion" and constantly minimized its impact on his and everyone else's life. Rose was struggling to understand just what "sexual compulsivity" meant. She knew I specialized in sexuality and had a lot of questions for me. Could he keep his promise never to do it again? Could this really get better or be "cured?" Was it interfering with his ability to be emotionally intimate? Should he get specialized treatment or go to a group? Since she had struggled with alcohol addiction and had wrestled it to the ground, I borrowed some analogies from the addiction model, thinking it might help her to understand what was happening and answer some of her questions about his sexual activities (oh, those unconscious motives). I emphasized that the analogy was convenient although not completely accurate, and it was important to understand that sex and alcohol had different underlying reinforcers and motivators. Unknown to me, Rose leaped on the analogy, translated Larry's problem into a sex addiction, and took it straight home with her. In hindsight, I suspect she was delighted that she had discovered that he was an addict too! Now she had some ammunition when he badgered her about her history of alcoholism, which he did whenever she wanted to be closer to him and have some emotional intimacy. It was an effective maneuver to distance himself from Rose.

It did not take long for Larry to call for an appointment. He wanted in on the action. Rose and I had discussed this as a possibility, although by this time we had established an alliance for individual therapy. I agreed to see him for a one-time meeting and then have a joint session with Rose for some feedback. Perhaps I could help facilitate getting some more couple therapy. I am generally an optimist, but in this instance, my ego got in the way when I thought I could get Larry to invest in couple work when my colleague could not. I was scheduled to see Rose again before I saw him, which would give us a chance to discuss more fully how she felt about my upcoming meeting with him.

It was at that meeting that I learned from Rose that she had used the term *sex addict* with Larry and how he felt about being labeled that way. I gave some thought to how I had cavalierly thrown out this somewhat hostile label to a man I had never met. Rose told me that he had become very angry with both of us. We talked about how this felt. She wanted me to know how Larry behaved. I knew I would have my work cut out for me when I met Larry. Imagine the hubris of some therapist hanging a label on him before even meeting him? He would show me who is boss! I also knew Rose was counting on me to wrestle him down to size and to help her manage her difficult husband. This would not be easy.

Larry strode into my office. He was a tall, imposing man whose sense of himself took up all the space in the room. He was angry and eager to win a fight with me. He was a man used to getting his way in all matters. Looking down at me from his imposing height, he put me down by reminding me I did not have a Ph.D., obliquely threatened me with malpractice, and dropped all the names of the people he knew in my field that he would call about me. Then he sat down.

I know therapists are supposed to be nonjudgmental, but then therapists are human beings, all legends aside. While being non-judgmental is a prevailing ethic that I can maintain without too much effort, on those occasions I lose it, I ask myself why. I had to try very hard to maintain an open, patient stance with Larry, not to get defensive or enmeshed in his anger. I experienced what Rose struggled with every day; it was difficult, without a doubt. I was hoping to salvage something, right the wrong, and be help-ful. I apologized and acknowledged that the term *sex addict* has a negative connotation for many people. Furthermore, I commented that I felt it was not a completely accurate description of many sexual behaviors. He responded that he called himself sexually compulsive. How dare I, merely a social worker, label him, espe-cially before I even knew him? Suddenly, I heard my Uncle Morty's voice murmuring in my ear: "If it smells like a herring, looks like a herring, tastes like a herring ... it's a herring!"

I took the heat and listened. When I could, I asked a few ques-tions. I had only a few chances, and was, truth be told, feeling a little intimidated and annoyed at myself for making this mistake. Larry was used to seducing women easily. But his hostility toward women was visible as he spoke; it belied his ambivalence about them. He was here to give me a thumbnail sketch of his history and tell me the facts of his sexual habits. I also think he hoped to bam-boozle me into helping him make Rose believe that he would never be unfaithful again. He was well-practiced in chatting up women. Perhaps he could con me. Age had also whispered in his ear, and it seemed that he, too, was genuinely determined to not be alone at this stage of life. In the same breath, and with a façade of bravado and pride, he told me that he had never been faithful to any woman in his whole life. Monogamy was not his cup of tea, but he would keep his promise to Rose this time. Everything was under control.

Underneath it all, Larry was desperate to keep Rose and not have another divorce. But I probably don't have to tell you that in spite of his ostensible pledge to be monogamous, I really was not confident he would be able to keep his promise. True to his character, he was out to prove he was special, different, the exception to the rule. He had organized his life around proving he was exceptional and entitled. He name-dropped the influential people he was friends with, told me how many women he had had, blustered about his professional life, and his power and wealth. He had a sense of entitlement that grated on me. I had some theories about his deep-rooted feeling of inadequacy and "not-quite-good-enoughness" that he covered with arrogance. Many of the women he had had affairs with were married; there had been no need to be emotionally involved with them. For many years he had thrived on secret liaisons and sexual encounters with no commitment. He had no desire to become emotionally vulnerable. These affairs fed his self-esteem and his erotic fantasies. Rose demanded emotional closeness and vulnerability, to say nothing of honesty. This was a tall order for Larry.

During his soliloquy, I found myself struggling with my own ego. My own therapy had informed me long ago that I had a need to be taken seriously, to be heard, and to be seen as competent. I told myself I did not need his approval. I should have caught myself "showing off" for Rose, and I should have anticipated that she might take it home to Larry. Hindsight and insight is always helpful. Rose's need was to have all the borrowed authority she could get in the face of her own sense of powerlessness with Larry. I thought I would be helping her, and perhaps I did. But I also was feeding my need to be taken seriously, to show off my wonderful diagnostic ability. How embarrassing.

But no one was going to impress Larry more than he impressed himself. He had been betrayed by the first woman in his life, his mother. She ran off with a lover when he was seven years old, leaving him with a paternal maiden aunt. His father disappeared right after he was born. Larry was an angry man, especially with women. For more than fifty years he had practiced being angry and keeping women at a distance. I am not sure anyone could repair that damage. This was not a problem of occasional infidelity. He had created quite a psychic dilemma for himself. While needing to be nurtured and loved by women, he was angry with them and unable to trust them. He had spent a great deal of time with women who were unavailable. He separated sex from love. When married, he could not remain faithful. He could not tolerate too much closeness; it was too dangerous for him. He might be rejected and then abandoned. He also had to feed his narcissism constantly with adoration from women whom he could seduce and leave before they became disenchanted and rejected him. Diagnosis: avoidant and narcissistic personality disorder. Five wives! "Sex is the consolation when you can't have love" (Marques, 2005).

Chapter 3

Anamnesis

Past history in present time

> I find history endlessly amusing, knowing as I do, that the record of any human community might omit stories of sexual abuse, murder, suicide ... Who knows—perhaps any region's most dramatic, most sensational stories were not played out in the public view but were confined to small, private places. A doctor's office, say. A white frame house on a quiet street.
>
> Larry Watson

Getting down to business and taking a history is a defining moment in the therapeutic relationship. I enter my client's life and hear their experiences in a particular and detailed way. More than likely, most clients have never had the experience of examining the details of their lives and sexual habits up close and out loud with another person. It is well to tread mindfully among the tender places; emotional landmines wait just below the surface. For the novice, it may be an anxiety-provoking exercise to think of the right questions to ask (Morrison, 2008). In the beginning, it is best to listen to the client's narrative and follow their lead.

In their ground-breaking text about the comprehensive treatment of sexual problems, Masters and Johnson (1970) observed: "The prevalent error in taking a sex history arises from the assumption that a 'sex' history is a thing of meaning apart from a medical or psychosocial history reflecting the individual as a whole. The separation of sex from consideration of the total human existence has become an unwitting habit." I might add the opposite is also true: Questions about the sexual areas of life must be part of any consultation for mental health issues. As noted in Chapter 2, it is essential to have some rapport with the client before sexual questions are asked and to contextualize sexual questions. Be clear with the client about why it is important to ask about all the details of their lives, as well as their sexual history and habits. Clients should understand that you ask these questions because you want to help and that knowing these details will result in applying the correct treatments. There is hope in the knowledge that these sexual habits are treatable, and hope is what is needed in large measure.

Taking a history, entering a person's life, making a diagnosis or a few diagnoses, is, in truth, an ongoing process in therapy. Practically speaking, it may take two or three sessions to feel enough information has been gathered to begin to zero in on treatment possibilities. "It is always important to note that each person's behavior is the sum of their total experience, including learned experiences, family history, psychiatric history and environmental influences" (Greenfield & Orzack, 2002). In reality, the evaluation of a client presenting with compelling sexual behaviors is not dissimilar from the evaluation of a client who wants help with any of life's problems (Leiblum & Rosen, 2000). Nevertheless, there are some unique issues to be considered in the assessment of sexual issues.

ENTERING A LIFE

The therapist who is armed with clarity about his or her own values and opinions—having spent time examining personal issues with family, relationships, and sexuality—might find taking a history a little easier. However, this clarity does not preclude the possibility that certain beliefs and assertions will be challenged by what you might hear. Nevertheless, experience and practice provide some perspective, acceptance, and ease about what may be heard and encountered with clients. If the therapist is comfortable with the issues, it goes a long way in helping the client be comfortable as well.

In the beginning, people will likely hold back details, or the therapist may neglect eliciting a sexual history, as we saw with Lloyd, who was treated for depression for a year without making too much of a dent in his symptoms because he had never discussed sexual issues with his therapist. We know that people are likely to minimize, deny or lie about their habits with drugs or alcohol, and the same will most assuredly be true with sexual habits. One would hope that the skillful therapist will get everything out on the table eventually. Some things take longer than others to acknowledge. I have learned to trust my instincts for ferreting out the hidden and forbidden. I follow Uncle Morty's advice: "If it smells like a herring ..."

For many years, my strategy has been to schedule the initial visit with a client without the spouse, partner, or family present, even when the request is for couple therapy. I will talk with the couple on the telephone and explain my strategy for an initial individual evaluation before seeing them as a couple. This gives me an opportunity to get a sense of each individual's personal perspective, context, and history. I tell people that this is not carved in stone, and if they are more comfortable coming in together for the first visit, I can arrange it. But in the past 45 years very few have preferred to make the first visit conjoint. After all, avoiding intimacy at any cost is generally at the root of the problem for which they are seeking help. On rare occasions, I still saw them individually after the initial conjoint visit.

I adapted this model from Masters and Johnson (1970). Their model was to use a "dual-therapy" team: A man and a woman would see every couple in their clinic. Each individual would be seen for an initial evaluation by a same gender therapist. The therapists would then compare notes from the individual assessment and plan the appropriate strategies for treatment. Then all four people would meet for feedback and discussion of the treatment plan. This conjoint meeting was called the "roundtable" meeting. In more recent years, the Masters and Johnson dual-therapy paradigm has been regarded as outmoded and cumbersome. It does not really improve the outcome and is more expensive and time consuming (LoPiccolo, Heiman, Hogan, & Roberts, 1985).

When I began my career, private practice was new for social workers. I worked in solo practice in a community where there were no colleagues in private practice, let alone anyone who had knowledge of sex therapy so I adapted the Masters and Johnson model to fit my own needs. I have continued to use the strategy of seeing each individual for an evaluation and then bringing a couple together for feedback and to develop a treatment plan. It works for me.

When an individual calls for an appointment and identifies the issue as compelling sexual behaviors or "sex addiction," I depart from my usual routine and schedule an individual appointment without including a partner or spouse. This may take a few sessions. Generally, I plan to meet the significant other at some point as the assessment evolves. Kafka (2007) also suggests that "the first principle for the evaluation of paraphilia-related disorders (or paraphilias) is to ask specific clinically relevant questions and to inquire without a spouse or significant other present." This model allows a person to feel they have the freedom to be open with the therapist without having to censor their narrative in front of a spouse or partner.

When I have made an initial assessment and have a treatment plan in mind, I request a visit with the significant other. Not only do I want to assess the partner, but I also want to get a sense of the strengths and weakness of the dyad. Many partners or spouses of people with secret sexual habits have mental health issues such as depression, low self-esteem, anxiety, poor impulse control issues, codependency, alcohol or substance abuse or have been sexually abused (Schneider & Schneider, 1991). I have found that many spouses or partners of the "identified client" will respond positively to a recommendation of individual therapy during the initial crisis. On some occasions it is not possible to meet the significant other. The client may not want to disclose the sexual behavior because he or she feels it would end the marriage precipitously, or the partner may be fragile and emotionally unstable, perhaps a suicide risk. Nevertheless, the conjoint visit is generally a useful, and difficult, experience that becomes the first step on a long road. Being in a relationship in which both people are willing to work together tends to bode well for the future of the couple.

It is also important to identify who your client is and to be clear why you have chosen to treat, for example, the husband rather than the both the husband and wife. If the couple is *not* your client, it may take a while to get the spouse or partner into individual treatment. Resistance may take the form of "Nothing's wrong with *me*; why do I need therapy?" It also may take time to find an available therapist with experience in this issue, so I offer to be available during the transition. Many couples fear being separated in therapy at this juncture because they are already frightened about divorce. I will deal with this subject in more detail in Chapter 9.

ASSESSING FOR RISK

Generally, I believe that treatment is best applied in the community where the client lives. If treatment is to promote self-regulation, it is best practiced within the client's usual environment and routine. Staying in the community precludes the client having to take a leave from work and being separated from the family, which could create other problems and more stress. However, there may be times when referral to a hospital, inpatient program, or residential treatment facility is necessary. During the crisis period of transparency and denial, it is essential to assess for risk as quickly as possible. Is this client at risk for harming himself or others? How out of control does this person feel both to themselves and to the therapist? How risky are their behaviors? Is the person a suicide risk? How close to the "illegal" line are the sexual behaviors? How exposed is the client and her family to health problems such as sexually transmitted infections, risk of losing professional licenses and thus financial security, risk of bodily harm, risk of adjudication or blackmail.

There are instances when a client may be a danger to herself or others and is particularly out of control or intractable. In these circumstances it may become clear that intensive inpatient therapy should be recommended as a first order of treatment. It must be emphasized to the client and, if possible, to the family, that an inpatient or residential treatment placement is not to be viewed as an end point to therapy. A consultation should take place with a psychiatrist when appropriate.

It is not unusual that people who are discovered to have sexual secrets may attempt suicide. When the secrets are revealed, the humiliation, guilt, and challenges to an already emotionally compromised psyche may create a situation in which the person views suicide as the best solution. Cooper and Marcus (2003) suggest that in these instances it would be appropriate to consider an inpatient facility. Goodman (1998) also suggests considering inpatient or institutional treatment under the following circumstances:

1. Significant medical difficulty
2. Significant risk of harm to self
3. Significant risk of harm to others
4. Demonstrated inability to provide self-care
5. Unavailability of a living arrangement in which improvement can occur
6. Need to interrupt an addictive cycle when office treatment has been unsuccessful

Gathering the details

I do not generally use a specific grid of questions for the initial interview. But for the inexperienced clinician, I would recommend following some of the screening question guidelines provided by Kafka (2000, 2007), Wincze (2000), and Coleman (1995). Clinicians might also want to examine James Morrison's book *The First Interview* (2008) to help determine their own comfort level when asking pertinent sexual questions. Using a broad brush, the following areas should be covered in a thorough evaluation:

> Family of origin history and current family constellations
> Developmental history
> Sexual or physical abuse
> Illnesses and medications (get a written list if possible), hospitalizations, accidents
> Mental health (client, immediate family, and family of origin)
> Substance use or abuse, including caffeine
> Detailed history of past relationships
> School history
> Work history
> Typical day
> Sexual history, including early awareness of sexual matters, partnered sex, and details of current sexual behaviors

My own style is to initially ask the client what brings them to my door. I prefer to hear the story as each individual tells it. Sometimes clients hedge the answer to this question, and I follow where they lead me. I can fill in the blanks as we go along. At some point in this first visit, I want to assess the nature and gravity of the sexual behavior and get a sense of how out of control the person feels. If there are no risky behaviors that demand urgency, I typically gather more general information about the client before taking a sexual history. This allows me to develop some rapport with the person before I dissect his or her sex life. In addition, it is not unusual that in asking what seem to be benign questions we inadvertently step into an emotional quagmire. For example, questions about families are certain to stir up something, not always positive. All families have some remarkable events that might result in a pause in the conversation. Eventually we will get to the sexual details.

Past relationships of the client are an important part of an assessment. I learned about the power and richness of this aspect of taking a history from William Simpson, M.D., a psychiatrist and psychoanalyst from the Menninger Clinic. About 25 years ago, I invited him to Vermont to give a lecture on psychoanalysis and sex therapy. As part of his visit, he attended psychiatry rounds with medical students and residents on the psychiatric inpatient floor of the hospital and interviewed a patient hospitalized for depression. In an amazing half hour, Dr. Simpson uncovered a pattern that the patient, a male in his thirties, used as his template in relating to women. Dr. Simpson asked the man to describe the first sexual relationship he could remember. He asked the first name of the partner, how he met the partner, how long the relationship lasted, what sexual behavior they engaged in, why it ended, who ended it, and how it felt when it ended. Dr. Simpson went on to the next relationship and asked the same questions. I remember vividly that there were eight women in approximately a nine-year period.

After the patient described the last relationship, Dr. Simpson asked him to tell us something about his mother. His mother had been cold, distant, critical, bossy, seductive, and an alcoholic—a carbon copy of all his previous female relationships! He had never known his father. The pattern of this young man's issues in relating to women became very clear. I learned a great deal from that revealing interview, and using Dr. Simpson's formula, have always elicited a history of all past relationships from my clients. It never fails to reveal an important blueprint of how the client relates to others and the quality of those relationships. You can follow the patterns of bonding and dissolution, loving and rejection, straight to the heart of the matter (no pun intended). The information gathered this way is very useful. Try it, you'll see.

Just as asking about relationships and understanding the ultimate significance of the multi-nuanced ritual of attraction, bonding, and termination, masturbatory habits are also a valuable source of information. Woody Allen, a well-known narcissist, once said "masturbation is making love to the person you love most." So it follows that masturbation, a sexual relationship with oneself, deserves the same examination as a sexual relationship with others.

The details will ultimately inform the treatment and provide a great deal of helpful information. It is necessary to ask questions that will provide an understanding about what sexual fantasies remain fantasies and what have been acted out. When did you begin masturbating? How often do you masturbate now? What is the most times you have masturbated in one day? When was the last time you masturbated that often? What kind of images or fantasies are most appealing to you? Have those images changed over time? Are they men, women, or both? What is the emotional context when you masturbate: bored, angry, lonely? Where do you masturbate: at home (in the bathroom with the door locked or in the living room when you think the family is asleep), while on the telephone, in the office, public restrooms, public spaces, in the car? Is your car parked, or are you driving? Where is it parked? What is the source of these images: your own imagination or people you see on the street, on TV, in videos or movies, magazines? Has the source changed over the years? What's the longest time you have spent online at any given time? When and where do you typically go online to cruise sexual images? Do you ever use these images or fantasies during partnered sex? Do you pay to view images online? Have you put pictures of yourself online? When and where? Who took the pictures?

The human imagination provides sexual fantasies and day-dreams of all kinds. But fantasies are fantasies, not behaviors, and it is important to distinguish one from the other. If a person has erotic fantasies of wanting sex with the same gender, does it mean the person is homosexual? Or if someone likes to hit or bite their partners during orgasm, does it mean they are sadomasochists? If a man tries on the clothing of a woman, does it mean he is a transvestite? We can enjoy a glimpse of a naked body, but it does not mean we are voyeurs. Sexual behaviors have many nuances, subtleties, continuums, and spectrums. Sexual fantasies may be problematic to the extent that some interfere with a satisfying lifestyle or the capacity for an intimate relationship, but for the most part fantasies are not problematic and serve only to heighten erotic pleasure.

"Personal expressions of sexuality are infinitely unique and evolve over time" (Cooper, Golden, & Marshall, 2006). In 1914, Sigmund Freud made the observation that we all have the potential to be heterosexual or homosexual. And in 1953, Alfred Kinsey's research validated that sexual arousal in response to a particular gender can be a fluid state, moving back and forth along a continuum over a lifetime. Psychoanalyst Carl Jung (1954) also identified the elements of female and male in all of us, calling them the *anima* and the *animus*. The plasticity of the brain provides us with the ability to flow in and out of various sexual attractions and sensual preferences (Doidge, 2008). The result of this flexibility is that human beings have the potential capacity for enjoying most sexual variations—even those more typical of the opposite gender—or whatever fantasy material the imagination can provide.

RYAN'S PROBLEM

Ryan's case gives us an opportunity to focus narrowly on assessment issues and consider the implications of the differences between fantasy and behavior. It also highlights the necessity of contextualizing sexual fantasies and behaviors and the need for a good understanding of the literature on many sexual behaviors.

Ryan was a pleasant looking, 44-year-old man of medium height, casually and neatly dressed. He had blond hair and intense blue eyes. His round face had an openness that was appealing. His fair complexion revealed that he blushed easily, and there was an earnestness and naïveté about him. He was forthcoming, open and got right to the point. He told me that his wife, Martha, was having trouble with the difference between sexual fantasy and sexual behavior. She accused him of abusing his two daughters, and wanted a divorce. He had to move out of his house a year ago, but the case, which had been dragging on for almost two years, was still not settled. Martha alleged that because he had sexual fantasies about women and masturbated with those fantasies in mind, he might sexually abuse his daughters.

"How could she *even think* he would do such a thing?" said Ryan. He could not imagine how she made the connection between adult sexual fantasies and abusing children. He said that although he had never done anything illegal, Martha had insisted he get three forensic examinations to determine if he was a pedophile. All the reports negated her accusations. Ryan eventually asked me to read these reports, all of which exonerated him. Nevertheless, the court had appointed a *guardian ad litum* to represent the needs of the children and ordered that visitations with his daughters, aged 12 and 14, must be supervised. Ryan hastened to assure me that he had not abused his children and that his daughters had affirmed this to the courts. However, his wife was still pursuing the issue during the divorce proceedings. Ryan came to see me because his lawyer and his family knew how upset he was and thought he should have his own therapist. He agreed it would be a good idea to have a place to vent.

Ryan had been married for twenty years to Martha, whom he met his senior year in college. Together, they built a successful business making specialty farm products for gourmet restaurants. As their marriage progressed and their business grew, Martha and Ryan each settled into their niches. In addition to running the business, he was a consultant to other farms attempting to bring their products to the marketplace. He was very shy and felt socially awkward, so he was glad he did not have to solicit business; people sought him out. It also meant that he did not have to have relationships with the people who hired him as a consultant, just give them advice. Martha's job was to market their products, so she had to socialize, which was her strong suit. It also included being introduced to a world of wealth, good food, and vintage wines. She began to drink heavily, which embarrassed Ryan. He had no idea how to handle this and distanced himself from Martha. As long as they were a good business team, he continued to avoid the problems they had as a couple.

When the children were born, the issues in their relationship became more evident. Parenting together required that they had to acquiesce to each other in front of the girls, even if they did not want to. Ryan thought they had learned to co-parent fairly well. However, as time went on, he became more lost in his fantasy world of women, who smiled at him from the pages of catalogs that came to the house for Martha. In addition, Martha distanced herself with alcohol, socializing as she marketed their business and engaging in several extramarital sexual relationships.

Martha traveled a great deal for business and had always left Ryan with the girls. He was very proud of his daughters, saying they were bright and the "joy of his life." He had a good relationship with them. Although his daughters confirmed he had never touched them inappropriately, they were angry with Ryan and suspicious because Martha had told them he was a "pervert" and "had trouble with his brain." They also hated the supervised visits with their dad because they were so superficial. Ryan never had any interest at all in children as sexual objects, never looked at them online, and was shocked that anyone would harm children that way.

One night when Martha was drinking, she threatened divorce because of his poor sexual performance. Naïvely, Ryan decided that if Martha knew his early sexual experiences it might explain his quick ejaculations. Perhaps she could understand him better so the two of them would have a better sex life, maybe agree to therapy. She had been chronically criticizing him for ejaculating too soon since they were married. When he talked about his sexual habits during adolescence and college, it never occurred to him that she would take that information and distort it to meet her needs. During the conversation they had about their sex life, Martha had confessed to him that she frequently had sex with men while traveling for their business. Ryan had never had sex outside their marriage. He was devastated and relieved at the same time. He was off the hook sexually and did not have to suffer the humiliation he experienced in a sexual encounter with Martha. Ryan paved his road to hell with good intentions!

Ryan had only two sexual partners in his life. The first woman he had partnered sex with was Jane. It had occurred during his junior year in college and only lasted two months. It ended because Jane said she liked Ryan as a friend but did not want to have sex with him any more. He was ashamed and humiliated by the experience. Ryan met Martha during his senior year in college. She was getting a degree in marketing, and he was studying business administration. She initiated the relationship and he went along with it, although he really had doubts about getting involved. He was flattered and scared at the time, but most of all he was relieved to be with someone who seemed to do all the work in the relationship. He would no longer have to feel weird and awkward while trying to date. Someone liked him and he liked her, at least well enough. Martha was a good sexual mentor and initiated him into the pleasures of partnered sex. He could let go of his insecurity and fears about his sexual performance. He was relieved to have a partner and to get on with his life. However, a few years into the marriage, Martha made it clear that she was never satisfied with their sex life. Ryan ejaculated too quickly to please her, and she constantly told him he was inadequate. They argued bitterly after they had children, and Martha, who also began to drink more heavily after the girls were born, seldom wanted sex with Ryan.

Adolescent longings

I took Ryan through the history of his sexual behaviors and preferences. It revealed a fairly common story. It all seemed to begin when Ryan was approximately 14 years old, about the same time he had a concussion. He remembers the day because he was not supposed to ride his bike for a few days as a punishment for not doing his chores. However, his parents were out, and he sneaked off to a friend's house and fell off his bike. "Hmm, a concussion. Interesting," I thought. I generally assess for accidents, but I am also curious about head injuries in people with compelling sexual habits and now routinely assess for them. I do this because I had heard Ray Blanchard, Ph.D., an expert on pedophilia at the Clarke Institute in Toronto, Canada, give a paper on self–related head injuries in pedophiles (Blanchard, 2003; Blanchard et al., 2003).

Even though my clients are not the same as Dr. Blanchard's, I ask all my clients specifically about head injuries. I am interested in this data because it may provide at least part of the answer as to why some people have compelling sexual habits when others are able to avoid them. At this time, it is pure speculation that perhaps head injuries may create a diathesis toward obsessions or compulsions for sexual behaviors. Nevertheless, to my great surprise, many of my clients during childhood, puberty, or adolescence who have legal and compelling sexual habits also said they had experienced a "wack in the head," as Blanchard describes it.

What Ryan remembered about his concussion was vomiting and a lot of blood, but he did not remember a long period of being unconscious or any residual effects. "Concussion occurs when the brain is shaken violently inside the skull, causing chemical changes that can damage large areas of the brain. The Center for Disease control says the nation is having an epidemic of concussions and that kids are a major part of that, suffering two million injuries each year" (Public Broadcasting System, 2007). And those are just the ones that are reported! J. Paul Fedoroff, M.D. (2003) also observes that people who have "social incompetence" are more likely to have had brain damage. I assessed that Ryan did have a high degree of social anxiety and naïveté about social relations. Researchers are currently pursuing the implications of neurodevelopment for many kinds of mental health and sexual problems. Perhaps someday science will uncover the significance of all this for people with sex in the too-much category.

While we do not yet understand the relevance of adolescents' head injuries, they become part of the larger picture when we put together all the pieces of a personal history. During this time, Ryan's friend showed him a hidden stash of "girlie" magazines in his father's garage. It is common for many of my clients to report having seen a hidden supply of sexually explicit material early in adolescence. Compelling sexual habits begin early in life (Goodman, 1998; Wincze, 2000). Somewhere in puberty or adolescence, people with compelling sexual habits may have discovered and devoured a hidden collection of sexually explicit material, books, magazines, or videos or may have been exposed to sexual acts. Sensing these images are forbidden, they are furtively examined and very arousing. The attending titillation and erotic feelings may result in masturbation and seem to be imprinted on the brain as an erotic preference.

Adolescent curiosity about things sexual is irresistible. The combination of a forbidden erotic experience and the fear of being caught can be a powerful erotic mix that may fade later in life or last a lifetime. Ryan felt very aroused by what he had seen and went home to masturbate to the images in the magazines. After he masturbated, he was left with guilt, shame, and fear, but he liked the orgasms. He found that he could not get these images out of his head. He was preoccupied with them all the time and began to feel obsessed with thoughts he was unable to turn off. The women in the magazines were in sexual poses, smiling at him, and were either naked or scantily clad. There were also a few pictures of men who had very large penises (at least compared to his) and were poised to have intercourse with these women.

When first exposed to adult magazines or videos, young boys will often compare themselves to the fully developed males in the pictures. Of course, they do not take into account that during adolescence their bodies are not yet fully developed or that the penises in the pictures might be enhanced in some way. Furthermore, at this time in their development, the vagina is generally unknown and mysterious territory. Young boys generally are not yet informed that the vagina is a muscle that adapts to whatever is in it, like a tampon, which makes penile size potentially irrelevant. This unexplored territory, therefore, is not factored into most young boys' notion of the reality of sexual relations. Thus, a sense of what I refer to as *comparative inadequacy* may stay with some boys into their adult lives.

Picking up on these seeds of sexual inadequacy and shame is a useful and important part of an assessment. Many of my male clients tell me that they have been upset and embarrassed in partnered sexual encounters since adolescence. This was not only because they believed their penises were very small, but also because they ejaculated more quickly than they thought they should. It is also common to have other coexisting sexual concerns such as erectile difficulties, arousal difficulties with partnered sex, or an aversion to partnered sex (Kafka & Hennen, 1999).

After discovering the magazines, Ryan often pedaled his bike back and forth to his friend's house. Ryan's penis rubbed on the bicycle seat as he pedaled to and fro, and he became aroused. The intensity of arousal began to build. He began to stop in the woods and fields on the road home and masturbated there. He heard the cars swish by and became frightened, but excited at the same time, that he might be seen. At these times he felt powerless, out of control, and very ashamed.

Ryan began to seek out images of women and women's lingerie in other places: on the streets, in the stores, and in magazines. Using these images, he would masturbate upstairs in the guest room when his mother had her garden club in for lunch. Ryan also began to bump into women in crowded places, and he was effusive in his apologies. He would ride his bike around town, trying to catch glimpses of women in their houses at night and fantasizing about women seeing him looking at them. He would become aroused by this voyeuristic fantasy and masturbate. He looked for women's undergarments on the clotheslines as he rode around and fantasized about wearing them, although he never took any. When Ryan was old enough to drive, he would park the car in places where he might actually be observed such as shopping malls. Sometimes he would spread the ejaculate on the door handles of cars and watch the person (usually a woman) get in the car. Fear accompanied arousal in Ryan's mind.

By his senior year of high school, Ryan was sure there was something very wrong with him. It was difficult to remember things, and he worried about his grades. He speculated that his constant preoccupation with sexual thoughts was interfering with his ability to concentrate and remember, but he was too ashamed to seek help. He did mention his memory problem to his mother, but she reassured him that he was getting good grades and shouldn't be upset about it. He seldom socialized, and then only with his pals who were on the same athletic teams. He did not date in high school. He could not figure out how to talk with a girl. It seemed that his mind was always flooded with sexual images. It took an extraordinary amount of effort for him to concentrate on his work and to memorize so he could pass his exams. Nevertheless, he succeeded very well in school and was admitted to an Ivy League college.

Ryan: The young adult

In college, Ryan did not join sports or clubs as he had in high school because he had to devote so much time to studying; he had the same problem memorizing in college that he did in high school. It was difficult to concentrate. As a result, he never made any male or female friendships. He felt lonely being so far from home and was chronically anxious. The college was very large. He speculated that you could fit three or four towns the size of his hometown on the campus. Ryan had a car at college, so his masturbatory forays into parking lots and public spaces escalated, but he had never been caught.

While in his early twenties, he dressed in women's clothes a few times. He was not aroused by the image he saw in the mirror, and he gave it up. It made him very anxious and uncomfortable, and it was not erotic. He was not sure why he tried cross dressing. He said in hindsight it disgusted him that he even *tried* to cross-dress. When I asked Ryan how he acquired the clothing, he said he bought it pretending it was for his girlfriend. It would not have been unusual for someone who wants to cross-dress to use his mother's or sister's clothing or to steal clothes from a clothesline. Ryan never stole clothing or used the clothing from anyone he knew.

Ryan wondered if he might be a homosexual. We explored this in more detail, and he said he had never fantasized about having sex with a man or was sexually aroused by men, although he thought his dressing up like a woman was homosexual behavior. I commented that many people who cross-dressed were married heterosexual males, and it was not necessarily an indicator of homosexuality or of gender-dysphoria (Carroll, 2007). He looked relieved. He liked his pals and felt more comfortable with them than he did with women, but he was not sexually aroused by them. In college, his masturbatory images were women in magazines or those he saw in classes that he thought were "hot." He imagined what it might be like to have sex with them; in his fantasy he "scored," but in reality he was very shy and anxious around the girls on campus.

Ryan told me that during his sophomore year in college he took a symptom checklist test that he found on the Internet that assessed for attention-deficit/hyperactivity disorder (ADHD), and felt that he fit the profile. ADHD is generally associated with inattention, hyperactivity, and impulsive behavior; it often coexists with troubled personal relationships, poor self esteem, and poor performance at school or work (Mayo Clinic, 2008). He asked the doctor at the college health service about it, but never followed through with a referral to the college counseling center for a more thorough evaluation.

It seemed Ryan still had a very busy mind, but I needed to collect more data before I signed him up for ADHD. These symptoms commonly coexist with hypersexual activities (Kafka & Prentky, 1998) and seem to respond to medication very well. Some medications, such as the selective serotonin reuptake inhibitors (SSRIs), generally used for other symptoms such as depression and anxiety, may also work well with ADHD symptoms. ADHD is typically treated with medications that specifically target attention deficit issues, such as Ritalin (methylphenidate) or Adderall (dextroamphetamine). It is always amazing to me to see how many of my clients respond to having medication that "quiets the mind." It brings much wanted relief and clears the way for growth and development.

As Ryan talked with me and answered my questions, I noticed that there was a calmness about him that belied the anxiety he talked about. He was somewhat detached from his story. It seemed well rehearsed. Like many people who have sexual secrets, Ryan had tried for many years to analyze himself and determine how he got this way (three forensic exams notwithstanding). Ryan thought that if he could understand what was happening, he might be able to change. But the sexual behaviors just escalated out of control, and he felt powerless to stop them. The result of this chronic attempt at obsessive self-analysis was that he was well primed to tell me how his sexual habits had developed.

Most people are desperate to figure out how their compelling sexual habits began. They are apt to go over and over the events in their past, tracing the development of their sexual behavior, searching for clues about its origins and hoping to find one pivotal event that can explain "why me?" It was no fun being Ryan. Sometimes he seemed to be dissociating. In Ryan's case, splitting off from bad feelings had become well practiced, a chronic way of dealing with life. Ryan was typical of many people with these types of sexual problems. He used sex as a way to avoid experiencing emotional pain, anxiety, conflict.

When I asked Ryan to tell me something about the development of his sexual behaviors and fantasies, he became a little more animated and connected. He looked me in the eye more often and spoke more freely. Perhaps he trusted me more and was eager to have someone who would support him and believe what he had to say. He told me that some of his sexual fantasies and frequent masturbation had stopped when he was in his mid- to late twenties, about the same time he was married. Some fantasies lingered, but his need to bump into women or view them in their houses had gone away completely. This made sense since there is evidence that frotteurism, which is defined as touching or rubbing against a nonconsenting adult, exists mainly between the ages of 15 and 25 (Fedoroff, 2003). It is rare to find people who prefer frotteuristic acts to the exclusion of other sexual behaviors who are older than 25.

While Ryan used to try to see women in their houses when he rode his bike home at the end of the day, he never went up to a house and actually looked inside because he was afraid he would be caught. Everyone knew everyone in his small town, and he did not want to be seen as "weird." He already felt that way all the time. When Ryan was a teen, he never masturbated where he could actually be seen. But the fantasy that people might see him was arousing and scary at the same time. It is essential to understand and to assess for the difference between people who actually exhibit their genitals to unsuspecting and non-consenting people in public places, for example the library or shopping mall, and those who might be called "public masturbators" who do not want to be seen but want to fantasize about being seen. Most exhibitionists have no desire to engage in any sexual activity with the people to whom they expose themselves. Most are married heterosexuals (Fedoroff, 2003). These nuances may be lost on many people, but they are very important distinctions to make.

The most Ryan had ever masturbated was approximately two to three times a day when he was an adolescent. This diminished as he got older, and by the time he was in college it was much less. He had roommates and shared a bathroom. For a while he only masturbated while in his car, but he stopped that when one day he thought someone had seen him and he quickly left the parking lot. A few years before the children were born, after he had been married for a while, he only masturbated at night in a locked bathroom or during the day if he was at home working alone, maybe once or twice a week. He never bought videos or adult magazines and did not go online to look at adult content sites. He did, however, examine the catalogs that came in for women's clothing and used some of the images in them. Martha found a few of her catalogs in the bottom of Ryan's closet and it caused quite a fight.

Martha also hired a detective to look at Ryan's computer, although Ryan had specifically told her that he never used the computer for sexual material. Nothing was found. He knew his propensity for sexual fantasies and had never allowed himself to follow the invitations that popped up on his screen. In addition, he also knew that his children used his computer, and he didn't want them to see anything bad. He could not believe Martha distrusted him so much and how much her "hatred" of him had escalated. He could not understand why Martha made these accusations. He was trying to be honest when he told her about all his adolescent sexual secrets. Nothing he told her had anything to do with children, but she was disgusted with what she had heard about his fantasies and behaviors.

As I moved through Ryan's history, I also learned some interesting things about his gene pool. He had two sisters, both of whom were married and had children. One had a child who had Down's syndrome, and the other had one child with Tourette's syndrome. His paternal grandparents both had alcohol problems, and he could remember his grandfather coming to family events drunk, becoming more and more out of control as the day went by. His parents did not drink, and he only had an occasional beer and caffeine in the morning. He exercised regularly, was in good health, never used drugs, and took no medications. Many mental health problems are inherited, but the data is not yet in about the implications of Ryan's gene pool.

I encourage people to think about our sessions during the week, to analyze what happened and perhaps to talk about the session with their spouse, partner or friend. I find it helps solidify what we are doing in treatment if a person thinks about the session between the meetings. It is also important for me to sit with the information I have for a few days and try to make some sense out of it. During this time, I begin to formulate the diagnostic implications for treatment purposes. I also make a list of the things I still want to know.

Driving home the day I met Ryan, the subtext of his history began to sink in. What stood out the most for me was the silent narrative, the losses Ryan had suffered in his young life. To be sure, he had accomplished a great deal in the "public expression" of his life. He was a college graduate with a master's degree and was successful in his business; he was a husband, father, and a nice guy. In our culture, we idealize childhood. It is ideally without impediments, provides security, support, and love. Sadly, for many childhood is far from this ideal.

While his home environment provided love and support, Ryan was tormented by sexual thoughts, and he felt driven by something he could not understand. He grew up feeling ashamed of himself and assumed he was bad. He was completely isolated in his misery. He thought if people "really" knew him, they would be repelled: he would be rejected, sent away to reform school, removed from his family and friends. He was chronically frightened and anxious. It is such a heavy burden for a young person to carry and surely had an impact on his development and psyche. And what about his capacity to relate to others, to trust, to give and receive love? Carol Gilligan, Ph.D., a distinguished psychologist who has authored much research and many books about child development, describes the psyche this way:

> In Greek, the word for "soul" is psyche. It also means "breath" or "life." This ancient word carries the wisdom that we are more than our genetic makeup, more than our life histories, more than our cultural lineage. Whether conceived as a divine spark or as part of the natural wonder of the human being, the soul is the wellspring of our minds and our hearts, our voice and our capacity for resistance. (Gilligan, 2003)

What had happened to Ryan's psyche? What was in his mind and heart while he was trying to develop into a mature human being, to take on adult roles and the responsibilities of life? I felt sad about Ryan's difficult childhood. I also wondered what it is about divorce, breaking the marital bond, that brings out the worst in us?

Between visits, I also spent some time thinking through Ryan's sexual history, sorting out his past and present sexual fantasies and behaviors. I ruled out that Ryan was an exhibitionist, a voyeur, or frotteur. He was not a transvestite; nor did he have gender dysphoria (Carroll, 2007). Ryan's three masturbatory sexual fantasies—exhibitionist, voyeurism, and frottage—had disappeared. This was in keeping with Fedoroff's (2003) observations that these fantasies typically fade away when people are in their twenties and early thirties. Many sexual habits of adolescence fade as people mature, although we do not have statistics on this issue as yet. Moser and Kleinplatz (2004) and their colleagues have observed that "while it is true that many individuals diagnosed with paraphilias recognize that their interests began in childhood, it is not clear how many who had unusual interests in childhood abandoned or changed those interests by adulthood."

This speaks to the importance of distinguishing between people who do and do not act out their fantasies. There are people who expose themselves repeatedly in public, as well as voyeurs who actually watch women when they are not aware they are being watched, and they are more likely to retain these habits through adult life. Voyeuristic fantasies are common, but they can also be precursors to violent sexual acts. Voyeurs have the potential to watch and then stalk a particular woman and may eventually rape her. Voyeurs may have many victims before they are caught and rarely seek help for their problem (Hollender & Callahan, 1975; Davis, 2003). It is important to note in an evaluation that Fedoroff (2003) has observed that "Men with TV [transvestic fetishism] almost never present with legal problems, aside from child custody disputes." Nevertheless, the research of Langstrom and Zucker (2005) reveals that up to 20% of individuals with transvestic fetishism have been involved with child abuse and 36% have committed exhibitionistic acts. Others can self-harm with autoerotic self-asphyxia and may be involved in sadomasochism. These details are important for the therapist to be aware of and to decipher. Being familiar with the literature on these various behaviors is essential to the process of assessment. The nuances of fantasy versus behavior must be understood. Ryan's life had been filled with masturbatory fantasies, and although his adolescent fantasies and behaviors had lost their grip on him, he still had fantasies and still masturbated occasionally in private.

Even though I ruled out some issues, Ryan still had other important issues that would benefit from therapy. It was apparent that he was struggling with social anxiety and incompetence, as well as relationship problems. This is not an unusual problem with people who have compelling sexual behaviors. Kurt Freund, M.D. (1990), a psychiatrist and scholar in the field of sexology, observed that exhibitionism, voyeurism, and frotteurism tend to occur together. He coined the phrase *courtship disorders* to describe the varying degrees of difficulty people with this trio of erotic preferences have in figuring out how to connect with and "court" potential partners. Freund describes this group as socially awkward, anxious, and unable to form friendships or romantic relationships. Today we might call this "social anxiety," or "intimacy disorder" or perhaps "attachment disorder." Whatever the label may be, it describes a problem with connecting to another person in an emotionally mature and satisfying way. Cooper and Marcus (2003) frame the issue of sexual compulsivity as a "relationship disorder."

It is worth considering that this specific cluster of behaviors is also frequently associated with Asperger's syndrome, a neurobiological and "developmental delay disorder characterized by social incompetence" (Fedoroff, 2003). People with Asperger's syndrome fail "to develop peer relationships appropriate to developmental level," and "lack social or emotional reciprocity"(DSM-IV-TR, 2000). There is a sense of being "odd" and naïve in some way, not quite fitting what one would expect of someone in that age bracket, not quite tuned into social cues from others, and not having appropriate social scripts for establishing relationships (Ray & Bray-Garretson, 2004). People with Asperger's syndrome are also very truthful, sometimes to their detriment and do not understand the art of social nuance. They may appear inappropriate in some situations. They often fail to pick up on social cues and thus may breach social boundaries by touching, hugging, or kissing people who are not expecting it.

Ryan was naive and socially inexperienced, which would account for some of his problems. I also sensed he was unaware of some social cues. When he entered the room he did not pick up on the cue to sit on the sofa opposite me but rather plopped into my chair. He did not notice when I tried to end the session and seemed naïve about social situations at work and home. At the same time, it was very impressive that Ryan had achieved success in both his education and career in spite of the level of preoccupation with sexual fantasies that he described over the years. While his symptoms might resonate with Asperger's syndrome, "resonate with" is not enough to make a diagnosis. But it is important to observe when social skills training might be in order.

Ryan's strengths were considerable. He was aware of his past impulse control problems and stayed away from the Internet as a source for masturbation. While Ryan was somewhat naïve about some facets of life, he was very successful at his job, oriented, and appropriate. Even with the stresses of an accusation of child abuse and the divorce, Ryan had not returned to his old habits. The frotteuristic, exhibitionistic, and voyeuristic fantasies appeared to be past history and not likely to reappear. Ryan also expressed what seemed to be a sincere investment in treatment and in understanding his sexual behaviors. For Ryan, adolescence was a time when he was "horribly depressed and out of control." As an adult, particularly during the divorce, he felt depressed and powerless in the face of his wife's accusations. Anxiety and shyness had also been lifetime companions. However, as an adult he was a successful consultant and developed a lucrative and complex business. He was a good father and provider. At the same time, Ryan was very angry, as well he might be. Accused of sexually abusing his children was horrific for him.

Treatment implications

After our session, I made some tentative diagnostic notes for Ryan and waited for our next visit: depression (dysthymic type), social anxiety, generalized anxiety, and difficulty with focusing on tasks, self-diagnosed attention-deficit problems, premature ejaculation, and masturbation with adult content. Poor sleep cycles. No adult content material on computer. No evidence of pedophilia. Alcoholic wife suing him for a divorce (GAF=70).

During his next visit, Ryan wanted to talk more about Martha and what had happened. He did not think I had a clear picture of what the accusation meant to him. Fair enough, let's hear it. Bottom line for Ryan was that Martha had often acknowledged that he was a very good father and now was accusing him of harming the girls. Martha typically had left him to care for the girls when she went on marketing jaunts. He was very worried that if they could not work out their differences, he would be denied seeing his children. He observed that when Martha drank a lot she was a "loose cannon." I reminded him that the girls had told the court that he was a good father and had never been inappropriate with them. The girls loved him, but the supervised visits were making them all feel awkward and on edge. Ryan was confused and angry and did not know what to do. He trusted his lawyer, who seemed to believe in him.

Martha's anger, on the other hand, kept escalating. What did she want from him? He told me about the routine they had developed now that he was no longer living on the farm. Ryan said he got up about 5:30 a.m. so he would have some time before he had to go to the farm. Some of his restrictions had been relaxed when the reports about child abuse were found to be negative. If he was allowed to, he would still take the children to school or at least see them before they got on the bus each day. If Martha was away, one of their employees, a woman who Ryan liked, would stay with the girls. Martha was inconsistent about how much, where, and when he could see the children after the *guardian ad litum* edict had been lifted.

Both he and Martha had had their own office space and individual computers when he lived in the house. Now he carried a laptop when they made their early morning rounds of the farm. They would meet with their employees about the needs of the day. He said they were lucky to have a good group of workers who were loyal to them. Then he would work at his apartment, taking phone calls and managing things online for their business and the consulting he did. Sometimes he would run or go swimming at the school when it was available for community swim. Most of his work could be handled at home, but sometimes he traveled, mostly within the state. He saw the girls for dinner three times a week. Sometimes he would come to the house and cooked with the girls and then they all would eat together. The girls did chores and homework, and then they went to bed about 9 p.m. All in all, it appeared that Ryan was a responsible husband, father, and businessman.

Ryan: The adult

Eventually, Martha left the house and the girls to open up her own marketing firm in Massachusetts. Ryan happily moved back into the house and was parenting full-time. So much for her accusations! Martha got what she wanted: half of Ryan's inheritance from his parents. He said it never felt so good to lose money. Humor gets you through so many things. Ryan still feels somewhat awkward around town with some people who still seem to doubt him. The emotional valence of these past few years will take a long time to diminish, and the impact of Martha's accusations will always be with him.

Ryan was highly motivated in treatment and ready to make changes. He took medication that benefited him a great deal. He was less anxious, more self-confident, calmer and slept well. He stayed in therapy for almost two years and now visits for occasional "booster shots." For a brief period of time he consulted a therapist who helped him with his social skills, and we followed through with some of her suggestions at our sessions. He looked me in the eye when he talked. His speech was not hesitant. With a quieter mind and less anxiety he could develop and mature. He and his daughters also went to therapy together to work on the residuals from his vituperative divorce. I suspected that opportunities for relationships would open up for Ryan. He wanted a relationship but he would do his homework this time before he got involved. He also felt more confident that he would have a lot more to bring to a relationship now. Therapy had also given him a chance to understand what his early experiences meant. I expected he would have more confidence now as a sexual partner. There was peace in the white frame house on a quiet road.

Chapter 4

Treatment
A time for action

I may advise, argue, badger, cajole, implore, or simply endure, hoping that the patient's neurotic world view will crumble away from sheer fatigue.

Irvin D. Yalom

TRACING THE ROOTS OF TREATMENT

Treatment for compelling sexual behaviors has its roots in the early twentieth century. In 1905, Sigmund Freud published *Three Essays on Sexuality*. Some of it was focused on an attempt to understand sexual "perversions" —the function they served in the psyche and their treatment. Freud viewed sexuality, in its broadest sense, as fundamental to human development, as well as a causative factor in the development of psychic disturbances. Freud's work, among others, paved the way for reframing these "perverse" sexual behaviors as illnesses worthy of scientific study and medical treatment.

This was a much needed shift away from the centuries-old belief that these behaviors were sinful and mitigated only by severe punishment. Sexual perversions were viewed as uninhibitedly pleasurable and purely ego syntonic, unimpeded by the ego, superego or defensive structures. "The sexually perverse patient repressed nothing, and acted out his unconscious in such a manner that he had little to gain by giving up his pleasurable symptom. As such, the patient had little or no motivation for change" (Travin & Protter, 1993). The pleasure of orgasm and erotic arousal is still viewed as a need driven by unconscious feelings that can impede or override the superego function and are often a vehicle for soothing and defending against a damaged sense of self.

Not long after Freud developed his psychoanalytic theories about sexual behavior, learning theorists began their work which, simply put, maintained that behaviors were primarily a product of environmental reinforcers (Skinner, 1938). In a nutshell, these theories asserted that if something was pleasurable, the inclination would be to repeat it; if it was aversive, it would be avoided. Orgasms, for example, are pleasurable and thus reinforcing. If you have an aversive or negative consequence, you might think twice about repeating the behavior. Building on learning theories such as Skinner's, theories of cognition formed the basis for behavioral therapy and cognitive-behavioral therapies.

Cognitive Behavioral Therapy (CBT), defined as the integration of cognitive and behavioral therapies, includes the work of Dollard and Miller (1950), Albert Ellis (1958), Aaron Beck (1967), and Bandura (1969), to name a few. CBT departed from psychoanalytically based therapies, which focused on revealing the intrapsychic root of a person's issues. CBT centered on changing destructive thought patterns, which would result in change of behaviors. It also integrated a focus on intrapsychic and relational issues. At the time, these learning theories contributed little to the knowledge base about the etiologies of perversions or paraphilias, but contributed much to the treatment of sexual behaviors of all kinds (Protter & Travin, 1985). Since their inception, there have been many variations of and modifications to these early learning theories.

In 1957, Albert Ellis, Ph.D., came out with his theories of Rational Emotive Cognitive Therapy (RETC). In 1958, he wrote *Sex without Guilt*. This work highlighted that rational thought about sex would change dysfunctional sexual habits. He also was the first to suggest that conjoint therapy would be helpful in solving couple's issues. Ellis's work coincided with both the work of Kinsey and Masters and Johnson. When Masters and Johnson (1966) observed how the body responded to sexual stimulation in the laboratory, it led the way to developing treatments for many types of sexual problems, such as lack of orgasm or rapid ejaculation. The behaviorists' theories of environmental reinforcers became the basis for sexual dysfunction therapy, or what is popularly called sex therapy (Masters & Johnson, 1974).

Since that time, treatments for sexual problems have been modified to integrate many other treatment modalities such as psychodynamic psychotherapy, group therapy, cognitive behavioral therapy, and psychopharmacology. In the period between 1975 and 1990, treatments for sex offenders relied heavily on behavioral theories and group therapy. More recently, these behavioral programs for sex offenders have adopted a more cognitive behavioral approach as well as a focus on intrapsychic processes and relational issues (Marshall et al., 1991). During the 1980s, clinicians became aware of sexual behaviors that were *not* illegal but deserved treatment. (Carnes, 1983, 1989; Quadland, 1985; Schwartz & Brasted, 1985) suggested group therapy for these types of behaviors and applied a cognitive-behavioral treatment modality.

It is interesting to note that while treatment paradigms have continued to evolve in the past century, the relationship between the client and therapist is still a central theme in most therapeutic paradigms (Goodman, 1998; Fernandez, 2002; Cooper & Marcus, 2003). It is also noteworthy that the assumptions about the etiology of compelling, unusual, or illegal sexual habits have a common thread from Freud's time to now.

Many theoretical formulations presume that sexual behaviors represent a warding off of painful feelings about the damaged self or a compulsion to repeat feeling states of a tarnished and traumatized childhood. From a learning theory point of view, it is also true that the pleasure of erotic feelings and orgasms is reinforcing and difficult to extinguish. And, more recently, it has been theorized that repetitive, pleasurable process or behavioral addictions are mediated by chemicals found in the brain. "Addiction occurs in the brain. Any behavior that produces pleasure will temporarily alter the brain chemistry and may result in a compulsion to repeat the behavior to attain more pleasure" (Sunderwirth et al., 1996).

Just as the labels for compelling sexual behaviors have been widely debated and are still unsettled, so, too, are theories of the etiology of these behaviors not fully understood. Nor is there a complete consensus about the components of treatment. Nevertheless, treatment strategies have integrated and extrapolated formulations and methodologies from many theoretical orientations. For example, we have threshed psychoanalytic theory, self-psychology, ego-psychology, object-relations, relational schools, conditioning and social learning theories, as well as theories of group process, sex offender treatments, psychoeducational interventions, and psychopharmacology to create a whole armamentaria to undertake the task of treatment.

Research on the efficacy of treatment for compelling sexual behaviors has flaws and lacunae because people with these problems are difficult to "capture" (Marshall et al., 1991; Goodman, 1998; Kafka, 2007). However, even without solid cause-and-effect outcome data for all treatment strategies, research has been able to examine the efficacy of some of the currently favored treatment components that are commonly and successfully applied to compelling sexual behaviors, such as a combination of psychodynamic psychotherapy and cognitive–behavioral therapy (Travin & Protter, 1993; Goodman, 1998; Kafka, 2007) and medication (Kafka, 1991; Kafka & Prentky, 1992; Stein et al., 1992). In the sex addiction literature, Patrick Carnes (1991) asserts that "individual psychotherapy with a therapist who is familiar with sex addiction," as well as all the behavioral and spiritual regimens that are associated with 12-step programs, is an efficient treatment paradigm. Freeman-Longo & Blanchard (1998) sum it up: "Research also seems to support that treatment has the best chance of success when it is part of an integrated program offered by those with at least some specialized training in this area."

With or without treatment, Goodman (1998) observes that while [sexual addiction] "tends to be a chronic, lifelong disorder, the frequency of addictive sexual behavior typically peaks between the ages of 20 and 30 and gradually declines." I have observed that sometimes sexual behaviors will stop during the initial crisis and sometimes there is a "flight into health" —a sudden and short-lived recovery or honeymoon phase during which behaviors stop, relationships get closer, and everything looks rosy. This does not portend or predict a permanent extinguishing of the sexual symptoms. It is important to point out that as therapy progresses insight into one's traumas, childhood, and relationships will be very important and useful. It is equally important that there be a commitment to other changes in order for the sexual behaviors to stop. For a deeper and more generalized change to take hold, the question of "Why would I want to change or stop my secret sexual life?" must be answered.

There is no doubt that working with clients who are confronting compelling sexual habits requires creativity, flexibility, and patience because each client has various needs, levels of intellect, and historical antecedents. We cannot predict how each person will respond to the treatments available. It is well for the therapist to have an eclectic approach that is well grounded in understanding sexual behaviors of all types. Treating an individual with secret sexual habits would preferably include a mix of psychodynamic psychotherapy, cognitive-behavioral therapy, psychoeducational techniques, and psychopharmacology interventions. Treatment strategies should be unique and diverse and are best applied in several venues—individual, couple, and group therapy; support groups of various kinds that may be self- or professionally led; and workbooks or other literature that might be added when appropriate. Yalom (1989) would urge therapists to: "Create a new therapy for each patient."

Overall, a highly motivated client with a truly integrated program of psychodynamic understandings and cognitive behavioral actions, as well as an appropriate application of medication(s), seems to hold the most promise for a successful outcome. In sum, given half a chance, treatment works. As with all types of therapy, a leap of faith is what prevails, even given a well-informed therapist with state-of-the-art knowledge.

GETTING THE TREATMENT PROCESS GOING

When we begin treatment, I try to educate my clients about the process that will take place. It makes sense to apply some structure to the abstraction of psychotherapy so it does not seem so open-ended to clients. There is a subtle but important difference between discussing the specific treatment methodology to be applied and the process of therapy itself. I find it helpful to motivate people to continue treatment by letting them know there are goals to reach and stages to go through along the way.

Scholars in this field, including Schwartz and Brasted (1985) and Goodman (1998), have spelled out specific stages for the treatment of compelling or addictive sexual behaviors. The 12 steps used in addiction programs can also be viewed as stages that point to a specific direction. Knowing there are stages to therapy gives people a perspective that the therapy goes someplace, that there is a map for this journey. In graduate school I learned about Erik Erickson's stages of life (1963). Then there were Elizabeth Kubler-Ross's stages of death and dying (1997), and Judith Viorst's (2003) journey "from 'I do' to 'till death do us part.'"

Since it is usually in hindsight that we recognize that therapy has taken us someplace, I frequently spell out the stages we will go through in treatment, reference the goals, and take time to look back at where we have been and where we are now. I find that this reflection gives sustenance for the rest of the journey. I have devised my view of the stages people pass through to meet their goals and tweak them depending on where the client is when they come in. These stages are:

1. The crisis of discovery and becoming transparent
2. Coming out of denial and wrestling with resistance
3. Examining and expressing emotions and feelings
4. Communication skills: Learning honesty and accountability with self and others
5. Self-awareness and self-regulation
6. Dealing with relationships: Past, present, and future

Many of my clients have problems with emotional intimacy, relationships, and attachment. I believe that psychodynamic psychotherapy based on the above issues will optimize the client's self-awareness and potential to engage in and maintain an emotionally intimate and open, healthy relationship. As we develop the client/therapist relationship, a therapist must monitor his or her feelings and reactions to the client. Introspection is, or should be, the stock-in-trade for therapists. We can do this through our own therapy, as well as in consultation with colleagues. Therapists bring a lifetime of experiences and emotional states—as well as cultural, political, and religious biases—to each relationship. If we want our clients to express their feelings, it behooves us to inspect our own reactions and feelings, as well.

In the effort to understand inner feelings and reactions, many therapists pay a lot of attention to the concepts of transference and countertransference. Most theoretical orientations encourage the use of these controversial and complex ideas in some form. Simply put, transference reactions are conscious or unconscious feelings from a past relationship or event that the client transfers to the therapist—a type of distortion or projection that can be negative or positive. The therapist, for example, is not really a client's authoritarian father or critical mother; it just feels that way sometimes. If the client reacts to the therapist as he or she might have reacted with an overbearing or critical parent, then the therapist can help the client understand this reaction.

Countertransference reactions are the therapist's unconscious and conscious projections and feelings that a client's behavior may evoke. For example, the therapist may become angry with a client who has had an affair because the therapist's partner or spouse also had an affair. Instead of being supportive, the therapist might act out unresolved feelings of anger by being judgmental or critical. Often people with compelling sexual behaviors feel so out of control that they will try to find ways to control many situations, particularly the therapeutic relationship. They might act out by being late, or not show up for an appointment and not call, leave their checkbook at home, change appointments often, not participate in the conversation, not return calls, etc. This may provoke negative countertransference reactions of anger or frustration in the therapist.

If I get bored in a session and my mind wanders off to what I will be doing on Saturday night, it is a strong reminder that I am not engaged with the client. Maybe the client is boring and talks too much or too long on irrelevant subjects. Here I am letting them talk away without pushing them to focus on the therapy and themselves. Uh-oh, I am not working hard enough, not keeping us on task. Am I wasting their money, taking up their time? Should we be examining why the client talks about everyone else but himself instead of considering a movie on Saturday night? It is, of course, important for me to refocus myself, as well as my client. Later on when I have time to reflect and make notes on the session, I may ask myself why I was bored with that particular material and discover it evoked an unpleasant memory from my past. I make a note to explore that material in more depth for myself and the client.

The therapeutic alliance that is created with each client should model an authentic and emotionally open relationship based on warmth, reciprocity, empathy and a consistent nonjudgmental attitude. Did I mention a sense of humor? It also requires that the therapist clearly set the boundaries from the beginning and keeps people on track about their goals. This includes spelling out confidentiality, expectations about appointments and fees, and explaining the duty to warn if something needs to be reported.

Keeping watch over boundaries, even very subtle ones, is important. For example, Ed was a new client and a very busy man. During the first month of our relationship, he showed up an hour late for an appointment and I could not see him. He was very frustrated. At the rescheduled session, he told me that he was sorry he had missed the appointment but that his wife, who kept track of his appointments, had told him the wrong time. It was a "golden opportunity" to point out that: (1) his relationship with me should not be mediated by his wife; relationships are straight lines with no go-betweens, (2) his therapy was his responsibility, (3) this was an opportunity to reflect on his ambivalence about therapy, which he had not yet been willing to "own up to," and (4) if he complained that his wife controlled him too much, why did he hand the controls over to her for his appointments? This moment in our relationship cleared the air and a good deal of the denial at the same time. It also clearly highlighted some important issues for Ed. In addition, it addressed the request from his wife that he not treat her as if she were his administrative assistant. She also would have to learn to stick with her goal to say "no" to requests to be his go-between. Furthermore, it helped them talk more about the control issue they struggled with.

Many people think they want to change but cannot motivate themselves to stop their behavior, no matter what the consequences may be. After all, the secret sexual behaviors are an escape from the pain and realities of life. Right from the beginning of therapy it is important to introduce the concept of lapse and relapse prevention. Recognizing that these habits are difficult to give up, we work on coping mechanisms that anticipate a lapse or relapse, which I discuss more thoroughly in Chapter 8. It is important for the therapist to understand that while the end-point of treatment may not be satisfactory to all concerned, some individuals and couples are able to adjust to a less than perfect outcome. Just as the treatment experience is unique for each person and situation, so too is each outcome.

Garnering resources

In order to recommend a truly comprehensive treatment plan, it is necessary for the clinician to cultivate the resources in the area and create a team for referrals. If there are no knowledgeable resources nearby, then it is useful to foster telephone consultation relationships with experienced clinicians outside the community. A clinician should build a knowledgeable team for various treatment options. For example, if medication is needed, we can call Dr. X, whom you can trust not to be critical and judgmental and who has experience helping people who have depression, anxiety, and obsessional thinking. And Ms. Z is a good family therapist who may be able to help you and/or couples deal with the family issues that have been raised, including sexual situations.

Like teaching a child to eat baby food, each adjunct therapy will be added slowly and mindfully, making sure the client can tolerate the next variety that might be added. For instance, it is reasonable to refer someone to group therapy who has social anxiety, but they might not be ready for professionally- or self-led group therapy until the social anxiety is better understood and perhaps medication has mitigated and stabilized the anxiety. There also may be no groups in the area. Would an on-line group be advisable? Well, it depends. Maybe the therapist could start a group. Couple therapy might also be added at a time when both individuals feel more on top of the situation and are able to attempt the open, honest, difficult, and intimate conversations that couple therapy requires.

Making treatment recommendations

When the assessment is well underway and the initial crisis, with its attendant turmoil, begins to settle down, I put together the treatment options. My clients have just begun to mourn the loss of secret spaces and perhaps started to identify painful affects in an effort to get more congruency between "private experience and public expression" (Jamison, 2000). People are also likely to be moving in and out of ambivalence about staying the course toward treatment. I factor in the immediate sexual behaviors, the coexisting mental health issues, psychosocial issues, as well as each person's unique cultural and biological contexts. Eli Coleman, Ph.D. (1995) reminds us that "Each case of CSB [compulsive sexual behaviors] must have its own individualized treatment plan; however, the greatest success in treating CSB is achieved when the patient is motivated and has the resources to engage in the treatment components."

After a few individual sessions, I share my impressions of "what ails" and the implications for treatment. I explain how the goals of treatment match the problem and how it will all fit together. This is an important psychoeducational intervention. Ideally, by this time I would have had an opportunity to meet my client's significant other, if they have one, and assess her or his mental status and view of the relationship. I generally do not have to pry out of any spouse or partner their feelings about the secrets revealed: feelings run high and anger drives. Validating and containing the anger well enough to get an evaluation of these issues require a balancing act on a very high wire. I also will have tried to assess the marriage or partnership before the situation erupted.

By this time, I will have met with the partner and client together to go over the diagnostic assessment and the treatment recommendations. However, this may not be possible at times because the significant other may categorically refuse to meet with me, making it clear that it is not his or her problem, the client may feel that his partner is too emotionally fragile to handle the situation, or feel that disclosure might end the marriage precipitously. However, most of the time I can convince the resisting partner to at least consider the idea that two people own the same marriage and sex life and need to work on it together. Generally, most couples are cautiously and anxiously open to a joint meeting at this point in the process. This reticence is healthy. I have yet to find one of these early conjoint visits to be a walk in the park.

To inject some optimism at this anxious time, it is well to emphasize that many people have been able to benefit from treatment, and it is likely that both partners will get to a better place than they are at the moment. But then, I remind myself that I am a stranger to these people. Who am I to expect they would trust me at this time? I connect the dots between the situation and my rationale for the choice of treatment strategies. I usually recommend individual treatment for both parties. I also tell them that from time to time that we might have a conjoint meeting, and that at some point it will make sense to have an ongoing relationship with a couple therapist.

The conjoint session also helps set out the boundaries and introduces the concept of the relationship system and how the client, their partner and perhaps the whole family may be involved in the solution as well as the problem. For example, while I may have an individual relationship with my client, the partner may want to call me about something that has happened. The ground rules are that I will only entertain telephone calls if both parties know I am being called and have discussed this together before the call is made. In addition, I may also introduce the issues that sabotage treatment. We also set some tentative goals at this session. It is helpful to have a couple do this together so we can reference these goals and use them to further the treatment process. It is important for all concerned to know that both the assessment and the assignment of treatments are ongoing, fluid processes and can be changed and developed as therapy continues.

Applying treatment recommendations

Turner, a 45-year-old married man, consulted with me because his wife found out about his Internet sex. He had rationalized his behavior as necessary because his wife would not have sex with him. He figured she would never find out about his habits. "What she doesn't know won't hurt her!" he said, defensively. He was masturbating two to three times a day and spending many hours on the Internet scrolling for sexually explicit adult material: mostly women with women and sometimes men with women. He had sex with prostitutes and sometimes massages with "a happy ending" when he traveled for work. He was chronically sleep deprived, depressed, and anxious. Sometimes he stayed up all night in his hotel room, scrolling around the Internet sites he found erotic. He drank a whole bottle of wine at those times and was not able to function well at the business meetings scheduled in the morning. His marriage was failing, he was spending large amounts of money for prostitutes, and his work productivity was falling off conspicuously. He had been threatened with both a divorce as well as job loss. Turner reluctantly acknowledged that help was needed—quickly.

Over a period of a few weeks, I told Turner what was known about his maladies, including his alcohol habits, and how we might work together on them. I also went over the salient and relevant issues in his developmental history, including an alcoholic father, a depressed mother who had been hospitalized several times and had shock treatments, and a sister who died of multiple congenital defects when he was eight years old. In a nutshell, the diagnostic considerations were that he was depressed and anxious; he abused alcohol; he was obsessed and preoccupied with sexual behaviors that carried dire consequences such as job loss and divorce, as well as possible blackmail, physical harm, or sexually transmitted infections. He said he seldom used protection when he had anonymous sexual encounters, so we discussed getting tested for sexually transmitted infections as soon as it could be arranged.

Turner was chronically angry and somewhat paranoid. He seemed emotionally closed down and narcissistic. Some of these observations could stem from the initial crisis or be long-standing character or personality traits. He was also chronically sleep deprived. I went over my diagnostic impressions and explained how these symptoms related to his sexual behaviors. I explained that therapy would include some immediate interventions such as a program to stop his alcohol abuse, ongoing psychodynamic psychotherapy, cognitive behavioral therapy, and perhaps medication. We also would explore the impact of his early childhood experiences.

During this time I met with Turner's wife, Lynn, for an individual session. She was in crisis as well. Then Turner, Lynn and I had a conjoint meeting. I reviewed with both of them what I had explained earlier to Turner and discussed how Lynn might fit into the treatment plan. She was relieved with the plan. Her whole world was falling apart, and she needed something to hold on to. We needed to roll up our sleeves and begin some interventions quickly if we were to save his job and marriage—what Kafka (2007) calls the "here-and-now issues." Contritely and ambivalently, Turner agreed to the plan.

With the cooperation of the human resources department, Turner was able to negotiate a month off from work. We found a week-long, daily, intensive alcohol program that he could attend, and return to if needed, and then planned a segue into regular Alcoholics Anonymous meetings. He did identify with growing up with an alcoholic father, which made it an easier decision for him to give up alcohol. He did not want his two teenage children to have the same memories. Turner's wife, Lynn, had an alcoholic mother so they both agreed to attend some ACOA (Adult Children of Alcoholics) meetings. It was an attempt by Turner to create some tentative solidarity with Lynn. She readily agreed to individual therapy and had been researching it herself. Lynn also welcomed that I offered her the names of some therapists familiar with the trauma she was experiencing.

Turner settled on using the computer only at the kitchen table because he had agreed to do some work at home while he was out of the office for a month. Lynn typically worked from home as an architect, so, at least at this juncture, she could be present while he began his struggle to "detox" from computer use and alcohol. I clarified that Lynn's role in all of this was not to act as the computer police or the alcohol monitor. The deal Turner made was that he would only use the computer for work. He and Lynn would share the same email address. He had never used the computer at work for anything but office matters since he knew that he would be fired instantly if he did. I pointed out that the compliance with this boundary at work boded well for him to be able to keep within other boundaries. He grimaced and did not look thrilled with this information.

After I got to know Turner a little better, I also recommended that medication should be considered. Another grimace from

Turner. Lynn asked me how that worked because I cannot write a prescription. I gave them information about the psychiatrist I work with and told them I believed that together we could diminish the power sex held in their lives. I acknowledged to Turner and Lynn that sometimes this would feel like a relief, and sometimes he would sorely miss his secret life and the solace it provided. For Lynn, developing trust and working on disclosure would be very difficult and fraught with ambivalence. Nevertheless, she felt strongly that the current crisis represented an opportunity to change a marriage that had become very unsatisfactory to both of them. They both knew something had to change!

Turner danced in and out of therapy for a few years but eventually settled into treatment, which was successful in many ways. Turner's wife and employer stayed with him. Medication had enabled him to be much more in control of his life. He was a nicer, calmer person, not reacting negatively to everything said to him. In the end, although his habit had greatly diminished, the magnetism of the Internet remained and he still went online at times. Lynn settled into acceptance about this because in other ways the relationship was significantly better.

Turner's depression and anxiety lifted. He was more accessible and was able to focus on work and other aspects of his life more reliably. He had actually been moved up in the management chain and was able to negotiate much less travel time. He was open with his wife about his feelings and temptations and had more empathy for her feelings. As Turner learned to talk about his feelings the relationship became more intimate. Lynn became more affectionate and sexual with him. Their sexual relationship became more connected and intimate, which both found satisfying. Turner learned that talking is foreplay! Turner had also stopped drinking. He had worked hard at leaving his old life behind and was lucky to get a second chance at his marriage and work.

COGNITIVE BEHAVIORAL TECHNIQUES

Keeping a log

Between treatment sessions I give my clients behavioral tasks to work on, based on cognitive behavioral techniques and tailored to the individual needs of the client or couple. The case material in this book discusses the use of logs and how they fit into the larger picture of treatment. For example, family "town meeting" nights help organize and focus a chaotic family life. These are scheduled once or twice a week and then reported on in sessions. Depending on the family situation, everyone joins in, including the children. Who has a dentist appointment? Who does day care chauffering? What's for supper? I need cupcakes for school next Tuesday. Who does the shopping? Or perhaps I will recommend the couple meet on a regular bi-weekly or weekly basis to discuss material I have suggested they read (see Chapter 8).

Early in the therapeutic relationship, taking into account how dire the crisis may be and how out of control the client feels, I generally assign the task of keeping a log. This will not only serve the client well, but gives the impression to family members or partners that "something is being done." Most important, logs generate a great deal of useful information. John Wincze, Ph.D., a psychologist at Brown University, observes that the log serves two purposes: "(1) It provides additional assessment information, which can serve as a measure of progress, and (2) it provides a therapeutic intervention by interrupting the automatic thought process that accompanies most atypical sexual behavior" (2000). Dr. Wincze cautions that the log be kept in a notebook with no name in it in case it is lost or discovered by someone. I tell my clients that there is also a lot to be learned even if they do not follow through with the task. After all, ambivalence, denial, and resistance show up in many ways and their presence always gives us something to work on.

I also suggest that the client not attempt to write the great American novel, with long descriptions of fantasies and sexual encounters. Some clients confuse this with "journaling" and feel overwhelmed by the thought of writing something every day. Be clear that this is a simple exercise with little actual writing. I have a sample log to offer the client, and we often "tweak" it to fit a particular situation or special needs. For example, Wincze (2000) suggests a simple table with four items: the date, the urge, the act and a comment about the urge or act. Under each column the client is free to put an "X" or "yes" or "no" and make a brief comment about the act. I have adapted Wincze's log:

1. Date: (e.g., Sunday)
2. Urge: (e.g., go on line; check out the videos in the adult book store; masturbate)

3. Fantasies/act/time spent: (e.g., masturbated- men having sex; masturbated- fantasies of being spanked- two hours; online 5 hours a night)
4. Emotional context: (e.g., bored, lonely, angry; rejected by wife, fight with boss)

This simple behavioral log is extremely helpful in capturing the cycle of the habits, triggers, length of time engaged on line or thinking about the desired sexual act, and other patterns. The cycle of "triggers" or feeling states that contextualize the sexual acting out will be important as we work on containing the unwanted behaviors. Awareness of the cycle will help in teaching the coping skills and self-monitoring designed to prevent a relapse. What emerges from a log is a map of the cycle of behaviors or feeling states that are more apt to produce sexual behaviors. It also allows me to see at a glance how a week has gone. The log allows us to add up the time spent pursuing fantasies and/or behaviors. It can put a client in touch with the reality of how much time their habit takes away from other things in life. It puts us both in touch quickly with what triggers the acting out. The log generally becomes a welcome part of the therapy for most clients, although sometimes there are some clients who are "hard sells!" It is generally very revealing and rich with grist for the therapeutic mill.

Jeff and his log

Jeff, a 52 year-old man, had been keeping a log since his first few weeks of treatment. I had known him for about two months. In the beginning, he resisted the log, then began to "journal" his sexual fantasies. We struggled with keeping it simple. His third wife had discovered that Jeff spent most of his time pursuing sexual encounters with anonymous women. She was leaving him.

Jeff had tried many remedies for his sexual habits, which were costing him a great deal in divorce court, to say nothing of his empty life. He had been in a month-long residential program after wife #2, tried abstinence from masturbation for a year, and reliably attended the local 12-step program for two years. The group disbanded but Jeff retained the same sponsor. Jeff still could not be faithful. When wife #3 left him after four years of marriage, he felt that maybe more therapy was in order. I was his third therapist but the first specialist in sexual matters. He was chronically depressed because of the difference between his public persona and his private life. He was also anxious and sleep deprived. The clock was ticking and life was passing him by. Keeping up a façade of bonhomie was always difficult, but it had become more tiring as he got older.

One day Jeff came into the office and proceeded to read a highly detailed and salacious sexual fantasy from his log about a woman he saw on the street. I also noticed that his fly was unzipped. Inwardly, I squirmed with discomfort and fixed my gaze on his face. I knew I had to say something, but I needed a moment to think what it would be. I thought about our struggle to keep the log simple. His *modus operandi* had been to impress women with a show of his superior intellect: reading them poetry, offering books he liked, writing small notes using esoteric and obscure vocabulary, and then seducing them. He was using the same strategy with me! It was very obvious that he was getting aroused by reading his log to me. I asked him to stop reading and acknowledged that I was uncomfortable. I asked him to zip his pants. I also explained that I felt that he had crossed a boundary with me. While he hurriedly groped for his zipper, I got up to refill my glass of water and give us both some space.

I took a deep breath and returned to my chair. I prefaced my remarks with faint praise for doing the log, saying how rich with meaning it was and how much we would learn from it. He smiled and nodded. Then I asked him how he felt when I asked him to stop reading. He hesitated and then with an angry outburst, he said, "I hated it. You humiliated me. I feel ridiculous. You are supposed to help me feel better not worse!" But he did not get up and leave (although maybe I hoped he would). He went on to tell me that I reminded him of his controlling mother and her vigilance about his homework and his controlling wives who nagged him all the time for the truth. Bingo! By asking him to keep a log of his behaviors, he interpreted it as yet another woman trying to control him and his sexuality. When I stopped him from reading to me, he heard his mother's critical, judgmental voice. He was angry with me and all the women in his life.

There is no doubt that I was discomfited by the experience. I also felt that he had given us both a great opportunity. I confronted him but did not judge him or reject him. Granted, it took some doing not to distance myself from him, and he knew it. He had taken a risk by expressing his anger with me. It was the first time he revealed his sincere feelings about the process of therapy and his mother, as well. He had an opportunity to have a real conversation with a woman regarding his feelings about women. By expressing my feelings about his fantasy, I also gave Jeff some insight about his impact on the women he pursued. We talked a lot about how his exploits affected women. He was a narcissist, and empathy was not his strong suit. Nevertheless, he was eventually able to connect the dots between his behaviors and their impact on the women he picked up. I called his pursuit of women as "wanting the 'come-'eres' and doing the 'go-'ways'." It was Jeff's unique approach–avoid game. It generally left him feeling empty, lonely, rejected, and humiliated. I followed the yellow brick road of my own countertransference, and we found his transference!

Seemingly unimportant decisions

Jeff was a master at seemingly unimportant decisions (SUDs). Marlatt (1985) also describes these behaviors as "apparently irrelevant decisions." Jeff was having great difficulty containing his predatory habits. He was always rationalizing how he loved to go downtown to the coffee shop and read the newspaper. Living alone, he felt less lonely downtown, where he ran into friends and colleagues and chatted with them. He was a writer and an academic and spent much time by himself.

Fairly on into the therapy, when he was more in charge of his behaviors than usual, we went over his log and discovered a SUD. Jeff decided he needed some special ice cream to take to a friend's house for dinner. It was Sunday and the dinner party was the following Saturday. If he went downtown he could get it at the place that sold that special ice cream. He had been avoiding downtown for some time, and we had been working on getting his social needs met more mindfully than "picking up" women. He figured he would just run in quickly, buy the ice cream, and get it safely back home to the freezer until the following Saturday. He was proud he was planning ahead.

He would often tell me that he "just happened" to see a woman at a coffee shop or while buying a newspaper and couldn't help chatting her up. Sometimes he would follow the woman, fantasizing he would get her to go to his apartment. But then, unable to make it happen, he would go home and masturbate with her image. It was a SUD to get the ice cream downtown when it was also sold at the supermarket near Jeff's apartment.

Jeff was always acting out his fantasies, and forever chasing women. When he had been married, he often chatted with his wife's friends or students at parties and waltzed them out the door to "see the view" or "get some fresh air." He usually managed to get one of these women into his apartment to see his poetry or literature collection and finally have sex with her. It was irresistible. After a while he was able to put these SUDs in his log and try to avoid them. He called a male friend to go to a movie, or called his sponsor in the 12-step group. But he wanted a woman for sex; masturbation was a lonely activity. On the other hand, Jeff was really working hard at containing himself and, for the first time, he was working on his past relationships and his childhood. It revealed a great deal and helped him put some things in perspective that had been thorns in his side (or his psyche) and kept him from having any really authentic relationships with women.

Why medication?

During the evaluation process, when I mentioned the possibility of medication, Jeff had initially made it clear that he would never "drug" himself. Nevertheless, I was increasingly convinced that it was one of the "missing links" in his treatment. He had been in a 28-day residential program, he had a sponsor, he had seen two other therapists, and he had been faithful to his 12-step program. With all this, Jeff had not been able to meet his goals for a satisfying relationship. Sex was driving his life. He had little impulse control. In addition, he had coexisting mental health issues such as depression and anxiety, which he continued to "medicate away" with orgasms. Medication might not help his narcissism and other characterlogical issues, but it might help with his impulse control, anxiety and depression. I was optimistic and eager to see what it might add to his treatment.

When I felt it was time for Jeff to consider medication, I nudged him about it. I told him that in spite of all the work he had put in to containing his habits, there was still something missing that he could use. "What is that? What do you mean?" he asked. Using a phrase I learned from the psychiatrist I work with, I said he was missing his "executive function." He was not driving—sex was. He had thus given his life over to women and orgasms, and yet he hated them for having so much power over him. His mother had been critical and distant from him while also being inappropriately seductive. Dad had left her alone with him when he was four. He had internalized her message to him as being worthless while at the same time she was being seductive.

Having a better understanding of the meaning of his past had helped a great deal in some areas of his life, but there was more that we could perhaps accomplish. He continued to be depressed and anxious. He did not sleep well and felt humiliated whenever a woman rejected him. He never stopped trying to look for sex (some may call it love) in all the wrong places. His goal for having a satisfying relationship was still not met, and at this point it did not look as if it ever would be. What did he have to lose by trying medicine?

Jeff was not alone in his fears and misconceptions about what medication can and cannot do. Skepticism keeps us safe sometimes. He saw it as another attempt to control him. What would he have left if he had no sex drive? What would he do if he lost the opportunity to feed his ego when he picked up women for sex and erudite conversation?

In treating people with compelling sexual behaviors, the family of medications most often used is the selective serotonin reuptake inhibitors (SSRIs). This group of medications includes Prozac (Fluoxetine), Zoloft (Sertraline), Anafranil (Clomipramine), Celexa (Citalopram), and Lexapro (Escitalopram), and the list gets longer every day. It is a popular misconception that these medications actually treat addiction. Technically, the medication targets the coexisting mental health symptoms and may give people more ability to manage their impulses and the need for sexual outlets.

We still do not know exactly how these medications work. What I have observed, however, is that they treat the accompanying depression, anxiety, obsessiveness, lack of impulse control, lack of ability to focus, and poor self-esteem that seems to accompany the problem of sexual excesses. People feel more in charge of their behavior; they get back (or become newly acquainted with) their own executive function. Sometimes more than one medication may be used. In addition, it is not unusual for a person to try several medications before they find a fit. For some it may be a trial and error process. Many people fear that they will be sedated or lose their sex drive. An open and honest discussion about what to expect when trying medication will dispel fears and myths. The client, the psychiatrist, and I become a team, meeting at intervals that make sense for the individual client. We want to preempt a negative reaction. Together we monitor the medication progress carefully, an approach that most often ensures a smooth and help-ful course.

I suggested to Jeff that medication might be able to provide a pause, like a comma in a sentence, before he acted. It had the potential to quiet his racing thoughts, help him feel more in control of his own life, sleep better, and feel more contented. Finally he agreed to have "just a consultation with no promises made" with the psychiatrist. That is how we generally approach the first psychiatric consultation. A consultation doesn't mean taking medication is a "done deal."

A team approach

Sometimes using the psychiatrist I work with is not an option because of distance or other concerns, so we may defer to the client's family doctor. Or someone may already be on medication when they enter therapy, so I work with whomever writes the prescription. In any case, it is important to work with the prescriber as a team, consulting together often, preferably in person or on the telephone, if necessary. As much as our schedules allow, we conduct telephone conferences with the client present. Ideally, the partner also participates in medication consults so he or she can understand that how the medication might effect both of them. This arrangement seems to work well for everyone involved. Both clients and physicians appreciate and welcome the collaboration.

The rationale for a team approach is that I am the primary thera-pist and see the client often, whereas the prescription writer will see the client at longer intervals for a shorter period of time. In addition, it is not unusual that during a medication visit the client is apt to say he's "fine" when that is not the case at all. Since I have been monitoring the effect of the medication with each visit, I will know if sleep becomes a problem, sexual feelings are diminish-ing, orgasms are difficult to attain, teeth are grinding, or the client complains of being too sleepy. If I think we should go up or down on the medication or change it, I suggest the client call the doctor and I call also. When we all meet, I might say, "Didn't you tell me you were not sleeping well?" or "Wasn't your wife complain-ing about it taking longer to have an orgasm?" A quick medica-tion check without the therapist does not generally reveal these same subtleties. A "medication team" approach is very useful, and I highly recommend it. As cumbersome and time consuming as it may be, I have become a "true believer" in this system, although twenty years ago, I was a hard sell.

Skepticism

Jeff asked the two questions that almost everyone inevitably asks when we discuss taking medication: "How long will I have to take medication?" and "What about the side effects, particularly sexual side effects?" I told Jeff that it is useful to delay the decision about "how long" until he experienced the benefits and changes from the medication. If there is a good response to the medication, the psychiatrist and I usually recommend a 12-month trial, unless, of course, there are problems. By then, a person will be well informed about the benefits of medication and can make a well-considered decision about continuing or discontinuing. If medication is discontinued after a period of time, it is possible that some of the emotional development that has taken place will "stick," meaning it may actually change brain chemistry, so some symptoms may not return. Medication is like a tool you keep in the closet should the faucet leak. If it does leak, you know where the tool is and that it will do the job to fix the leak.

Regarding the question of side effects: forewarned is forearmed. First we discussed what to expect in general terms. The person taking the medicine is often the last to observe the changes. I often notice very subtle things fairly soon after the medication has begun, and will point them out. For instance, eye contact may be better, a person may seem calmer when we discuss certain issues, be more relaxed and able to sit in one place comfortably, perhaps sleep better and feel more rested. Clients often tell me that their spouse notices that they have more patience, are less reactive, less anxious, happier, calmer and better able to focus on tasks. I prepare my clients for side effects, but it is my experience that clients seldom have them—or at least only mild ones in the beginning. Some of the things they might encounter may be that one cup of caffeine or one glass of wine might seem like two or three. A person may feel jittery or have more of a "buzz" when he has a glass of wine or a cup of coffee or even a bag of M&Ms. Stomachs may be upset: "Can you tolerate it for a few days and see if it goes away?" Same for mild headaches: "Will Tylenol or aspirin work?" Almost always these early symptoms leave after three to four days.

Some people get very anxious when they have early, mild symptoms and cannot tolerate them. We may drop the dose back or stop the medication and maybe try another. Most of my clients sail through with no side effects, or transient ones that are generally tolerable and have very helpful results. It is not generally predictable how well medication will work, or even if it will work at all. We start with a very small dose and slowly move up. I also explain that if someone does well at a high dose of the medicine it does not mean they are "really crazy" or "emotionally disturbed." It is important to keep in mind that we are all different, and how our livers metabolize anything, even pepperoni pizza, will be what predicts the dosage. There are also lots of medication choices, so if one does not work another may be substituted. If necessary, individual doses can be fine-tuned, bumped up or down to eliminate unwelcome symptoms or increase the benefits. As far as anyone can tell, these medications seem to cause no permanent damage and are not addictive.

Listening to people's fears about medication contributes a great deal toward assuring a successful outcome with a particular medication or treatment. This skepticism is not only healthy but useful. Let's not forget the social and political valence that some medications have, like birth control pills, morning after pills, and pills for emotional conditions, and erections. When SSRIs began to appear on the scene about 20 years ago, there was also much controversy and debate. Peter Kramer, M.D. (1993), a psychiatrist at Brown University, wrote *Listening to Prozac*. Prozac was among the earliest of the SSRIs. There was a controversy about whether or not it was a good idea to change people's personalities, if indeed it did.

Elizabeth Wurtzel (1995), a young depressed woman, wrote about her experiences with depression and medication in *Prozac Nation*, giving the public a view of what it was like to struggle with depression. Depression was finally getting on the map and people were at least talking about treatments, even though some of the conversation was disparaging. I have watched the evolution of medication for emotional distress for 45 years and am pleased that there now is a whole new family of medications to treat emotional dilemmas. Forty or fifty years ago, people (mostly women) who were "nervous" or had "nervous breakdowns" were often sedated and became addicted to the few medications available at that time. Clients need to know that the SSRIs act on the brain differently than sedatives, that they won't feel numbed out or sedated. But they do quiet the mind.

Tinkering with the psyche, the personality, and enhancing sexual capacity is upsetting to some people. It became acceptable to treat psychotic, hallucinating, catatonic people in institutions, but not the people that were once labeled the "worried well." These labels included people with depression, anxiety, obsessive habits, phobias, and post traumatic stress disorder—people who seemed functional but were in great psychic pain. They held jobs and walked around carrying their struggles inside. Emotional problems were looked upon as character flaws rather than difficulties worthy of medical treatments.

Today, medications are advertised on television and in magazines and newspapers. This can be overwhelming and frightening to people trying to make decisions about what medications to take. We often hear that the Federal Drug Administration (FDA) has recalled some medications because of harmful, irreversible, or fatal side effects. I think back to the time when oral contraceptives were developed and used widely. Some women had strokes or blood clots while taking them. Still, oral contraceptives did not disappear from the market. Neither have the pills for erections disappeared when recently a small number of men who took Viagra had associated ophthalmological problems. It all speaks to the importance of careful medical attention and perspective when considering the costs and benefits of any medications. New medications are discovered every day. How can we decide what is good for each of our unique needs and body chemistries? Certainly a thoughtful consultation with a physician is a good beginning. Many of the SSRIs have been around a while so they have a track record. It is reassuring to know this when people are anxious about long-range effects of medication.

I have also learned that most people look very carefully at other people's experiences with medications. If a client has a relative or friend who had a negative effect from a medication, it might make the client wary. If someone's mother took Prozac and did well with it, that might be a reason to take it. On the other hand, perhaps someone is trying to individuate and separate from her mother, and doesn't want to be anything like her or do anything her mother did. Maybe an older brother had schizophrenia, and growing up with him in the household was a nightmare for the younger sibling: doctors, special school, medications, time and attention consumed caring for him to the exclusion of the younger child's needs, and embarrassment. The client might ask, "Am I getting a mental illness too? Why do I need medication? What does this mean?" It is important to fully understand the meaning and implications medication might have for each person. If I neglect or miss some of these implications, my client might struggle with the medication or perhaps stop taking it when it might have been really been helpful.

Sexual side effects

And what about the impact of medication on sexual behavior and desire? Not only is it a very good question, but it is the $64,000 question! Jeff heard that these medications have some impact on sex drive, which had been so central to his life. He found it impossible to contemplate what would happen to him if he lost his sex drive. He told me that is why he had resisted even the idea of medication. I am not surprised. Straightforwardly, I validate that he might experience a difference in his sex drive but not necessarily a complete loss (although truthfully, it may seem like a loss initially).

My perspective from working with many people who have decided to try medication is that a change is more than likely welcome for most, although for some it is not, and for still others it is somewhere in between. Sexual desire is personal and subjective. When someone has been as highly sexualized for a very long time as Jeff was, it may be too frightening to experience a change in sex drive or desire. It is important that the client knows that if he experiences something he does not like, it will not be permanent. The medication can be tapered off or the dose can be changed.

I told Jeff that while the psychiatrist and I am there to consult with, he is the expert on his body and psyche, and he will get to decide for himself if the medication serves him well. He will decide if it is welcome when he has the "executive function" over his sexual desire. Is it a return to "normal" sexual desire? For that matter, what is "normal" sexual desire? I used the analogy with Jeff, as I have with many clients, that if you have been driving down the road at 100 miles an hour and you see the police, you will most likely slow down to 65 mph. It may feel as if you are creeping along, but 65 mph is still pretty efficient to get you where you need to go. You might enjoy the road and scenery more. It's a matter of getting used to the new landscape that emerges.

I have observed that clients will feel more comfortable with the change in libido and the lessening of the erotic pull to act out sexually. The ability to focus, to concentrate, to notice how good it feels to cuddle, to get a hug, to enjoy a conversation, to have connected and intimate partnered sex begins to fill in the empty spaces. It may take some time to experience a new kind of sexual desire that feels comforting, connected, and in control. Everything in life is relative.

There is also another sexual side effect that is fairly common with the SSRIs—the length of time it may take to ejaculate or have an orgasm. This is usually dose related, and can be reversed. While initially this also may feel like a frightening loss, it will often have a positive side. Many men who have been masturbating a great deal complain that during partnered sexual encounters, they ejaculate too soon (often an objective issue). Or they may have spent a lifetime feeling inadequate about their sexual abilities. Some are so anxious about their capacity to delay ejaculation that they cannot even get an erection. Lasting longer may be welcome for some.

Certainly approaching a sexual encounter without anxiety is welcome, too. But sometimes partners complain if orgasm is delayed. Not only will some take that as a rejection and a sign that they are not attractive or sexy enough to produce an orgasm but also it may result in soreness or an irritated bladder, aching legs, etc. The dose can be tweaked, and foreplay may need to be lengthened. Longer foreplay is usually welcome by both parties. As long as the couple is willing to partner with these changes, they can have positive effects. Orgasm is not the only goal in a good sexual encounter!

Dealing with sexual side effects from medication requires much support, creativity, and reassurance from the therapist. I point out subtleties, nuances, and small details. It is important to keep in mind that clients with compelling sexual habits have not done much introspection or focused much, if at all, on how they feel. It requires much patience to help the person achieve a good understanding of the benefits and down sides of medication, but it is definitely worth the time and effort.

It is central to the overall treatment process that a balance be established between leaving the old habits behind and gaining new coping skills, resting into the new place and experiencing the comfort it provides. While some people really welcome not feeling sexually driven all the time, others may find it difficult to get used to a change in sexual appetite. I emphasize that this change does not necessarily mean their sexuality is gone. It may mean we have to tweak the dose, or wait a while to see how things play out in partnered sex.

Because they have been uninhibitedly feeding their appetite for sexual stimulation over a long period of time, clients may find it very difficult and just plain frightening to deal with the change medication provides. It is my clinical experience that a majority of my clients will eventually settle into a different, less driven range of arousal and comfort with partnered sex. In addition, the reciprocity of the partner who begins to trust the changes in feelings and connection that occur with treatment and medication, contributes to reinforcing the rewards of a less frenzied, more intimate emotional and sexual experience. So the answer to the $64,000 question is, "You have to wait and see." We will work on solutions when problems appear.

Giving medication a go

Jeff eventually decided that he wanted to have a consultation with the psychiatrist. The first consultation is usually an hour. We then taper down to 30 minutes and sometimes 15 and space the visits at intervals that seem good to the client. However, the client always gets to decide how much time he or she needs. As it worked out, Jeff had a very good result from taking medication. Most people, Jeff included, find it a relief to have a quieter mind. His thoughts were not always racing, and he could focus better on tasks. He spent much less time having sexual fantasies, and when he was out and about and saw a good-looking girl there was a pause during which he was able to talk himself out of pursuing her attention. The moment between thought and deed lengthened. This gave Jeff a chance to consider his own needs and desires for sexual outlets. Sex was no longer the "drug of choice" when he was feeling insecure.

Medication also helped Jeff recognize more quickly what the consequences of his behaviors might be. He no longer felt out of control. With less anxiety and defensiveness, Jeff was able to dig deeper in psychotherapy as well. He began to understand his own past in a way that was more useful. We worked together for a few years. Jeff continued to weigh the costs and benefits of medication over time. He did not have a partner, but lately he was trying to talk to women without an agenda for sex. It was awkward and surely a new skill, but he was at least willing to see that it might have benefits. Three divorces had finally made him think about checking out what the woman was all about before he had sex with her. He was learning how to "do his homework" before he made any sexual commitments. What he wanted at 52 was someone who could hold up for the "long haul." He finally developed a good relationship with a woman he had known for many years but who resisted his sexual invitations. She was a friend and an intellectual equal. Now they live together.

Chapter 5

"I sing the body electric"
Techno-sex in the postmodern world

Ebb stung by the flow and flow stung by the ebb, love-flesh swelling and deliciously aching,
Limitless limpid jets of love hot and enormous, quivering jelly of love, white-blow and delirious juice.

Walt Whitman

THE COMPUTER CHIP REVOLUTION

The computer never fails to fill me with a sense of awe and wizardry. It both delights and frightens me. I describe it ambivalently as *terribly wonderful.* I use it tentatively, never knowing what will jump out at me, where it will take me, and when it will fail me. I always imagine that this might have been how Alice felt when she fell down the rabbit hole into Wonderland.

There is no doubt that the computer and the Internet have transformed the world. They have changed the way we communicate with each other and what we communicate about. They have also exposed us to sexual material most of us could not even imagine and have changed how we think about sexual interaction. In the 21st century sexual material is in our face even if we don't wish it to be. Although Walt Whitman wrote about sex in a very explicit way, his poetry, and other sexually explicit material that predated the computer, had a less intrusive, more consensual presence than the Internet and media do today.

Sex and sexual topics are the most frequently sought after sites on the Internet (Griffiths, 2001). The Internet has had a great impact on how we meet and mate as well. Sexual activities on the Internet can be life-enhancing and educational or disruptive and illegal. Along with other social forces like the women's movement, the computer chip revolution has spawned still another sexual revolution. The Internet and its possibilities scurry ahead of us like the rabbit scurrying through Wonderland as Alice tries to keep up with him. The Web has infinite capacity to deliver sexual material. Like cells in a Petri dish, sexual content on the Internet divides and mutates rapidly. It feels out of control. New technology— BlackBerrys, iPods, Palm Pilots, as well as cell phones with all kinds of enhancements such as cameras and TV access—proliferates and gives us unlimited access to the Internet. It is difficult to escape these intrusive personal (or not so personal) information systems. In this post-modern techno-era, the Internet, video games, movies, TV, cell phones, camcorders, and DVDs all provide challenges to the way we seek sexual gratification.

Internet commerce in sexually explicit material, some legal and some criminal, is very big business, generating millions of dollars for those entrepreneurs who, like Danni Ashe in 1997, have brought their talent to the task. To make these hefty profits, sexual sites need to attract and retain large numbers of people. Writing in *The New York Times* in 2001, columnist John Schwartz reported that from December 1999 to February, 2001, the number of individual visitors to online adult sites grew 27%, meaning nearly 22 million visitors grew to 28 million visitors in only fourteen months! Think what it must be today! Even though less than 1% of visitors to adult sites actually pay for a peek, these sites are still turning a tidy profit for the industry.

Eight years after Schwartz's 2001 report, Brad Stone (2008), writing for *The New York Times* about the porn industry, described that it is still the "pervasive and resilient-to-recession online cash venture." Stone reported that Richard J. Gordon, who started a payment processing company for Internet porn in the '90s, has made and continues to make millions of dollars because these pay-for-a-peek sites "continue to have its roots in sexual entertainment." Gordon has a close business relationship with a Japanese man, Wataru Takahashi, who promotes the sexually explicit Japanese animations that have become very popular and easily seduce both the curious and serious users.

Postmodern relationships

Since the Internet has entered our lives, our imaginations are the only boundary. Anyone can engage in any kind of sexual adventure they can imagine anywhere, anytime, with anyone without ever leaving the house! Gunther Schmidt, M.D. (1998), a German psychiatrist, has some interesting observations about what he calls "postmodern sexuality" in the Internet era. He describes modern sexuality as "fragmented, disrupted, de-essentialized, episodic, and potpourried ... a huge supermarket told in a 'language of excess' and 'hyperbolic madness,' [it is] 'glitzy-glossy,' high tech, and consumerist." He continues:

> On top of this come the untapped and bewildering opportunities offered by the Internet and cyberspace that fire the imagination of sex visionaries and culture critics. We are promised world wide babble, sharing in inventing and acting out pornographic tales, joining in virtual orgies, or ... having long-distance intercourse with one or several partners. One can take over any role one chooses on the virtual scene, adopt any identity: man, woman, gay, lesbian, old, young, for weeks and months, as long as the game continues.

Most of the sexual frenzy we see today is more talk and Madison Avenue hyperbole than reality. While we might expect that this sexually open, no-holds-barred society we live in today has changed what people actually do in the privacy of their bedrooms, it really has not substantively affected the average person's sexual practices. A comprehensive survey of the sexual practices and beliefs of Americans was conducted in 1994 by a team of social scientists and researchers at the University of Chicago, headed by Edward Lauman, Ph.D. The survey included 3,432 people, which in 1994 was the most comprehensive study ever done on sexual practices since Kinsey's research (1948, 1953). The study revealed that Americans are in a somewhat different place than those surveyed by Kinsey, but not substantively. The Lauman study, which preceded the proliferation of sex on the Internet, revealed that the average couple only has sex once a week and that the sexual behavior of choice is vaginal intercourse. In a nutshell, the truth is people today are not having as much partnered sex as the media would have us believe and, for the most part, couple sex is pretty much a mainstream event. On the other hand, many are looking at every imaginable kind of sex on line and masturbating with these images as the stimulus.

Monogamy and adultery have taken on different meanings today as well. President Jimmy Carter once said that "anyone who looks on another woman with lust in his heart already committed adultery" (Scheer, 1979). Many people would not agree with President Carter; if they did, it would mean that almost everyone commits adultery! Is looking at another woman or man and "lusting in your heart" really adultery or being unfaithful? There are also many people who would agree with President Clinton that he did not have sex outside his marriage. It was not intercourse, merely oral sex. Many people think oral sex is "not really sex." Isn't that what all the people who take "abstinence pledges" think when they have oral sex? We all have our own standards and opinions when it comes to sex. This can be a real problem when two people own one sex life and have strong differences of opinion about monogamy, adultery, and masturbation.

With the Internet there is no need for human contact, for an eye-to-eye intimate conversation, in order to have a sexual encounter. For some, unfettered and uncommitted sex is the glue that binds them to the glowing screen. It replaces a connected relationship with a real person. The Internet has taken the erotic experience to a place we never would have thought possible. It has also created problems we never could have predicted. For most people, real-partnered sex still figures in the bonding equation, but in different ways than it did in the past. For others, the use of online sexual experiences becomes a way of life—a substitute for real-time sexual relationships, an escape from life's realities. It allows avoidance of emotional intimacy and acts as a drug to medicate away the fear of closeness with spouses or partners or any human being. It certainly can "unglue" a relationship. John Bancroft (2002) characterizes the postmodern relationship this way:

> [Relationships] seem to last as long as both partners are satisfied with the personal bonus it provides. It is, therefore, by nature, of uncertain duration and often short-lived. It reflects each individual's commitment to his or her own personal growth and well-being as well as a negotiated, and hence more equitable, way of relating to one another. Within such relationships we can see how sex can contribute to intimacy, serving to bond the relationship if it works well, weakening it if it does not.

WHAT DRIVES THE INTERNET CONNECTION?

David Greenfield and Maressa Orzack (2002), researching the issues of cybersex, describe "problematic online sexual experiences" to be, at least in part, "the result of the synergistic relationship between the psychoactive elements of the Internet, including reinforcement, disinhibition, excitement, and anonymity, and the level of stimulation provided by the specific sexual material." Put in less scientific terms, fear of discovery, coupled with the forbidden and the erotic, overrides many inhibitions. In a garage with a cache of magazines, or on the Internet, the same triggers could pull almost anyone into a lifetime of secrets and lost opportunities for themselves as well as their families. We just haven't figured out yet what precisely makes one person vulnerable and another impervious to this synergistic combination.

Al Cooper, Ph.D. (1997) suggested that the unique combination of accessibility, affordability, and anonymity fuel sexual activity on the Internet. These attributes make sexual activity on the Internet not only attractive and available, but also intrinsically difficult to contain. In reality, these attributes are an illusion. For example, not all sites are free or affordable. An obsessed user can be online for many hours accumulating large credit card debt that can threaten financial security. In addition, there are considerable costs in terms of quality of life, employment loss, and wasted time. Anonymity, or the implication of secrecy or anonymity, also serves to heighten the pleasure of Internet sex and entices users to experiment with activities most would never consider off-line. These days even a relatively unsophisticated but determined partner, spouse, family member, employer, or a highly trained legal investigator will be able to track someone's Internet use and expose sexual pursuits. Exposed, the user may be found to have a more profound problem than anyone (particularly themselves) imagined.

Sexual activity on the Internet has the potential for escalating out of control and becoming problematic for all users—even when the online sexual activities are legal. Since a whole generation has been born for whom the computer is as ubiquitous as the telephone was to my generation, problematic use of the Internet is becoming widespread. The world is connected to the computer for every type of business and all world affairs. In addition to the Internet being essential to the world infrastructure, sexual pursuits online and the synergy of gaming online has spawned a whole generation of users who have developed serious problems because of Internet use.

It is interesting to note, however, that while women now use the Internet and access websites as frequently as men do, statistics showed that "men dominated certain types of websites (e.g., government, financial, sexually explicit materials), and in general used more types of sites than women" (Wasserman & Richmond-Abbott, 2005). This corresponds with the fact that more men than women have compelling sexual habits (Kafka, 2007) and are caught on the Web using sexually explicit material. It is nearly an epidemic. This research also revealed that women are more likely to use the Internet for cooking, religious purposes, and purchasing products for the home. Wasserman and Richmond-Abbott also predict that in the future more women will expand their use of the Internet. Some people cannot resist the synergy of the Internet. It is a way to evade the issues that keep some feeling inadequate, anxious, and depressed, perhaps on the brink of suicide. Cooper and Marcus (2003) observed that while "Freud once said that 'dreams are the royal road to the unconscious,' sexual behavior seems to be the fast track to unspoken, perhaps unrealized, feelings."

"Cybersex," "cybersexing," or "cybering" are terms used to describe online sexual activity, with the goal being erotic titillation generally ending in orgasm. While there is no such thing as "typical" cybersex, the more common types of online sexual activities include cruising the Internet for sexually explicit images such as pictures, stories, or videos; using instant messaging or entering chat rooms (with or without cameras) to flirt and have sexually explicit conversations; finding people to meet off-line for liaisons that may result in a romantic relationship or be solely for sexual contact and experimentation (Cooper, Golden, & Marshall, 2006). Telephone sex, although it predates the Internet, shares many of the characteristics of cybersexing.

With the advent of cameras on telephones and Web cams that can be set up anywhere, pictures can be made of people without their knowledge or consent, then loaded onto a computer and sent anywhere. This has become a popular activity. All Internet activities have the potential to become problematic and perhaps illegal and dangerous. For example, meeting with people off-line can be either safe or dangerous. It can expose a person to assault, blackmail, or sexually transmitted infections. It behooves everyone to be discriminating when they arrange to meet off-line, to be clear about the purpose, and to create a safe venue for the meeting. The therapist ought to be assessing these off-line meetings for risk.

It is also useful to be aware of the more common cons and scams on chat line venues. For example, the person who eventually wants to meet and borrow money is a popular con. The scams are infinite and very clever. Does a client ask the age of the person he or she is chatting with? If the anonymous chatterer says he or she is over 18 years old, a client may feel he has covered the legal obligation, but it is a very slippery slope. If age is not discussed, the client may find the person he's speaking with is a computer detective trolling for pedophiles. It may take many sessions to assess the details of Internet use. The details are important: who? what? where? and when? Logs are very useful if a client really wants to "work the program."

Cooper et al. (1999) and Carnes et al. (2001) describe and categorize various types of cybersex users, which is a useful framework for formulating diagnostic and treatment strategies for people attached to the Internet for sexual stimulation. I have adapted and combined their categories:

- **Recreational users.** This seems to be the largest group. There are two subtypes:
  a. *Appropriate recreational* users may be looking for information or education about sexual topics or just ways to enhance their sex life.
  b. *Inappropriate recreational* users are not obsessive or compulsive. They use sexual material such as jokes, cartoons, or screen savers that are inappropriate at work or at home with friends or family. They seem to have poor social skills, with no sense of socially acceptable boundaries and social customs. They may tell jokes at inappropriate times to get attention. Perhaps they may be found to have symptoms that resonate with Asperger's spectrum.
- **Discovery group:** These users are just beginning to use the computer compulsively and have no prior history of inappropriate sexual behaviors or fantasies. The Internet "triggers" or hooks them and they become dysfunctional users.
- **Predisposed group:** There are a significant number of people who have a preexisting disposition for sexual obsessions, compulsions, or other mental health conditions. For them, the Internet has provided another outlet for problematic sexual behavior to escalate and significantly interferes with their lives.

- **Lifelong sexual compulsives:** This group of users has a lifelong history of problematic sexually compulsive behavior. There are three subtypes:
  a. Some in this category will use the Internet as another way to act out their sexual compulsions.
  b. Some find that the Internet is a less risky place for them to act out their fantasies and behaviors.
  c. For some, the exposure to the possibilities on the Internet challenges their emotional resources as well as their impulse control. They escalate to even riskier behaviors.

Sorting out Internet dilemmas

While the focus of this book is on legal behaviors, I don't believe that any discussion of the Internet and sex can avoid the issue of pursuit of children on the Internet. With the help of the Internet, children are lured from their homes, abducted, sexually abused, and murdered. This happened in Vermont in June, 2008, but it happens daily everywhere on the globe, even though the majority of these instances do not make the headlines. It is a complex issue that never ceases to horrify and stir everyone up—as well it might. The politicos weigh in, advocates for preventing child abuse weigh in, ordinary people are mobilized to stop these horrific acts, and families still continue to grieve.

There has been much valuable research on perpetrators of child abuse in an effort to understand why they abuse children and learn how to treat them effectively (Marshall, Fernandez, Marshall, & Serran, 2006; Schwartz, 2002). In the end, even with the greatest vigilance, these crimes against children continue. It is a highly complex and egregious problem with no one answer or one solution. One of the cases I discuss below highlights the necessity for objectivity and well-informed diagnostic thinking when dealing with accusations of child abuse. The other case is a more usual scenario and highlights how someone can get caught up by the Internet as a way to escape the stressors of life.

CAREY

I was called to the psychiatric ward in the hospital for a consult on a 30-year-old woman who was afraid she was a pedophile. Carey had just been admitted for attempted suicide and had severe obsessive compulsive disorder (OCD) with painful and distressing ideations, as well as an obsessive attachment to her computer, cell phone, and iPod. When I met with her, she had a telephone hooked over one ear, a laptop clutched tightly to her chest with her arms around it, and an iPod with its ear piece in her other ear. She slept with the iPod on. She said it was the only way she could get to sleep. The question I was asked to consider was: "Is this woman a pedophile?" The staff was mobilized by the case and we were to have rounds to discuss its many implications. The resident briefed me on Carey's history and the attending physician discussed the medical implications of her admission. Then I interviewed Carey.

Carey was a single, pleasant-looking woman of above average intelligence who designed software. Her eyes were frightened, but she was able to focus on the interview. After her sister recently had a baby boy, Carey began to look at infants on the Internet. When she visited her sister, she was fascinated by her nephew Tyler's genitals, and sometimes when she was changing his diaper she was afraid she might touch his penis and damage him. She was never aroused by these incidents. In fact they scared her, and she felt so ashamed and guilty that she refused to go to her sister's house anymore, fearing that she would harm the child.

Carey worried constantly that she might abuse Tyler. She began to research child abuse online and convinced herself that she had all the symptoms of pedophilia. She was very upset and worried about going to jail, but thought it might be the best place for her. Carey was ashamed and felt worthless; she could not face her family. She obsessed about these ideas constantly and was tortured by her thoughts. Carey had a history of depression. At the same time, she also had been successful at work, dated a little, and had good friends that she socialized with. She had a younger sister and brother, and she had sometimes helped her mother take care of them. She had no memory of ever having been abused or of abusing her siblings.

Her history with the computer was also interesting. As a software designer, she used the computer all day, every day. She found herself unable to leave it alone even when she left work. She needed it for everything, even ordering a pizza. If she wasn't connected to the telephone and computer, she became very anxious. She took them everywhere and shyly admitted she even took them into the bathroom and that she had cut her hair very short so she could shower quickly. Carey wished she could learn to contain her need for being "wired" all the time. She was hopeful the admission to the hospital would help her distance herself from all her "gadgets," as well as help her be safe with children.

Carey also obsessed that she would be arrested and became agitated whenever the main door to the psychiatric unit was opened, feeling sure that someone was "coming to get her." During our interview, Carey asked me many times if I thought she was a pedophile. I reassured her that we would get it all sorted out soon and that it did not appear to any of the staff or to me that she was actually a pedophile. I explained that the obsessive compulsive disorder appeared to be driving the disturbing thoughts she was having. Medication would quiet these disturbing thoughts.

Her family was close, supportive, and very concerned. Her maternal aunt was diagnosed with bipolar disease and had committed suicide. Carey's younger brother also had OCD but it was attached to obsessively washing his hands and fear of germs. After talking with Carey for about an hour and a half, I agreed she had severe OCD and other serious psychiatric problems, but I did not think she was a pedophile. There was no indication that she had ever actually abused a child.

It is always a clinical challenge to sort out what actually happens when someone has intrusive thoughts. The staff discussed all the implications for this case. It was a multi-discipline group, and we examined the issue from all sides. "What if she really was a pedophile?" Everyone was concerned that we make the right decision. Ultimately, everyone was satisfied she was not a pedophile and that psychiatric treatment would be useful. I recommended two articles to the staff that I found very helpful; they addressed the issue of obsessive compulsive disorders and sexual ideations (O'Neil, Cather, Fishel, & Kafka, 2005; Warwick & Salkovskis, 1990). Some people have thought disturbances and psychoses and obsess about child abuse or doing others harm, although they do not act on it. It is best to consider the difference, however scary it may be.

MITCH

I was not prepared for the man I met in the waiting room. When I spoke with Mitch on the telephone, I did not imagine the tall, handsome, confident, socially poised, and very charming man who walked into my office. On the telephone he sounded very tenuous and quite anxious. He had been referred by a colleague, who conveyed a sense of urgency and distress. Mitch carried his laptop into the office and opened it as he sat down. No one had ever brought a laptop to my office. Turning the screen toward me, he said, "Look at these pictures and tell me what you think. How old do these women look to you?"

I was somewhat hesitant to see what was on Mitch's screen. I mobilized myself, got my reading glasses, and left my chair to peer more closely at the screen. I used the time to figure out what to say while I examined the female images smiling at me from the screen. Instead of answering his question, I asked Mitch, "How old do *you* think they are?" "No, no," he said, "*you* have to tell *me* what you think." So I asked him how old he *wanted* them to be? Somewhat impatient with still another question from me, he answered that his wife thought they were teenagers and was about to divorce him because he looked at these sites on the Internet. He repeated: "It's weird, so weird; they look like grown women to me; I cannot figure out why she is so angry with me."

Mitch had been looking on the Internet for sexual stimulation for a few years. In hindsight, Mitch had been in the grip of desire for about twenty years. He fell into the category of users who had preexisting sexual obsessions before he went online. His use of the Internet became problematic a few years before he sought help. It had begun to interfere with his relationship with his wife. He told me that he had recently become scared when he realized that the female images he viewed on the Internet were becoming younger and younger. However, he became defensive and denied it when his wife had accused him of looking at teenagers under 18.

At work, he was used to talking and joking a lot about sex. He was a flirt and was inappropriate a lot of the time. His wife was critical of how much he looked at other women, and she often checked where he had been on the Internet. She felt insulted, rejected, and betrayed. Mitch knew he needed help. He had volunteered, without prompting, the answers to the two questions I am always interested in learning about at the beginning of therapy: What brings you to therapy? What do you hope to accomplish? Mitch was motivated to get help with the escalating behavior he knew had implications for his wife and their relationship. He was a physician, and there was also a possibility that he could lose his license if he did not change his habits. He knew it was against the law to view people under the age of 18 in a sexual situation or chat with them online for sexual purposes. He was worried that the girls he saw online were younger than 18. I also thought they were younger than 18, but it was difficult to be sure. Producers of the site intentionally create ambiguity about the ages of the models.

In spite of the anxiety I had heard on the telephone, in person Mitch seemed confident and sure of himself. He was also open with me, answered questions easily, and seemed determined to make the most of this first session. While he had every right to be full of himself, he was not. He was a warm, kind person with whom it was easy to engage. He wanted to understand fully what was happening to him, to try to change his behavior. He described his wife Eleanor as his best friend. He loved her very much and did not want to lose her. He knew it would hurt her if she knew the extent of his sexual habits.

Mitch's timing in seeking help was interesting. Mitch was almost at the end of his fellowship in thoracic surgery. He had received an offer from another hospital on the West Coast. However, he was hoping that they could remain in here. If the hospital did not make him an offer, they would be moving within two months of our first visit. Ambivalence shows itself in many ways. Mitch was no exception. He was torn between keeping his secrets and giving them up. Albert Camus (1957) once said: "Believe me, the hardest thing for a man to give up is that which he really doesn't want, after all."

Mitch's assessment

We agreed on some short-term goals because of the uncertainty of his stay in here. I would do an assessment that might take a few sessions, meet with his wife, and then we all would meet together. I would give them some feedback about the findings, and discuss what the treatment possibilities might be. He asked if I could refer him to a therapist if he decided to move, and I reassured him that I would find some colleges to recommend and help him make the transition if it became necessary.

The assessment revealed some interesting issues. Mitch was eager to share the details of his family history, his health, and his relationship with his wife. He painted an idyllic picture of his mom and dad and two siblings. His parents were supportive and kind, although they definitely were "on the job" with discipline when it was needed. They socialized a lot and alcohol was served, but he didn't seem to think that his parents had a problem with alcohol. He was the middle child of the three children; one of his sisters was three years younger and the other five years older. When I asked about significant illnesses or traumas, he remembered having been knocked unconscious playing ball when he was nine or ten years old, and had lost his memory for a few hours. Interesting—another head injury to add to the list.

Mitch dated a lot in college and had many sexual adventures. He met Eleanor in college and while she was his "main squeeze," he was not faithful to her. He had trouble committing to the relationship, and after college they separated for a few years. When Mitch was in medical school and felt more focused on where he was heading in life, they resumed their relationship and married. He described Eleanor as his soulmate, and was glad they both had taken the time to figure out what they meant to one another.

Toward the end of the first session, I learned that Mitch and his wife not only drank a lot, but that they both occasionally used marijuana. He told me that Eleanor's father and brother had serious alcohol habits. I took him through the details of his habits, and some were troublesome. He used to drink every day and a great deal on weekends. In college he had been stopped twice for a DWI and lost his driver's license for a while. He was grateful he had not had any accidents, and since then was careful not to drink and drive. Other than those incidents in college, he had never been in trouble with the law or suspended from school. During his residency, he became aware that if he drank in the evening, he felt groggy and bad the next day so he became careful not to drink when he was working. The medical school and hospital were very vigilant about staff drinking and substance abuse. He and his wife smoked pot only on rare occasions, maybe three times a year if they managed to have an overnight without their three-year-old daughter, Molly.

As the hour was winding down, I was disarmed to see that Mitch suddenly had tears in his eyes. He sat forward on the couch and asked me, "Will you be recommending that I stop drinking?" I asked him about his tears. He said that he just could not face the fact that he had such a serious problem with sex and that he would have to give up alcohol too. He had done quite well in life so far and did not want to think of himself as a person with problems that he could not control. Yet here he was sitting in a therapist's office! I suggested that the person who was so successful would also be the same person who had a great deal to bring to the task of treatment. Becoming a surgeon is not easy. It is also difficult to be a husband and father but he seemed to be up to those tasks. Mitch said that he hoped he was, but he felt he was running out of strength.

I wondered if this statement was a veiled suicidal thought or an expression of exhaustion and depression. I asked, "What does it feel like to be running out of strength?" Mitch said he was tired all the time, and worried that he would not be able to stop drinking or give up the erotic "buzz" he got from the Internet. The Internet was a place he escaped to when his life was too hectic and demanding. Alcohol and the Internet were the only ways he could relax. While he wanted help, he was afraid there would be no way to escape from all his responsibilities, no pleasure in his life. I commented again that running out of strength must seem very frightening. "What would giving up look like?" I asked. He had never thought about committing suicide, but he did think about going away, not practicing medicine, living in a small town and owning a hardware store. I would see him again in a few days. In the meantime, if he felt as if he was running out of strength between visits, I was available. While I did not believe Mitch was suicidal, he certainly was depressed, anxious, and overwhelmed.

Mitch's secrets

During the evaluation period, Mitch and I examined the many details of his sexual habits, always paying attention to the context within which they developed and were acted out. Mitch had been highly sexualized for a long time. He talked and joked about sex frequently, flirted whenever he could, and loved to establish eye contact with attractive women when he was out and about. Scanning for "eye candy" was a common behavior for Mitch. A few times a year when he went to conferences, and after he married Eleanor, Mitch engaged in sexual liaisons that he described as "one-night stands." These encounters happened before Molly was born, and alcohol often played a big part. He found his work very stressful, and his relationship with Eleanor was complex and often troublesome. While he really enjoyed being with his daughter, fatherhood had been unexpectedly difficult for him. It became easy to escape to the Internet. Online, an erotic buzz could be accessed any time; it fit easily into his lifestyle.

Mitch is not alone; many people have the same issue when looking at teenage bodies online. They become frightened when they realize that they are developing an ever more voracious appetite for erotic stimulus from ever younger bodies, and that those "young women" may be less than 18. Many have no idea that their sexual experiences online may be monitored by the law. Some people figure that if the images are on the computer, and thus available to everyone, it is permissible to view them. Or, they think there will be no problem if it is a "first offense." The legal system does not equivocate: A minor is a minor. While looking at these pictures may not necessarily mean that a person is a pedophile, we need to consider that the exploitation and manipulation of these children is unequivocally damaging to them even if there is no contact with them.

I asked Mitch about the details of his online sexual activities (OSA). He viewed young women (of an indeterminate age) and adults, men and women in consensual sexual acts, and sometimes women with women. "What was the longest you've been online for sexual activity?" "Five or six hours." "How often did that happen?" "Every few weeks, when I'm home alone." "How often, in a week, are you pursuing sexual interests on the computer?" "For short periods of time if I'm alone, three or four times a week." "Did you need the stimulation from the net to be able to have sex with Eleanor?" "No." "Are you going to chat rooms?" "No." "Have you ever been involved in any kind of nonconsensual sexual acts off-line?" "No." "What about children? Have you ever considered sex with children or been aroused by children?" "I've been waiting for you to ask me that; I know you have to ask, but it scares me. Your question expresses my own worst fears; this is very difficult for me. I can't even imagine being aroused by children, but to be honest I am confused because those girls on the screen look like they could be under age." We sat quietly for a few moments, letting it all sink in.

Breaking the silence, Mitch began to talk more about his Internet use. He looked at things he would never want to do, but he was curious to see how far people would go: "sadomasochism, cross dressing, obese women, stuff like that." He thought he was pretty "vanilla" compared to some of what he saw online. He had no desire to act these things out, but it offered an interesting way to escape from reality. Sometimes he just could not stop looking around even though he thought he had wasted a lot of time. He looked at retail outlets for lingerie and sex toys. He wished Eleanor would wear sexy lingerie, and be willing to try a vibrator sometime. Orgasms relaxed him.

Mitch looked away and said, almost to himself, that he supposed getting on the Internet had become much the same thing as turning on TV when he was young. Every time he went into a room that had a TV, he would turn it on, whether he wanted to watch it or not. He wasn't sure what that was all about. Perhaps it was a compulsive habit. He needed something to fill in the quiet space, to avoid his own thoughts. I asked myself if Mitch was escaping from something then as he is now, and what that might be? I queried him: "What do you think you were avoiding?" He left the session with the unanswered question hanging in the air.

At our next visit Mitch told me that he was offered a position at the hospital where he had his fellowship. They would stay in Vermont. He and Eleanor were very pleased; they could get on with their lives, buy a home, and put down roots. He asked if he could remain in therapy with me. I responded that I was happy that their dreams had come true and said I was pleased he wanted to continue our work. We were just at the point where Eleanor was going to come in for a visit, after which I would meet with them both to go over my findings. Now we could really get to work!

Mitch and I talked about how his typical day went. He was up and off early when he was working and put in long days. Sometimes he was on call and needed to leave home in the middle of the night. He was often tired. He tried to help Eleanor as best he could, but his job left little time for that. When Mitch was not actually in the operating room, he had sex on his mind a great deal of the time. Mitch often went online after Eleanor fell asleep. He liked being alone, developing a fantasy, and following it through to orgasm. On the Internet, Mitch did not have to deal with Eleanor and her rejection. They had not had sex with each other for almost two years after Eleanor discovered he had been on the Internet while she was pregnant with Molly. Eventually, they resumed their sexual relationship, and she became pregnant again. But she was still so angry with him that they seldom had sex. Sex on the Internet was a soothing, relaxing experience, with none of the complexities of partnered sex.

> If I do that (masturbate) I can start when I like, come when I like and stop when I like; I needn't bother with foreplay, or romantic lighting, or tender nothings murmured in her

ear; I don't have to guess what she might like, or discuss afterwards how it was; I can go to sleep when I feel like it. (Schmidt, 1998)

Mitch also used the computer at work and at home for educational and household purposes. He went online to take care of household accounts, contact friends and family, and research information for work. However, he figured the majority of the time he was online was for fantasy material for masturbation. He had never used the Internet for sexual pursuits while at work. He knew he would be dismissed, and inherently felt it was unprofessional. He had drawn some boundaries for himself and stayed within them. Boundaries set by the client always are good things and need to be validated and promoted. It bodes well for a positive outcome. Now that he was on the full-time staff of the hospital, he felt more secure and serious about his role. His flirting and joking about sexual things stopped. In hindsight, he was embarrassed about having been "such a jerk."

I went back to the question that was still hanging in the air. What might Mitch be avoiding when he turned on the TV or went on the Internet? He said that he withheld some information during the history of his sexual development. In the midst of uncertainty about my role in his life, he did not want to let go of this particular secret. He had, consciously or unconsciously, tried to finesse getting into a real therapeutic relationship by coming to see me when it was possible he was moving away. He also feared that if he shared his secrets they would lose some of their erotic power. Given the light of day, secrets can lose something. As we know, the magic combination of forbidden, hidden, and erotic sexual events provides psychological and physiological payoffs that have a hold on people in a way that not much else does.

I was pleased that Mitch was engaged enough in our relationship to be able to share his secrets with me. What unfolded was a piece of Mitch's erotic history that had begun when he was 12 or 13 years old. It was not such an unusual scenario. He had already discovered masturbation and wet dreams, so he had been introduced to orgasms and the pleasure of sexual feelings. Jane, the sitter, was 17. After his younger sister was asleep, they would play video games and watch TV until bedtime.

One day while Mitch was sitting next to Jane, who had her arm around him, he furtively felt her breast. Since she did not move or object, it became a regular event. He fantasized about it, waited for her visits, and found it very arousing. He said he was "hugely hormonal" at that time in his life, and could barely contain himself until the next time Jane was there. It escalated when Jane invited Mitch to touch her breasts again, and they engaged in sex play with their clothes on, touching genitals. He then began to masturbate in private to the rerun of this event whenever he could. He never told his family about it because he was too embarrassed. Besides, it felt good even if it was also very confusing.

When Mitch tossed these events off to me as "not abusive" and "not really worth mentioning," I was sure that they were more important than he could admit to himself. Many men will categorically deny that these type of experiences with baby sitters or teenage girls who were older than they were, perhaps a teacher or coach, were not abusive, although as adults they would question the ethics of such sexual behavior. In 1998, the *Psychological Bulletin* printed a controversial meta-analysis of 59 studies of college students who had reported that they had been sexually abused as children. This study concluded that the effects of childhood sexual abuse "were neither pervasive nor typically intense, and that men reacted much less negatively than women" (Zernike, 2005). Mitch would find out what effect this experience with Jane had on him as therapy unfolded.

First times

Mitch grew up much attached to the erotic power of that early experience with his babysitter. I think how often over the years I have heard about the power of the first erotic experience, and how that power never seems to diminish over a lifetime. These moments almost never include vaginal-penile contact. They are, instead, usually about the first kiss, fondling of breasts, or other sex play. The power of this passionate and naïve groping seems generated by a compelling mix of fear and hormones; it is the forbidden fruit that is always so sweet in the tasting and gets sweeter still in memory. Mitch never had a desire to act out this childhood scenario with anyone in real life. However, as he became older, Jane stayed the same teenage girl in his mind. In his own fantasy world, these clandestine events still had the highest erotic valence for him. The teenagers he viewed online were sexy but not as much as his own memory of Jane. Under the stressors from work, growing responsibilities in the operating room, his marriage, and being a new father, he was feeling shaky. He wanted to regress to the good old days when he was taken care of. He began to look for ways to be soothed or distracted from his daily worries.

Mitch felt guilty about his sexual fantasies. He was ashamed of cheating on Eleanor. On the other hand, he rationalized that his online sexual activity was because sex with Eleanor had become almost nonexistent after the first pregnancy, and he did not think it was "adultery." While he knew a lessening in sexual appetite is typical after a pregnancy, Mitch felt badly that he did not take the responsibility to work through his sexual habits and make a commitment to negotiate psychological and sexual intimacy with Eleanor. Eleanor's discovery of Mitch's Internet habits also compounded the problem. She was beginning to realize that his flirting and eye contact with other women was of epic proportions. She did not know about his affairs.

Suddenly, Mitch looked at me with an expression of fear on his face and said pointedly, "I hope she will never have to find out." So I asked him, "Is that a question for me?" It sure was. I told him, "What you tell me here is confidential." I also told him my philosophy about honesty: that it has its place and time. Mitch had resolved never to have sex with another woman since Molly had been born and had stuck to it for two years. I said I supported his goal to never deceive Eleanor again. There was much to explore and understand about the function and meaning of those affairs in his life. It would need some work to learn how to avoid doing it again, no matter how much he wished to avoid them. We talked a great deal about his role in the marriage and his responsibility for the way it was working out. Eleanor was also in individual therapy at this time.

As I have mentioned before, in many cases it is necessary to contain sexual behaviors from the very beginning of the therapeutic relationship, particularly if the reality is that the person feels out of control. Mitch's sexual fantasies had begun to gobble up his life, and he really wanted to get things under his control. Everyone was in agreement that his computer use needed to be curtailed. The computer and everything it stood for in their marriage was abhorrent to Eleanor. He was able to use the computer at work appropriately, so I likened this to his being able to exercise some boundaries at home, as well.

Treatment

Treatments have to be realistic to work. While one approach to containment of online sexual activities is total abstinence from masturbation, fantasies, and computer use, I am of the opinion that this is unrealistic. When goals are set that are unrealistic, they have the potential to reinforce a sense of failure and shame. Mitch could be discriminating about his computer use, but it was not likely that this would stop him from having sexual fantasies. While Mitch never used the computers at the hospital for anything but work and did not roam the "red light district" online when Eleanor was around, he could be in his secret world in his mind whenever he wanted. While it is a goal of treatment to understand and refrain from unwanted behaviors, it is equally important to learn to cope with fantasies that might lead to a relapse. It was also very important that he continue to look inside and figure out who he was.

Eleanor's job required long hours on the computer, and she often brought work home. While it may be sensible for some people to move the computer to a place in the house where everyone can see the screen, this does not work in every situation. For example, putting the computer in the kitchen may make others in the household feel intruded upon. Family members should not become involved in policing someone else's computer use. Considerations should be: Is there room in the kitchen for the computer? What happens when everyone goes upstairs, or into the den? What about laptops that can be taken anywhere and everywhere? Why can't blocks be put on the computer like they do for children's safety? Computers can have blocks but there is no "perfect" blocking situation; some people can undo them, and they may slow down the computer as well. The computer is so central to people's work these days that, in reality, it will be the clients job to create their own boundaries on the Internet.

Mitch began to keep a log, which became the "price of admission" to each of Mitch's sessions. He was somewhat resistant at first because he felt as if it was going back to kindergarten. "Kindergarten?" I asked quizzically. He thought about it for a while and said it was just his gut reaction. I pushed him a little, and he said that he had been involved in so many complex and difficult learning processes in the past several years that this seemed too simple to be that important. This was another case in which it took a while to sell the idea of keeping a log.

While eager to be a "good" client, Mitch was also in a hurry and he was not used to going inside and keeping track of feelings. In his frame of reference, problem solving was done swiftly and decisively: Open a chest, repair a heart and sew the person back up. A log seemed simplistic and plodding. When someone shows up without one, we figure out why. It is difficult to write down what has been going on in your head every day. It can be very painful to look at our secrets, and sharing them with someone else may be even more painful yet. The shame is palpable. Denial is not relinquished easily; it may take some time to get honest, even on paper. I am content to wait as long as I see someone is trying to learn how to look inside. Eventually this exercise teaches people to be honest with themselves, to monitor their feelings and thoughts on a day-to-day basis. Ideally, self-monitoring will become a lifetime habit. Keeping a log puts most people in the driver's seat and in control of where they are going.

Mitch finally began keeping a log of his daily behavior, and he was proud to show me that he had not had OSA all week. The next week he used the computer for sex only once; the third week he said he had been so good, that he had "treated" himself with an hour online while Eleanor was sleeping. This is a common situation when people begin therapy. It's like going on a diet. After doing well for a while, the dieter rewards himself with a hot fudge sundae, then feels guilty. I said to Mitch with a touch of irony, "It must have felt good to treat yourself: only twice in three weeks, not so bad. How did it feel after you masturbated?" He quickly picked up on my irony and said he felt happy at first but then felt depressed and angry that he would never be able to control himself. I asked him to tell me about his anger. He admitted he was angry about "this whole process—therapy and everything." I wondered if he was warding off the possibility that I would also be disappointed if he had lapses. He acknowledged that he was worried about my reaction. "Tell me more," I said. He thought about it for a while, and told me that he spent his whole life trying to be perfect and please his parents. His parents had expected a lot from him and his sisters, and he never wanted to fail them. So how did I fit into this picture? Had I required that he be perfect as well? What does perfect mean anyway? We had a lot to talk about. Mitch eventually learned that he could trust his own instincts about what was perfect for him, and he did not always have to please his parents or me—metaphorically or in reality.

After a while Mitch got to like the exercise of sitting down each night, creating a quiet moment for some reflection and writing down where his head had been all day. Initially, it was a useful way for him to observe how flooded his head was with erotic thoughts and fantasies. He thought about how difficult it had been to focus on surgery and not wander off. He also began to observe his emotional triggers: "Every time Eleanor nags me about drinking, I want to masturbate." "When I feel depressed, bored or lonely, I turn on the computer and start scrolling around." "I am often bored, even though I have so much to do." "Why do I feel lonely when I have a wife and little girl who love me?" "I am always worried I will not be able to get an erection with my wife, so I try to get stimulated on the Internet."

There it all was: the denial, the feelings, the rationalizations. Writing down feelings makes it difficult to hide from them. Looking at the "dailyness" of sexual thoughts, we can get a reality check on how much time is spent in wondering, for example, when the next orgasm will happen, preparing for a sexual event or encounter, engaging in the encounter, and then covering the tracks after it is over. Keeping sexual secrets is difficult and time-consuming work. It takes up a lot of space in the mind and leaves other things unattended. With the log firmly in place, Mitch was learning about self-monitoring. Slowly, defenses and denial began to fall away.

ELEANOR

Eleanor told me that she had been sexually abused by her paternal uncle when she was about 10 or 12 years old. Sexual abuse is common in the history of spouses or partners of people with sexual behaviors that are out of control. My own working theory about this is that there is something about the highly sexualized spouse that is familiar to the sexually abused spouse. This resonates with attaching to the trauma. Eleanor had never told her mother. Her mother had died suddenly in a car accident when Eleanor was just about to enter college. The birth of Molly, and now her pregnancy with a second child, had awakened many unresolved issues with her mother. Her father, who remarried, was an alcoholic and had always been distant and rejecting. Eleanor was the eldest of four children, and was burdened with the care of her siblings because her mother had been depressed and drinking for many years before she died. Now she was the primary bread winner while Mitch went to medical school.

Both Mitch and Eleanor had very demanding jobs. Theirs was a complex but common situation. They had created their own stasis over the nine years they had been married. It was a delicate balance. While there were times when sex felt good and connected Eleanor had kept herself emotionally and sexually safe by distancing herself from Mitch even before she discovered Mitch was on the Internet. He protected himself from Eleanor's rejection by seeking contact with other women, whether fleetingly on the street, in an affair, or virtually on the Internet. He was searching for connection with women who welcomed his touch, keeping the connection to the feelings he had as a young boy with a baby sitter: nurtured, not responsible, and eroticized.

Eleanor felt confused and upset. On the one hand, she was relieved to have Mitch less interested in her sexually; but yet she felt rejected and jealous of the women online. Because she had been sexually abused, Mitch's sexual needs frightened her. They resonated with how powerless she had felt when her uncle assaulted her. In addition, Eleanor complained about the stress of not only being the primary income provider for many years of their marriage, but also the primary caretaker of Molly and their home. However, she had difficulty relinquishing the power and control it gave her, which she needed to feel safe in the relationship.

Eleanor and Mitch

When I met with Eleanor and Mitch together, I pointed out that much marital glue was still in place in spite of this crisis. I offered them my perspective from working with many couples, that they would feel differently about these events as time went by. For now, Eleanor needed a safe, supportive place to call her own. She was pregnant and, therefore, felt even more vulnerable than usual. Eleanor was glad to have her own therapist at this time, but she was also encouraged and validated to hear my thinking about their marriage. We all decided that while they were settling into individual therapy I would see them together occasionally. When they were ready to do couple work on a more regular basis, I would recommend some therapists for them.

I helped Eleanor explain to Mitch how the sexual abuse experiences with her uncle came alive when he went online, scanned for women when they were out and about, or flirted with them in her presence. She explained to him that his sexual behavior evoked the feelings of powerlessness when her uncle abused her. These reawakened feelings made her feel angry and afraid when Mitch objectified women by "gawking" at them. Mitch was shocked and admitted that he had never considered the impact of his behavior on Eleanor from that point of view. This admission and understanding went a long way with Eleanor.

I brought up that they both had significant family histories of alcohol use, and that they might think about the implications of this history in their own marriage. I asked them to think about how it felt to them when their parents drank. Eleanor said that while she did not drink at all during either pregnancy, she did think about their alcohol use and observed Mitch's habit. I suggested it might be helpful for them to go to an ACOA meeting together or read a book about it and and see what it had to offer. I recommended Elkin (1984) and Knapp (1997).

I explained the reason behind the recommendations to Mitch and Eleanor—the skills I was trying to put in place and why I suggested some work to do at home. In each case, I need to be realistic about expectations. I do not expect that each person can utilize the "ideal" we read about in professional articles or books. I cautioned that there is no such person as the average person or therapy that works just the way it does in print. For instance, if someone does not like to read, it is not useful to recommend a book.

Mitch worked very hard for a year. Through writing his log and reflecting on its content, he began to see the patterns emerge. In addition to the log he decided to keep a journal, a habit he had developed in college and medical school. His log helped him realize that when Eleanor felt he was preoccupied and distracted a great deal of the time, she was right. Mitch usually attributed it to his work, a problem in the operating room, or the busy life they had, including getting Molly to and from day care on time. Being so preoccupied also resulted in being forgetful, which was troublesome. Mitch was now beginning to see where his mind was a great deal of the time. He learned that his preoccupation isolated Eleanor because he became distant and disengaged from her.

Eventually, he also began to realize how his sexual behaviors were triggered by certain emotions and feelings. He found that he went to the Internet when he was angry with Eleanor and when he was overwhelmed at work, stressed by too much to do, and when he had a lot to drink. This is a very common list. People don't express their feelings of discontent and anger because they are afraid of conflict, and Mitch was the champion of avoiding conflict at any cost. But burying his feelings and trying to be perfect came at a high cost to him and his relationship with Eleanor.

Their usual points of conflict seemed to be nagging, sex, or money, although we discovered over time that in reality it was more about fear and abandonment. Sometimes Mitch was angry about things that had nothing to do with Eleanor, but it was handy to blame her. Mitch worked hard at being able to express to Eleanor how he felt. She was working at hearing him and, at the same time, not feeling responsible for what she heard. Mitch desperately wanted to get off the treadmill of feeling angry, stifling the anger, then using an erotic encounter to soothe his feelings. Eventually he became pretty good at preempting the cycle. If he had a lapse, he went only to unambiguously adult sites. He learned to interrupt a fantasy when it began to involve teenage girls.

Mitch accomplished this with two useful techniques: (1) identifying the emotional triggers and avoiding them by talking about them to Eleanor or writing about them (2) imagining an aversive event that might occur as a result of his behavior—for example, the police showing up at his door, losing his license, or Eleanor discovering him at the computer looking at sexual sites. Sometimes he would also recall his feelings when he was with the babysitter. While that was an uncomfortable place to revisit, it helped him put things in perspective. He did not want to continue his erotic connection to the babysitter. While he did not feel he was sexually abused, he did feel that it was certainly inappropriate for the 17-old sitter to be sexual with a 13-year-old boy. He would be careful and vigilant with his own children. While I was not invested in his viewing this event in any particular way, it was important to me that he understood how it was connected to his life at this time.

I suggested to Eleanor and Mitch that they begin to make time for one another on a regular basis, and have a predictable "date night." They also needed to learn to talk about ordinary family issues—to make plans for the week; decide who drives Molly, who makes dinner, who gets groceries; discuss plans for the future, such as house renovations, etc. These types of conversations might refocus their attention and develop a feeling of partnership for family issues. I was working on a team approach. Building on this skill, I would then invite them to talk about their relationship, how it felt to be in therapy, issues with their family of origin, and sharing their inner feelings. These conversations aimed at creating closeness and the emotional intimacy they both said they wanted. Hopefully, they eventually would be in the same life boat, rowing in the same direction.

As time went on, these suggestions seemed to work pretty well. Eleanor learned in individual therapy that Mitch's sexual habits were not her fault and were not because she was sexually inadequate or Mitch found her unattractive. It was about him. Her anger began to dissipate, and she became more accessible. Mitch had more feelings and thoughts to share, and felt more connected to Eleanor. He was increasingly aware of how his sexual habits resonated with her and connected to her sexual abuse. Both Eleanor and Mitch worked on understanding their family-of-origin dynamics and how they impacted on their relationships in adult life.

Because of his log, Mitch also was able to gather some data about his drinking habits. He noticed that after drinking, he was particularly disinhibited and aroused. Maybe he really did have a problem. He and Eleanor had made a deal that since she would not drink during pregnancy, he would not either, ostensibly showing solidarity with her pregnancy and together symbolically protecting their child. This provided a much better context for this pregnancy compared to the first pregnancy when Mitch had been sexually acting out.

Mitch was inclined to feel that when he saw the patterns and understood the triggers for his behavior, he was "done" with therapy. I reiterated that just containing the behavior, at least some of the time, is not the end. Although it should be regarded as a giant step forward, in truth it is just the beginning.

Mitch had refused to discuss medication with me when I first mentioned it. It could wait, but I kept an eye on his anxiety and depression and his ability to forgo the computer for sexual stimulation. Was his mind quieter? Did he have fewer sexual thoughts? It is not uncommon for clients to refuse medication or be very skeptical about it. Many tell me that their behavior represents a character flaw that they should be able to manage without medication. Usually we have a conversation about medication several times throughout therapy. As I discussed in the previous chapter, most people come around to trying it and experience what it can do for them. For the most part, it has proved a great help. Many are very relieved to be more in control and achieve a more peaceful state of mind. I waited to see what would change after a few months of therapy and when Mitch stopped drinking. Just before the baby was born, about five months into therapy, Mitch told me he was less anxious than he could ever remember being. Everyone was happy when William, a healthy 8 pound, 4 ounce baby, was born.

A few months after William's birth Mitch began to be more anxious. He said he was having trouble with his thoughts again, and found himself wanting to go back on line, to flirt and have an extramarital sexual encounter. He identified that having a second child brought back how he felt when Molly was born. He felt overwhelmed by the responsibility for another child, as well as rejected by Eleanor, who devoted all her time and attention to the baby. Mitch said he guessed it was time he grew up. I wondered what he meant by growing up. He knew that he should be able to do without Eleanor's attention and nurturing. The baby needed her. But he felt isolated, depressed, and anxious nevertheless.

Mitch explored this scenario for a while, talking about his feelings of being the middle child. He never felt he had quite enough of his parents' attention, often feeling isolated and alone. He thought his sisters received much more attention and love than he did. It surprised him that having children could reawaken such feelings. This discussion went on to result in helpful insights for Mitch. It allowed him to let go of the distortions about himself and his family that he had carried for many years and gave him a clearer lens through which he could view his family life. I mentioned medication again; he said he would think about it. That was progress!

In the next session I asked about any left over business from the last session. While he had been pleased with all the revelations about his family and felt more grounded by the understanding he had achieved, he wanted to explore the topic of medication. A friend of his was on Zoloft (Sertraline) and telling everyone how it changed his life. Mitch had been thinking about something I had once said about recent research using scans of human brains. This research is beginning to reveal that there might be a neurobiological basis for compulsive and addictive behaviors (Maas et al., 1998). He said he wanted to work through his emotional issues but also wanted to know more about the role biology might have in his problems. He did not like the current return of symptoms and was scared by them. He acknowledged that there were times when he still felt out of control. It was almost like a tic; he would be going along fine and suddenly found himself unable to avoid masturbating or establishing eye contact with a woman. His son's birth was a stressful event, but he was also able to see the larger picture. Things were going very well, yet there was still room for improvement. He thought medication might help. I cautioned him that while I thought medication would likely help him exercise his "executive function" better and he might feel more in control, it was not a magic pill for stopping sex on the Internet. He would still need to manage his urges. He was ready so I gave him the name and number of the psychiatrist to whom I refer clients. The medication served him very well. He was less stressed, happier and calmer. He felt more in charge of himself than he could remember.

Eventually Eleanor and Mitch also went for couple therapy. Mitch checks in with me once in a while for reinforcement. He and the family are really doing well. The Internet has loosened its grip on him. Life has become full of other choices. He and Eleanor have become a real couple. They have gotten some help with childcare and housekeeping. Eleanor was able to quit her job and market herself as a consultant, and is able to fit work into her life schedule rather than fitting her life into a work schedule. Mitch and Eleanor are considering building a log home in the woods. It is as close to the hardware store as he can get right now. But who knows what the future may bring?

Chapter 6

The legal side of sex
A cautionary tale

STRONGER LESSONS

Have you learn'd lessons only of those who admired you, and
were tender with you, and stood aside for you?
Have you not learn'd great lessons from those who reject you,
and brace themselves against you? or who treat you with
contempt, or dispute the passage with you?

Walt Whitman

No one wants the government peeking into our bedrooms or listening in on our conversations or looking at our emails. If we cross-
dress, masturbate, or have oral sex, should we be vulnerable to the
heavy hand of the law? When sex enters into the discussion, we
can never know how anyone, even those we would expect to be
impartial, will react. Nevertheless, social attitudes about sexual
behaviors, which vacillate over time between abhorrence and tolerance, influence the shape and substance of laws about sex. These
laws, as well as definitions of sexual behavior, are an ever-evolving
process, subject to the vagaries of the political, religious, and social
milieu of the time. Each culture or community can determine for
themselves if a particular sexual behavior is legal or illegal, functional or dysfunctional, good or bad.

In 1994, Judge Richard Posner and Katharine Silbaugh, an attorney and professor of law, wrote a book capturing as best they could
the hundreds of constantly changing laws dealing with sexual
behavior. In their introduction to this compendium they noted:

> When law tracks the moral beliefs held by all or at least the
> vast majority of the members of society, as is true of the laws

prohibiting murder or theft, people do not have to "know" the law in order to comply with it; they have only to follow their conscience. Given the diversity of moral opinion regarding sex in the United States, conscience is not a sure guide to legality any more. No longer is it "obvious" (if it ever was) that sexual relations between consenting adults of the same sex is a crime, or that the age of consent to marriage should be lower for females than for males, or that marital rape is not a crime, or that adultery and fornication are crimes.

WHAT IS INTERCOURSE?

Nor is it "obvious" these days how we define sexual relations or behaviors, or even what we mean by the term "sexual intercourse." My interest in how people perceive or define their own sexual behaviors and how these definitions match up to the definitions of society and the law began 35 years ago when I met Nick and Babs. They were referred to me by a physician at an infertility clinic, who believed they were ostensibly infertile because they had never "consummated" their marriage. He was told by Babs and Nick, who had been married for five years, that they had never had intercourse. The physician told me that he had examined the woman and her vagina and could find no physical barrier to penile containment. He wanted me to help them learn about intercourse and consummate their marriage. He was confident Babs would then become pregnant.

When I met Babs and Nick, they told me they had intercourse frequently. The contradiction between the referring physician's information and their self-report was confusing. When I asked them about the details of their sexual relationship, it finally became clear that the only sexual behavior they both enjoyed, and thus had ever practiced, was oral sex. He liked cunnilingus, and she liked fellatio: they had orgasms this way. As far as they were concerned, they had consummated their marriage and had *intercourse* frequently.

Neither were interested in vaginal-penile containment. Nick and Babs wanted the infertility program to inseminate Babs with Nick's sperm. They could give me no reason why they did not want penile-vaginal containment. There was no pain or trauma in their history. Moreover, they made it clear that they did not want to discuss it. I met with them a few times. They were a pleasant, well educated couple who had lives that were satisfying and productive. They wanted a family. Who was I to interfere with what was nirvana to them? So I contacted the doctor at the infertility clinic and set him straight about what they wanted. While it was relatively new territory for everyone at the clinic, the physician obliged them and inseminated Babs with the Nick's sperm. They were very satisfied with the results: Babs became pregnant and sent the clinic a picture of their daughter. As it turned out, I learned a great deal from this encounter. Things are seldom what they seem.

A few years later in 1979, I gave my first professional paper at a national meeting of the Society for the Scientific Study of Sexuality (SSSS) on the definition of the word *intercourse*. Babs and Nick's sexual preferences and the doctor's decision to frame it as an unconsummated marriage, set me thinking about how each of us perceives and defines our own (and others') sexual behaviors. I was curious about the definition of intercourse and the concept of unconsummated marriages. What little information I found on the subject in books or journals was archaic. The articles and monographs I dug up under the very suspicious and watchful eye of the medical school librarian referred to the absence of intercourse as the cause for nonconsummation of a marriage—defined by some cultures as the inability, or failure, to produce a child, and always considered to be the woman's fault. It simply did not occur to the authors of these papers that men could also contribute to the nonconsummation of a marriage. In many cultures women were divorced and even killed if they did not provide a male child. We now acknowledge that men also can be infertile, incapable of ejaculating or getting erections, or unwilling to have sexual relations—all possible reasons for inability to consummate a marriage.

I also turned to the dictionary for answers to my questions about the definition of intercourse. The first dictionary I looked in defined intercourse as coitus, and when I looked up coitus, it was defined as *intercourse*. Not much information for the uninitiated there. So I consulted several more dictionaries, finding nothing more enlightening in any of them. I finally came across Dorland's Medical Dictionary, 25th Edition, which described coitus as "sexual connection per vaginum between male and female." While I thought this was a little vague, I found it to be closer to describing the traditional view of sexual intercourse than any of the other scientific tomes in which I had searched.

30 years later, I checked again to see if anything had changed. In the 28th Edition of Dorland's Medical Dictionary, written in 1994,

and the 30th Edition, from 2003, coitus was still defined as "sexual connection per vaginum," but the definition of intercourse was more specific: "1. coitus, 2. any physical contact between *two individuals involving stimulation of the genital organs of at least one*" (my italics). It took about 35 years for the dictionary to catch up with the notion that many people may consider oral sex or mutual masturbation to be intercourse! This dictionary definition of intercourse, however, does not jive with the current custom of modern teenagers, who limit themselves to oral sex in the belief that they are *not* having intercourse: thus, they still consider themselves virgins. Maybe that is why many adolescents feel they can sign up for "abstinence" pledges. And what about Bill and Monica? Did they have intercourse? Or was it even sex? Why didn't someone just look in the dictionary?

If you research canon law, civil law, criminal law, or military law, you might find different definitions of intercourse or sexual relations. Canon or religious law, for example, defines intercourse as "penetration however slight" of the penis into the vagina. Many people might not agree with that definition. I have worked with people who felt that their relationship or marriage was not consummated because there was barely any vaginal containment of the penis, because of premature ejaculation, vaginismus (an involuntary closing of the vaginal muscles that precludes containment of the penis), inability of a partner to get an erection, or even because someone does not have an orgasm!

Military law skirts the issue of homosexuality by mandating "don't ask, don't tell." Is it because of the particular sexual practices that homosexuals use when expressing their sexuality? I wonder how military law would be applied if heterosexual couples were open about their oral and anal sexual practices? Why are those behaviors okay if two people are heterosexual but not if they are homosexual? Has anyone asked? It is difficult for me to even imagine the government attempting to control and legislate adult consensual sexual relations! I often wonder about the strong homophobic reactions that sweep our culture and that incite many to protest marriage between two people of the same gender. Here we are in the 21st century still arguing about it! Perhaps it's because people of the same gender have sex for the sheer pleasure of it, sex for the sake of love. They don't need any other agenda, like procreation, to make it "legitimate." Maybe some people are just jealous.

One might ask why it is important to figure all this out. Who cares any way? From my point of view, it is very important to understand how each person subjectively experiences a sexual event and how they label it. Of course, it is central to the therapeutic process that we understand what we are treating and why. But it is also essential to examine these questions carefully when the law attempts to interpret what people do with their bodies and how it impacts on others. If sentences and punishments are to be meted out, do they fit the crime? And what crime, if any, has taken place? It is not always good that justice is blind.

Legislative bodies can make laws about sexual behavior, but any judge may decide how to interpret the language in a particular statute and may give a law a particular spin that was not intended by the lawmakers. Thus, even when our sexual behaviors may be consensual and legal, someone may distort and condemn them in a court of law. At the same time, legislators often make laws that take the "one-size-fits-all" approach. Haven't we learned that this is a faulty premise on which to base anything? Each individual has unique needs that should be considered each time a sentence is handed out.

Regulating sexual behavior is largely the domain of individual states. And sentencing standards differ vastly from state to state. The same crime in one state may result in serving a year of jail time, and in another state may result in 30 years to life in prison. Or there may be federal sentencing guidelines that a judge is bound by that do not fit the crime or the needs of the individual and community. Laws about some sexual behaviors are frequently challenged, often found unconstitutional, and may be impossible to enforce, but the law may continue to remain on the books.

Sometimes it may be helpful to consider sex laws before making a move to another state! For example, in 2003 Texas made sodomy (oral and anal sexual practices) legal. The law had originally been designed to target homosexual behavior and attempt to make it illegal. However, because oral and anal sex is also enjoyed by heterosexual couples this law was eventually removed from the books. Sex between two people of the same gender may be considered illegal in one state and not in another. Most of us agree that as consenting adults what we do with our own body and with another's body in private is no one's business. Nevertheless, each state has a right to make it their business. It is likely that most of us could have been arrested at one time or another somewhere in the United States for sexual behavior that may be part of our usual erotic repertoire, such as mutual masturbation, oral sex, or having intercourse with the woman on top. We even could have been arrested for sleeping in the same bed with someone to whom we were not legally married! The pictures we look at, our sexual fantasies, how we dress, and even what gender we think we are continues to be scrutinized by the law. With no probable cause, simply because it wanted to, the federal government announced in 2006 that it wanted to examine what each of us "Googles."

CONFUSING GENDER ISSUES AND SEXUAL ISSUES

In 1952, Robert Sherwin, a leading legal expert of his time in the field of sexuality and the law, represented Christine Jorgenson, an American citizen who grew up as George Jorgenson. Christine went to a clinic in Denmark for sexual reassignment surgery. She felt that she had always been a female trapped in a male's body and wanted to become an anatomically correct woman. Only after surgery could she feel whole and consistent with what she knew to be true about herself: She was a woman. Why did she even need a lawyer? Shouldn't we be the experts on determining our own gender? However, genital reassignment surgery raised many legal issues that Mr. Sherwin was called upon to negotiate.

Ms. Jorgenson had a gender identity issue, not a sexual behavior problem. Nevertheless, it caused a storm of controversy because transgenderism was a little-understood phenomenon 30 years ago. Although scientific research has revealed gender issues to be human conditions that are often successfully treated with genital reassignment surgery, these issues still raise eyebrows. Several years ago I was asked to testify before the legislature as to the legitimacy of this phenomenon, and the necessity of surgical treatment. A decision had to be made about whether Medicare, i.e., the government, should pay for the surgery in the state of Vermont. It was approved. Many condemn tinkering with our bodies and gender in this way and believe that it is a sin rather than a gender issue. For some it seems to stir the pot of homophobia.

While we are on the subject of gender, clarity is necessary when we discuss the issues of someone who is a transvestite (a person who enjoys wearing the clothing of another gender) and a person who considers a change in their physical gender or even a person who refuses to label him- or herself as one gender or another. According to Langstrom and Zucker (2005), the majority (about 75–89%) of transvestites are heterosexual males, with a small minority who are homosexual and bisexual. There appears to be two types of transvestites or cross-dressers. One group identifies itself as having the core personality characteristics of women but have no desire for feminization through hormones or surgery. Dressing up in women's clothing is comforting enough for them. The second type would prefer to be feminized with hormones and perhaps surgery and has a strong interest in taking on the role of female.

Transvestism is not intrinsically illegal or sexual behavior. Hal, who would have preferred to be Helen, was harassed by his neighbors. He just liked to wear women's clothing and did not want hormones or surgery. The police knocked on his door one day because people were complaining about his appearance around town. The police acknowledged that it was not illegal to cross-dress but said they just wanted to "check up on things." Hal felt vulnerable and eventually moved to a big city where he would be more anonymous and have more opportunity to meet people similarly inclined. "Men with TV [transvestism] almost never present with legal problems, aside from child custody disputes" (Fedoroff, 2003).

A small number of men who cross-dress (about three percent) have transvestic fetishism, which is sexual arousal and erotic attachment to the clothing of the opposite gender. Transvestic fetishism is different from transvestism, which is done for the purpose of feeling or being feminine. A transvestic fetish may be associated with some illegal behaviors such as child abuse. It can also be associated with other sexual behaviors that are not illegal but may be dangerous, such as autoerotic asphyxia. It may also be associated with frequent masturbation and sex with multiple partners. All these scenarios are time consuming, at best. Therefore, both for legal and mental health reasons, it becomes important to differentiate between the subtleties of being a transvestite, having transvestic fetishm, and being a transgendered person.

Carol Tavris, author of *The Mismeasure of Women* (1994), raises some important issues as we try to answer these difficult ethical questions.

> We need to untangle the moral issues from the psychological issues from the legal issues. You may not like something, but does that mean it should be illegal? If we have laws that are based on moral notions and developmental notions that are outdated, do we need to change the law?

CHILDREN AS VICTIMS/CHILDREN AS OFFENDERS

We know that the brain is not fully developed during adolescence. We also know that each of us develops and grows at a different rate. Will sex with an "older" woman, such as a teacher or caregiver, for one boy who is 14 or 16 be the same for another boy? What is the context of these events for each boy? How developed or mature are they when the sexual encounter occurred? What will be the meaning of these sexual liaisons for each of them as they grow up?

When a woman or a man abuses a child, it is a serious offense. While I chose not to focus on illegal sexual behaviors in this book, these behaviors are part of the experience of many people I treat. Collecting data about how many children have been abused is a challenge and subject to many limitations. However, David Finkelhor, Ph.D., a leading researcher of child abuse, concludes that "at least one in five adult women in North America experienced sexual abuse during childhood and one in six males (16 percent) but a more conservative estimate for men would be 5% to 10%." Finklehor (1994) also observes that boys are more likely to be abused by women, and girls are more likely to be abused within the family.

Not everyone agrees that every case of a 16-year-old boy and his sitter or teacher is child abuse, or two children fondling each other's genitals constitutes a sex offense. While there are undoubtedly negative consequences of such exposure to sexual exploitation, there are no real cogent studies available at this time that show direct cause and effect. What we do know, however, is that many people with compelling sexual habits, legal or illegal, have also been sexually abused as children. It does *not* mean that people who have been sexually abused are destined to become abusers, perpetrators of crime, or have compelling sexual habits. Far from it. Research concludes that "only a small percentage of individuals who have been victims of child sexual abuse will victimize other children" (Moser et al., 2004). I have found that clients who have been sexually abused as children are not always set up for a lifetime of misery, crime, or mental illness as a result of the abuse. There is a spectrum of adaptation in these instances. We all adapt to trauma in our own way.

A headline in the newspaper one November morning in 2005 grabbed my attention: "Don't lock child offenders up for life."

While the article, written by attorney David Berger, did not refer exclusively to sexual offenses, its general premise applies to all crimes committed by children. Berger wrote:

> A recent report by Amnesty International and Human Rights Watch reveals that 2,225 child offenders in the United States have been locked up for life without any possibility of parole. Fifty-nine percent are serving life without parole for their first criminal offense. A 'one size fits all' approach to criminal justice ignores children's inherent ability to change."

This inherent ability to change is particularly highlighted when my clients share their childhood histories. These stories are often replete with sexual experiences from a very early age. Many of these experiences were not upsetting or harmful to anyone, and it is impossible to predict what impact, if any, they may have on a child. Our discussions of these childhood experiences are all in hindsight. We look back from an adult perspective. We attempt to ascribe adult labels and meanings to childhood developmental tasks. Sexual interests are fluid: Some things that might have been compelling during adolescence may have faded in adulthood.

The law, however, does necessarily account for a child's "inherent ability to change" when it sets up federal mandatory guidelines for particular crimes. In January 2004, Federal District Court Judge Gerard E. Lynch had to sentence 18-year-old Jorge Pabon-Cruze, a college freshman in Puerto Rico, for selling images of child pornography on the Internet. Jorge had set up a chat room using the screen name "Big Thing" and sent images of child pornography to people who answered his chat room advertisement. Judge Lynch, using mandatory guidelines legislated by Congress, sentenced Jorge to ten years in prison. A conservative and centrist judge, Lynch denounced his own sentence: "This is without question the worst case of my judicial career," he said. "An unjust and harmful" sentence has the potential to do disastrous damage to someone who himself is not much more than a child." Judge Lynch also noted that had the teen's crime been having sex with a 12-year-old, as opposed to swapping downloaded child porn images, he would only have faced a five-year sentence (Weiser, 2004).

This is an example of how Congress has taken the purview of sentencing decisions away from experienced judges and given the power to make these decisions to prosecutors. People who abuse children are at the bottom of the pecking order in society. We have moved forward in our thinking of drug and alcohol abuse and see it as a treatable issue. We still have a long way to go when it comes to making reasonable decisions about how to help people who have legal or illegal sexual habits that do not benefit society or themselves.

I cannot bring myself to call a child or adolescent a "sex offender." Whether adults like it or not, children and adolescents have sexual interests and engage in sexual behaviors. We all know that this age group is subject to acting impulsively, needy of peer acceptance, immature, and not fully developed neurobiologically or socially. When you look back on your childhood, who were you? Would you want to be judged now for some of the things you did when you were young? I wince at the thought when I examine my own life!

It is imperative to understand the psychological and social contexts of sexual behaviors at every age when trying to take a history for treatment or making a report for the courts. For example, an adult evaluator may interpret certain sexual behaviors as excessive or compelling when the behaviors may reflect that teenage boys, in particular, are preoccupied with sex at this stage in their development. Or a teenage boy may exhibit his genitals or body, which might be interpreted in many ways. An evaluator may ask what exactly is being exhibited: the penis, the buttocks, the chest, total nudity, partial nudity? Does the child have privacy to experiment with his body or is this the only outlet he has found? Is the audience consensual or not? Is it in front of a group of peers who have challenged him or dared him to show his parts to them? How great is his need to be accepted by peers? Does the child have a loving, nurturing home, or is he in need of guidance from a kind adult? If the evaluator is looking at an adult's history that involved adolescent sexual behavior, it is important to find out at what age the behavior stopped, if it did. Does adolescent exhibitionism, for example, determine a lifetime habit of exhibiting oneself or deserve a lifetime label of "sex offender?"

At one time or another, we all may look back and identify the things we did, preferences we had, and feel somewhat unnerved by our childhood or adolescent escapades in the world of sexuality. We may be glad we have "outgrown" these experiences. But some of these erotic experiences may have remained deeply ingrained in a person's sexual repertoire, like Mitch and the baby sitter, for example. Should we hunt up this adolescent babysitter and accuse her of child abuse? *I* don't think so but others may disagree. Did she have a lifetime of abusing children? I doubt it.

Boundary violations of children can and do have a profound impact. While some children do not consider themselves victims when they have had sexual contact with an adult, others have been deeply affected by the betrayal of trust. How a child or adolescent experiences a boundary violation depends on the child and the circumstances. For some it may have negative or significant psychosexual effects and for others none, or somewhere in between. Who was sexual with them? How old were they when it happened? Was it a peer, a teacher, a relative, a trusted friend? How often did the child experience this activity? Was it violent, physically painful, and scary? What type of violation took place? Will adult anxiety about childhood or adolescent sexual conduct produce reactions to these behaviors or events that will be more harmful than what has actually taken place?

Doctors Moser and Kleinplatz, and their colleagues have written and thought a great deal about contextualizing child and adolescent sexual behaviors and have observed that: "Guilt laden or anxious responses to child or adolescent sexual behaviors or conduct may be more problematic to the child and adolescent than the actual sexual behaviors" (Moser et al., 2004). This is not a popular view in our culture today, and many misunderstand it as an acceptance of the exploitation or violation of a child. Some prefer to think that any type of sexual exploitation will be harmful. Far from excusing boundary violations, the clinical view of Moser et al. recognizes that the issue is not that simple. There is no black and white; one size does not fit all.

Little research exists about what children and adolescents actually think about sex and what behaviors they engage in. When faced with what might be unusual sexual behavior in a child or adolescent, we often do not know how to deal with it or even help the child deal with it. It would be difficult to imagine someone like Kinsey, for example, being allowed to systematically interview children and adolescents about their sexual behaviors in today's political climate. This reticence about looking at and understanding childhood sexual habits probably stems from the myth that if children are exposed to any kind of information or discussion about sexual behaviors they are likely to experiment with these behaviors.

This implies that knowledge about sexuality is dangerous. Sex education programs funded by the federal government are based on this erroneous supposition. Research has revealed that the sexual educational programs based on abstinence-only models, the only ones approved of and funded by the federal government, have failed abysmally (Edwards, 2003; Wilcox and Wyat, 2003). Abstinence from sexual relations is interpreted by many teens to mean that oral sex is okay but vaginal-penile containment is not. You can decide for yourself whether or not oral sex equates with sexual abstinence. What is unequivocal, however, is that knowledge about sexual behavior can protect both children and adults and is not inherently dangerous. Nor does it inherently provide license for sexual acting out.

While the media promotes, celebrates, and invites adult "sexiness" (whatever that is), there may be a dangerous subtext to the invitation. Some people become "hooked" while others may be able to avoid the obsession with sexiness and sex in general. At the same time that the media is hyping the joys of being sexual—or at least *looking* sexy—we seem to be more interested in relating the dangers of sexual activity to children, hoping in some convoluted way to prevent or delay sexual experimentation.

We should be vigilant about the messages we inadvertently give when we educate children and adolescents about sexuality, making sure the information is relevant and appropriate to the child's needs. As Derek Polonsky, M.D. pointed out in a personal communication: "What I find problematic about most courses/books [about sex] for kids is the message—you have sex—you get sick—you die. It is rare that you read—sex is fun and very exciting—which is why so many people do it!" We expose children to what I call a "danger-based" sex education, which largely covers the negative consequences of sexual activity such as pregnancy and sexually transmitted infections. We are still struggling to understand what is normative or within usual limits for sexual behavior. Yet we sure know how to bring the law down on sexual habits that have even the appearance of being unusual or appear to violate boundaries.

About 15 years ago, a public defender asked me to evaluate an 11-year-old boy. Dylan insisted on "mooning" or exposing his buttocks to his neighbors in spite of many interventions. His mother had died when he was six years old and his dad was trying hard to raise him as a "good boy." I wonder how we decided that children aren't intrinsically "good" in the first place. When they do things that we do not like, does that make them "bad?" Perhaps they are telling us something is "bad" in their lives, and we need to understand what their behavior is saying. Regrettably, people were not "listening" to Dylan's behavior. Dylan was sent to a work camp and labeled a sex offender. I do not think I will ever be able to forget Dylan. I suggested that he be evaluated for Tourette syndrome or perhaps Asperger's syndrome and certainly be treated for his anxiety and depression, kept at home, and given more support systems to help him and his dad. I advocated for a change of sentence. However, not only was Justice blind in this case, but she was deaf as well.

Chapter 7

Some call it love
Unique sexual issues of women

> I marvel at how mixed up people get when it comes to love .... It seemed like I was now thinking of Zach forty minutes out of every hour, Zach, who was an impossibility. That's what I told myself five hundred times: impossibility. I can tell you this much: the word is a great big log thrown on the fire of love.
>
> Sue Monk Kidd

Traditional beliefs about women influence mental health and medical treatments, as well as social policy and legal decisions. Until recent times, most theories about women's bodies and sexuality have been developed by men, and much of our knowledge about human illness and treatments has been extrapolated from studies on men. Fortunately, within the past twenty years, women's health has finally been viewed as intrinsically worthy of serious research. While we are moving in a positive direction of focusing medical and social research on the unique needs of both genders, the prevailing ambivalence about women's sexuality seems to remain constant. It is important that we look beyond the conventional stereotypes of women and understand women's sexuality, health, social, and political needs in a broader context.

To contextualize the diagnostic and treatment issues shared by women with legal or illegal compelling or obsessive sexual habits, we must cultivate a historical perspective. While there has been some progress in the treatment of men with compelling sexual behaviors, the research and literature about the unique experience of women with excessive sexual behaviors is still deficient. We know more about women who are the spouses or partners of men who struggle with compelling sexual behaviors than we do about women who have these sexual behaviors (Kasl, 1989; McCarthy, 2002).

Women and men seem to have different motivations when it comes to sexual behavior. It is a generally accepted point of view in our culture that romance and the opportunity to form a relationship is what motivates women to seek out sexual encounters. The sociobiologists would argue that there is a biological imperative to reproduce, the purpose of which is to assure that the human race will continue to thrive. While more research needs to be done in this area, Kafka (2007) suggests that women first seek "relationships and 'connection,' with sexual behavior as a secondary factor." This does not mean, however, that every woman is sexually motivated in this way. The women I work with seem to validate Kafka's observation and are more likely to be obsessed with romance and seek love and a permanent relationship—a bond that would include, for the most part, producing children.

A simplistic formula would be that women seem to look for love by having sex, and men seem to avoid love by having sex. Men appear to be more genitally and orgasmically motivated, and more often want anonymous sex rather than having to deal with a relationship. While this may appear to be a stereotype, it does have some statistical backing (Cooper et al., 2000; Missildine et al., 2005; Kafka, 2007). The research of Whitney Missildine and his colleagues at the Center for HIV/AIDS Education and Training in New York has supported the cultural assumptions that "men tend to seek more sexual partners over a lifetime than women, indicate a stronger desire for casual sex, and report desire for physical release and arousal as a primary motive for sex."

Generalizations notwithstanding, it is central to therapy to understand the unique and personal meaning of each client's motivation and psychological context for sexual behaviors, whether they are designed to connect or distance themselves from other human beings. My clinical observations, however, reveal that most women and many men are seeking to fulfill the need for human contact, intimacy, and the fulfillment of dependency needs—even when they seem to be holding each other at a distance.

WOMEN'S SEXUALITY IN HISTORICAL CONTEXT

In addition to being conflicted about sexuality in general, society has always been particularly and consistently ambivalent and restrictive about the sexuality of women. For centuries, men have tried in vain to solve the mystery of what role women played in creating life.

Women have absorbed ambivalence and oppression since Eve tempted Adam in the Garden of Eden. Eve, the seducer and temptress, took the rap for being the sole perpetrator of "original sin." Men have been desirous of women's sexual favors and, paradoxically, been frightened and mystified by women's sexuality. Therefore, in most cultures, men have attempted to regulate and control women's behavior. Unusual, cruel, and dangerous ideas about women's bodies and their sexuality have been foisted on women in all cultures and societies. For many centuries, the widespread medical and religious view was that women were sexually insatiable and their bodies dangerous. Women's menstrual fluids and genitals were viewed as dirty or dangerous.

Women are still blamed if the pair bond does not produce children (particularly sons), if there is adultery, and for other evils that sex is thought to convey. When men have affairs or are disinterested in having sex, women will often believe it is their fault. Men collude with this perception and often blame their spouse or partner for their own failures at monogamy. Therapists must not lose sight of this distorted belief system, which perpetuates a myth that has been around for centuries. Men are still off the hook for these behaviors. In addition, women have yet to be assured full ownership of their own bodies. We have a long way to go before every person is free to choose with whom they will share their bodies and for what purpose.

Even when the founding of the United States seemed to promise parity in the new-world social structure, women were viewed as unsuitable to participate in all the rights and privileges of the newly created democracy. They were deemed too undependable and emotional—victims of their biology. Eve's role as perpetrator remained firmly in their psyches. At that time, the Puritan ethic promoted the teachings of the Old Testament in which sex was not merely a concession to humans' baser instincts—it was an unambivalent commandment of God: "Be fruitful and multiply." Women had to follow God's bidding, which was to be married and produce children. It was expedient for the male elders of the community to emphasize this aspect of religious belief, because not only would a wife be commanded by God to be sexually available, their many progeny would also ensure the Puritan position in the new world. But while they were busy having children and raising families in the wilderness, women were learning to be strong, independent, and assertive. They had to walk across the mountains of the West and settle the frontier. These women were the great grandmothers of the suffragettes (Gotwald & Golden, 1981).

By the nineteenth century, attitudes toward women and their sexuality took another turn. Science had solved the mystery of how life began, and as the globe began to shrink cultures met and mingled while exchanging ideas about life and religion. In 1848, a determined group of women in Seneca Falls, New York, took up the banner for women's rights, and began the women's movement. These women created *The Declaration of Sentiments,* which asserted women's rights to economic power, political power, and power over their own bodies (Merryman, 1999).

Meanwhile, the Victorians of 19th century England were in a frenzy of sexual repression. Sex was seen as draining energy. Sex was viewed as necessary in order to reproduce, but dispensable and sinful for any other purpose. Passions were denied, the body hidden and dehumanized. The Victorians indulged themselves in excesses of prudery. Piano legs were covered because a view of an ankle or leg was considered an impropriety, as were tours of art museums made in mixed company (Gotwald & Golden, 1981). Medical treatments were applied for sexual behaviors that men deemed excessive. Women who were sexually assertive were viewed as "potentially hysterical," in need of medical treatment that might include a stay in an asylum for the insane, sedation, or removal of the clitoris or uterus. If a woman was diagnosed with hysteria, as a cure she might have been masturbated to "paroxysmal convulsions," a euphemism for orgasms, by the same physicians who were condemning masturbation as a morally evil behavior and a risk to one's health (Cornog, 2003). And these were just a *few* of the remedies.

In the late 19th century, Freud and his colleagues developed the "talking cure" for mental and emotional disturbances. Listening to their patients

> these men of science unearthed the dark secret and the pervasive effects of the childhood sexual victimization of women. However, the discovery of this aspect of the underbelly of human behavior (specifically abusive human male behavior) was far from celebrated. Instead, awareness of the sexual abuse of female children was suppressed by the societal ego of Victorian times that could not tolerate this internal cultural conflict. (Guidry, 2002)

Freud had actually linked childhood victimization and mental health symptoms. But he retracted and obscured his theories because it was expedient for him to pander to the Victorian sensibility and political climate of the times. No one wanted to believe that men (and even women) would abuse a child. It was not until the women's movement in the 1970s that the issue of childhood sexual abuse was taken seriously, and we began to come to grips with the real problems this abuse presents for women and men.

At the end of the 19th century and through the roaring '20s, sexual behavior and female/male relationships were scrutinized by Freud and his colleagues. Before these men of science revealed the workings of the psyche, the body's role in providing sexual pleasure, as well as sexual problems, was thought to be simply an inevitable consequence of human anatomy and biology. When the psyche was revealed as the root of some human behaviors, it became a simple equation of "mind over matter": fix the mind, the behavior will be fixed as well. Neuroses and pathologies of the mind were in vogue, and psychoanalysis promised many cures for the foibles of humanity. At the beginning of the 20th century, it appeared that all a woman needed to do was to be psychoanalyzed and she would be released from the sexual inhibitions that the Victorian era had imposed on her!

During World War I, the women's movement quietly began to gather steam. During this period, women also began to attend to the task of getting the privilege to vote and promoting birth control. The post-war period of the roaring '20s saw skirts shortened, hair bobbed, bodies and bosoms liberated. Women had been filling men's jobs and roles during the war and wanted the same rights and privileges to continue when the war was over and the men returned. Women's roles began to change dramatically. By the time World War II began, women were already taking on what had been traditional male roles. Many women became the major breadwinners while also tending to the machinery of war. Rosie the Riveter, an airplane assembly worker, became a national heroine. She provided a model for the new roles women would fill in modern life.

Still, when the war was over, many women were encouraged to give men back their jobs and to retreat to an idealized version of the role of mother and wife. They were encouraged to become passive recipients of the New Deal. Paradoxically, the economics of the time also began to require households to have two incomes.

The media in the '50s and '60s reflected the prevailing uncertainty about the role of women in society. This was also the time when the birth control pill arrived on the scene. Women finally had an opportunity to take control over their reproductive decisions. The arrival of The Pill, an oral contraceptive, along with the media's attention to women's liberation, encouraged women to take charge of their own lives. However, this reproductive freedom did not dilute the double standard about sexual behavior. Women were still encouraged to be faithful, passive wives and mothers who could now be available for sex without having to worry about becoming pregnant.

The '60s also saw the passage of the 1964 Civil Rights Act by Congress, which was mainly directed at ending racial discrimination but also prohibited discrimination based on gender. Of course, as always, not everyone approved of the liberation of women. Amos Oz (2003), writing about life after World War II, shares his Aunt Sonia's view of what it was like for women growing up during the years just before and after the great war:

> Your life is your own only for a short time: from when you leave your parents' home to your first pregnancy, we had to begin to live our lives only around the children ... . True, even then there were quite a few women who made careers for themselves and went out into the world. But everybody talked about them behind their backs: look at that selfish woman, she sits in meetings while her poor children grow up in the street and pay the price. (Oz, 2003)

These were pretty confusing messages around which to build an identity. Women born in the '40s and '50s had confusing road maps to follow. Who were the role models for girls born in those years? How did we form our ideas about what kind of a woman we wanted to be? At that time in history, women were like our pioneer ancestors, who climbed over the mountains to new frontiers without really knowing what they would find on the other side. We were the great-grandchildren of the suffragettes.

The women's movement that began to simmer in the 1840s fomented many accomplishments over the years. Finally, in 1973, women gained more control over their reproductive rights when the U.S. Supreme Court agreed that *Roe v. Wade* would become the law of the land. At last women's legal right to an abortion would be viewed as a woman's private decision. This decision was largely influenced by the National Organization for Women, which mobilized conservatives who have consistently attempted to remove this right. It will take much vigilance to preserve this precarious privilege.

Even in these postmodern times the "double standard" continues to intrude on how women view their own sexuality. Recently, Randall Peterson (2008) wrote an article in *The New York Times Magazine* section about the politics of virginity on college campuses. At Harvard University, Peterson interviewed Janie Fredell, a member of the organization called the True Love Revolution. "The more she studied and learned, the more Fredell came to realize that women suffer from having premarital sex, 'due to a double standard,' she said 'which devalues women for their sexual pasts and glorifies men for theirs.'"

To sum up where the women's movement is in the beginning of the twenty-first century, I like Carol Groneman's observations about how the sexual revolution and the women's movement have "netted out" so far:

> Even though the sexual revolution appears to have changed the double standard about who gets to enjoy sex or how much sex is "normal," a deep ambivalence still exists in society toward female sexuality. The old double standard has been replaced by a more nuanced and complicated set of beliefs. Women still find themselves in a double bind: expected to be sexual, but not too aggressive; tolerated as lesbian, as long as not too butch; assumed to be sexually experienced, but not more experienced than their male partners. (Groneman, 2000)

LESSONS FROM THE YOUNG

These days, one of the ways I keep my ear to the popular culture, keep current about sexual attitudes, and keep my finger on the pulse of the double standard is when I occasionally see an adolescent for an evaluation of their sexual behavior. Although I do not specialize in adolescents I know enough about adolescent development to do an evaluation for the courts when complaints of sexual behavior are involved. I hear the adolescent's concerns, the cultural references, and vocabulary. Parenthetically, I also value these infrequent opportunities to see how the younger generation is doing.

In addition, I relish the opportunity to remind the court system that adolescent sexual behavior should not always be regarded as ubiquitously and patently pathological. The context and meaning of adolescent sexual behavior must be understood and taken into consideration before any judgments are passed.

In this vein, not too long ago I winced as I heard a 14-year-old boy describe a 12-year-old girl as a slut. My thought was that things still haven't changed much: The guys are still taking themselves off the hook for their sexual behaviors. I asked him if he would tell me what he meant by the word slut. His eyebrows and shoulders shot up in surprise. His face registered dismay. What was I, dumb? I thought I'd wait for a moment to see what he would say. He waited and hoped I would figure it out by myself. To end the stalemate, I suggested that the word could mean many things, and I wondered what *he* meant by it. He said it was when a girl "asked for it." Uh-oh. We had a lot to talk about after that: taking responsibility for himself, his sexual behavior, and his view of that 12-year-old girl, for starters. I hope he got it—for the rest of his life.

Once again, I was reminded that the double standard is still alive. There are many who are ready to call a woman a slut, whore, or "nympho" if she asserts her sexuality. Or, on the other side of the coin, she may be called a prude if she is not passive and accepting in the face of a man's sexual needs. Boys seem to learn that girls "ask for it." I know they don't discover this notion all by themselves. Marshall et al., (1990) summarized the work on rape tolerance by Hall, Howard, & Boezio (1986) in this way: "Social Factors such as beliefs about what constitutes sexual violence have greatly influenced the general acceptability of this behavior. Rape tolerance, or the extent to which people minimize the seriousness of sexual assault, has been seen through the denial of trauma to the victim, blaming the victim for provoking or precipitating the incident and questioning her credibility, as well as denying the extent of sexual assault."

In Western culture, one constant that we seem to cling to is the issue of consent in human sexual contact. Not that we have always agreed about what consent means or how to define it. Perhaps we never will. However, at this time in history, much of Western society seems to subscribe to the standard of consent as a central and necessary ingredient in human sexual relations. Still, there are some individuals, as well as some cultures and religious groups, that consider women and children property and therefore not worthy of being asked for consent. However, we generally considered that consent cannot be given by animals, dead human beings, or minor children. But what about minor children experimenting with other minor children? Are they breaking the law? When they ask each other, "if I show you mine will you show me yours?" are they "sex offenders?" Even when we think we are sure about consensual sexual behavior, legal and ethical debates continue. Alan Werthheimer, Ph.D., a political scientist writes, in his book *Consent to Sexual Relations* (2003): "We can all agree that "no" means "no." The difficult question is whether "yes" means "yes." All sexual behaviors take place in a particular context: cultural, historical, developmental, psychological, legal, religious, familial, political, and social. I am sure I have left out some. It is evident that it would be an egregious error to ignore the many contexts of any sexual behaviors, particularly when judgments are made or treatments are applied.

WOMEN WOULD NEVER DO SUCH A THING!

When I was in graduate school in the early sixties, we learned that women, for some reason, did not have fetishes or paraphilias, let alone sexual habits in the "too-much" category. As a matter of fact, that was the only thing we learned on a sexual topic! I remember feeling sort of smug at the time. There is still mythology around the notion that exaggerated expressions of sexuality, or even criminal sexual behaviors such as pedophilia and rape, are the exclusive purview of men. In addition, many may think that women do not have fetishes, do not masturbate to magazines and videos, will not go on the Internet for sexual purposes, or have affairs.

Not only are we very ambivalent about women as sexual human beings, our society promulgates the myth that women are passive and nonassertive, waiting for a man to initiate her into the rites of sexual activity. It is very difficult for our culture to conceptualize that women have sexual behaviors that are illegal or marginally legal. Since laws reflect social policy and prevailing public beliefs, society has been in denial that women, too, can cause sexual harm and can have sexual excesses that disrupt their lives. The legal system and often the psychiatric system reflect this bias. So ingrained are these notions in our culture, even today, that they permeate the law's approach to women as perpetrators of sexual crimes as well as the mental health and psychiatric treatments women receive. These myths are kept alive and passed on by our culture. "A myth is a fixed way of looking at the world which cannot be destroyed because, looked at through the myth, all evidence supports that myth" (Weldon, 1999). We must be vigilant for opportunities to challenge these myths, these "fixed ways of looking at the world." Today, research and the media are revealing that women are not only involved in the sexual abuse of children, but also have sexual behaviors that are disturbing to them, feel excessive, or are disrupting their lives and the lives of their loved ones (Davin et. al., 1999; Fedoroff et al., 1999; Cooper et. al., 2006). Research shows that "men are statistically the predominant perpetrators of sexual crimes and have a statistically higher number of non-criminal, but disruptive sexual behaviors. The male-female prevalence ratios of PRDs [paraphilia related disorders] are estimated at 5–1" (Kafka, 2007). In addition, Coleman (1992) observes that the reason more men have sexually compulsive behaviors than women is perhaps culture-based, because women's sexuality still appears to be viewed and defined from a male perspective.

It is a shift for many to think that women may be pursuers as well as being pursued, victimizers as well as victims. In the movie *Notes on a Scandal* (2006), a female teacher seduces a male student, a subject that has been followed in the media as cases appeared in courts all over the country in roughly the past 10 years. While there is not an epidemic of women teachers seducing their students, it is not an uncommon event. I would speculate it has been happening for centuries but never discussed. Some men may not define this kind of sexual relationship by women as dysfunctional or illegal. For example, Mitch, whose problems we examined in Chapter 5, did not regard his experiences with his female baby-sitter as sexual abuse. She was 17 years old, and he was 13. However, when he began treatment, we would find that this violation of Mitch's boundaries has had implications throughout his life. We would not even have to ponder the effects of this event if the gender roles were switched.

Myriam Denov, a leading researcher at the Department of Criminology at University of Ottawa in Canada, has pointed out that even though there have been some changes in legal approaches in both the United States and England, there still is a strong gender bias in laws dealing with the issue of rape or even "indecent exposure." "Gender bias continues to exist in laws concerning sexual offenses, highlighting the ways in which the criminal law sustains and reinforces traditional sexual scripts, implicitly denying women's potential for sexual aggression. Even if a victim comes forward to report a serious sexual offense by a female, criminal law may not have the language to represent such a case, or the political will to prosecute it (Denov 2003).

Denov's research reveals that there are many cases of child sexual abuse by women perpetrators that not only go unrecognized by the law but also by mental health professionals as well.

> Traditional sexual scripts, particularly the perception of females as sexually passive, harmless, and innocent, appear not only to have influenced broader societal views concerning sexuality and sexual abuse but also to have permeated the criminal law, victim reporting practices, and professional responses to female offending. (Denov, 2003)

In a study released in 2005, the federal Department of Education discovered that "forty percent of the educators who had been reported for sexual misconduct with students were women." (Zernike, 2005). And, as the Internet permeates our lives, a study by The Crimes Against Children Research Center has discovered that women were the harassers in 19 percent of the reported incidents of aggressive or distressing online events experienced by children. While there is resistance to the idea that a woman could sexually abuse children, the number of legal cases against women who have engaged in sex with children has been rising slowly in the past few years. (Finkelhor et al., 2000)

There are many instances when the sexual difficulties of women have been ignored by mental health providers who simply could not imagine that a woman seeking help could, for example, be a child molester, a sexual predator, have sex with a different man every night, or be an exhibitionist or voyeur. Neither is it unusual that a woman might want help with these issues but can not bring herself to speak of them. Clinically, it is important to recognize that women, as well as men, have these types of sexual behaviors. Therapists should be comfortable asking about them and then know what to do to help.

As a society, we do not look comfortably at the harmful face of sex. Women often do not seek help for sexual abuse, sexual harassment, or even personal sexual problems. Many suffer in silence, feeling that no one will believe them. In addition, many men do not find it easy to talk about being sexually abused because such abuse is not "manly." Mitch did not consider that his relationship with the babysitter was abusive, although as an adult he thought it was "not right." Our culture projects weakness and shame on men who have been sexually exploited. Women in particular may have great difficulty giving voice to the traumatic events in their lives. They may act them out silently in ways that are harmful. Eating disorders and self-harming behaviors such as cutting (which are more common in women than men), alcoholism, and sexual behaviors such as sadomasochism and multiple, anonymous sexual encounters, are some of the more common ways women may give voice to their sexual victimization, physical abuse, or neglect (Southern, 2002).

Keeping in mind that the data on the frequency of compelling sexual behaviors is still sparse, women are more likely to be involved in compulsive masturbation, multiple sexual partners (including prostitution), severe sexual incompatibility with a spouse or partner, and sadomasochism (Kafka, 2007). In addition, while these behaviors may be considered more romantic or psychological and not specifically sexual or genital-related behaviors, others have identified "love addictions," obsessional fixations," and "crushes" that have the possibility of undermining good partner relationships and causing emotional, lifestyle, and legal problems that warrant attention (Hollender & Callahan, 1975; Kasl, 1989; Carnes, 1991; Coleman, 1992). Women who have CSB frequently have coexisting mental health issues such as alcohol or substance abuse, anxiety and depression, lack of sexual desire, sexual abuse, or physical and emotional abuse and childhood neglect.

THE BALANCE OF POWER IN A RELATIONSHIP

The power in relationships is generally perceived differently by women than it is by men. Just from a purely physical point of view, men are generally bigger and stronger than women, so the sheer physical balance is not equal in most relationships. However, the physical mass/power quotient is important to notice in any relationship—be they same gender, heterosexual, or therapist and client. This difference in size may have implications when we least suspect it. I remember an instance when it became a very important part of the therapeutic equation.

I was consulted by a colleague who had been working with a couple on their sexual relationship. Therapy was not going well. I pictured my colleague, an imposing figure who is more than 6 feet tall and large-framed. I asked him to describe what the couple looked like. The husband was a powerful man, the CEO of a large company, and almost as tall as the therapist. His wife was just 5 feet tall. The presenting problem was that the wife was not able to have orgasms, had low sexual desire, and was depressed. There are many issues I could have raised, but my instinct invited me to ask my colleague to close his eyes for a moment and imagine how he might feel in a room full of tall, powerful, competent men if he could not get an erection. He quickly figured out the woman needed a safer place to work out to these problems and referred her to a female therapist. She was quite relieved. He reserved the couple work for later, and helped her express her reticence and fears about being with these two men in one small room, focusing on her sexuality. Issues with power show up in many ways in the therapist's office.

Currently, the TV series *Mad Men,* based on the advertising industry in the 1960s, has become very popular. It is a perfect tutorial about the abuse of power and sexism in corporate America at that time. In the movie *The Devil Wears Prada,* it is the female boss who emotionally harasses and bullies her employees. While in this century there are laws about sexual harassment, it is has not disappeared; it is just more subtle. The abuse of power in relationships comes alive in my office when I discover that someone in a position of power and trust has sexually exploited or abused my client. Neither men nor women are exempt. It may be a relative, a parent or stepparent, therapist, teacher, farm hand, doctor, lawyer, religious leader, or anybody you can think of.

Exploitation does not necessarily have to be sexual to be harmful. It may be an abuse of power for emotional, political, economic, or social reasons. It may take place within the confines of a family or within corporate or religious structures in the larger community. For example, within the family, it may take the form of one sibling physically assaulting another sibling, or a wife or husband who is a tyrant and is physically and emotionally abusive. Abuse of power in any form takes its toll on the psyche. Therapists need to assess this in the history of a client with any type of sexual problems but particularly in those with compelling sexual habits. Therapists also must take great care not to exploit the power with which clients often endow them.

TWO WOMEN: FOUR LIVES

We will now focus on the experiences of two women: Lisa, a heterosexual woman married to Rich for 15 years who had many affairs, and Eileen, a lesbian woman in a new relationship with Susan. Lisa and Eileen were struggling with exaggerations of sexual expression and sexual secrets: parodies of relationships that were ultimately disappointing and dissatisfying. For many years, both women had been seeking (in all the wrong places) some version of what they thought of as love. When I met Lisa, she was looking for a total makeover for her husband while having multiple one-night stands with other men. When Eileen finally met Susan, she wanted to change her ways.

Lisa and Rich

Lisa was a *limerence* junkie looking for the *methadone man* (Erian, 2005). The word *limerence* was coined by Dorothy Tennov, Ph.D. (1979). I love it. It has an onomatopoeic resonance with its meaning of that "twinkly-moon-June-spoon" feeling that occurs when someone falls in love. The heart pounds, feet don't touch the ground, and life is beautiful. Tennov (1979) invented the word because there was a "need for a term for a type of love that differs from other conditions also called love." It is not the equivalent of sexual desire, but it is unquestionably sexual. It describes the state of mind when a person fixates on someone with whom a bond is intensely desired. The ideal situation would be that the intensity of limerence would be reciprocated, and then, when the intensity diminishes, be replaced by another kind of love, the comforting and friendly love that many couples enjoy over a lifetime.

> Stendhal, a French writer who was a soldier in Napoleon's army, observed there is no greater human happiness than that which is bestowed on the limerent person when reciprocation seems likely. But the person in limerence is also vulnerable to protracted emotional suffering. Unhappy loves have been

implicated in major historical events at least since Helen of Troy and up to and apparently including Monica Lewinsky. (Tennov, 2001)

The pursuit of limerence is a full-time preoccupation for many people. They want that wonderful limerent feeling all the time. Who wouldn't? But the obsessive pursuit of limerence can create unimaginable carnage, and usually ends with a rude awakening. Lisa seemed to be searching for multiple limerent relationships. How could her husband Rich compete with them? I am of the opinion that while sex in a long-term relationship or marriage can become more satisfying with age, it cannot compete with the erotic charge of limerence or the excitement of a forbidden and secretive affair. It was my guess that Lisa was having relationships with married men, or multiple anonymous sexual encounters with men while she was out and about with her friends, or both.

It took Lisa two years to come out of denial about what really bothered her. When she initially contacted me, she said she wanted to know how to put more romance in her marriage. "Perhaps," she requested, "you could recommend some books, or techniques, or something?" I offered an appointment and asked if her husband might also like to be involved. I commented that two people share the same sex life so I often found it helpful to talk with both of them. "Oh, no, no, no," she said. It was *her* problem. She flatly refused to involve her husband Rich. She scoffed when I suggested that two people own the same sex life. She said that there were some things she needed to talk about and work out first. Fair enough.

Lisa was an attractive and talkative woman who could have easily passed for a 20-year-old. She was 45. She was a triathlete, tall and in good shape. She carried herself and dressed in a way that said she was comfortable with her body and proud of it. It undoubtedly attracted many envious stares from others, men in particular. She was also a part-time bookkeeper. She told me that she just was not "in love" with her husband any more. I asked her to tell me more about what she meant. She answered: "I don't know. I just think he's the best guy, but he doesn't turn me on anymore; he's not exciting."

I tried to engage her more by asking some questions about her family, as well as the history of her relationships before her marriage. She listened to my questions, shrugging most of them off quickly, and denied that she had any problems with sex in any previous relationships. She was insistent that she had worked through her issues with her mother and father, listened to tapes promoting health and a positive attitude, and that is what worked for her. She did not really want to talk about her family or her past. She just wanted some techniques to get the spark back in her marriage.

Lisa told me she liked to go out with her girlfriends, liked dancing, liked flirting, and then went home. She had once been picked up for a DWI, and she and her husband had an agreement that she would either call him for a ride, take a cab, or ask a friend for a ride if she had too much to drink. But alcohol was "not really a problem," she said. She "had it under control." Her husband did not like to socialize, hated dancing, and even disliked her friends, so he never came with her. Sometimes it was very late when the parties were over, so she stayed with a friend rather than wake Rich up.

I did my damndest to get some real data, but her "positive attitude" just ran right over it all. I learned a long time ago that denial serves a great purpose, and if I chipped away at it too quickly, it would be fruitless. Let this unfold as it may. I listened to her talk about herself, which she seemed to enjoy a great deal. She told me about the motivational tapes she had and how they helped her. She told me that her life was fun and outside of her husband being a "stick in the mud" everything was perfect. He loved her, and she loved him but was not "in love" with him. She did not want to hurt him, but she had to be honest with him about it because she simply did not want to have sex with him.

I decided to take her at face value (what else was there to do?) and suggested a few books and resources that might offer some advice about helpful sexual techniques. If they were not useful, I was available to offer what I could in the way of therapy. We had two visits, and Lisa disappeared. I had an inkling that there was a lot more to this than met the eye. I hoped that the questions I had asked allowed her some room to at least consider the answers. Maybe one of the questions might strike a cord. Patience can be its own reward.

Several months later, I had a call from Rich, Lisa's husband of 15 years. He reminded me about his wife's visits and asked if he could also visit with me. I asked him if Lisa knew about the call, and he said he had asked her for my number. Rich was a tall, dark, handsome 45-year-old lawyer who specialized in criminal law. He was really upset that his wife did not love him anymore. If there ever was a "strong, silent type," it was Rich. He was right out of central casting! It was very difficult to get him to talk. He did tell me that their sex life, when they first met, was very exciting. He did not understand why it fizzled, or why Lisa was not interested in having sex with him anymore. He had no sexual performance or desire issues but still worried that he was inadequate in some way. When I asked, "What makes you think you are sexually inadequate?" he answered, "Why else would Lisa tell me she does not love me?"

I was struck by what I could only characterize as Rich's unusual naïveté. Given that he was a criminal lawyer, something did not seem to fit. He came from the Midwest and was raised on a large wheat farm with little contact with the outside world until he went away to college; maybe that is what explained his guilelessness. He was really puzzled about why Lisa did not want sex with him. It seemed strange to me that a criminal lawyer would not be more suspicious about what his wife actually did when she went out all night. I was curious to know more about it. I gently asked if he thought there might be someone else. Ignoring my question, he described what Lisa did in great detail when she went out and about with her friends. He just thought that maybe if he learned to dance and party a little more she would like him better. I believed he really had wondered where she was going and did suspect she was seeing someone else but could not face it. At the end of the hour, he recited his secret fears to me. He almost whispered that he thought she might be unfaithful but really was not sure. I offered to talk with him individually again in a few days. He was ambivalent about returning by himself and said he would think about it and call me. He was in such pain from what he speculated was Lisa's unfaithfulness that he could not speak to me about it.

Again, some time went by before I heard from them and then they wanted to come in together. Nothing had changed. Denial was still in place. Lisa had invested Rich in listening to her tapes, and he had agreed. He also would acquire a positive attitude toward life, and it would solve their problems. I guessed he would do anything not to have to look at the real reasons behind Lisa's feelings and to keep the boat drifting along smoothly. I tried to get to the hurt Rich felt, but he would not ask Lisa for comfort or reassurance. Nevertheless, Lisa did acknowledge that she was sorry she hurt him and that she loved him but was not "in love" with him. Every time she said that to Rich, he cringed and I winced. I said to them, "I wonder why you, Lisa, say that so often and why you, Rich, allow her to say it to you, if you both know it hurts so much?" Both of them shrugged their shoulders and agreed to think about it. They thought about it for a long time. A year went by before I heard from them again.

It had been about 2 years since Lisa had first contacted me when I heard from her again. This time she was ready to look inside. Sometimes it takes a long time to be truthful with yourself, to face denial squarely. "When the mind is ready a teacher appears" (Gordon, 1981). As I had suspected, Lisa was a *limerence junkie*. Her opening statement to me this time around was that she had "never been faithful to anyone in her life." Maybe this time we could get somewhere.

The distinction people often make between feeling "in love" and "loving" someone has always captured my imagination. Steve Levine (2007) talks about love being both a noun and a verb. Many people have come to my door with this dilemma. Usually when someone tells me that they are not "in love" with their partner or spouse anymore but they still "love" them, I suspect an affair. When I poke around a bit, usually another lover is discovered. It is a way to split off erotic feelings of sex from the loving feelings of psychological intimacy. This was true for Lisa, although she had a variation on the theme of "just having an affair." It had taken her two years to own up to her problems with fidelity, but Lisa was finally ready to explore the lessons she thought she wanted to learn.

Lisa was an only child of parents who divorced when she was 6 years old. Her mother had many men in the house. She also had a terrible relationship with her mother, who projected her own sexual acting out onto Lisa. She began calling Lisa a "whore" and "slut" when she began to menstruate and wear clothes that were typical of the teen scene at the time: short skirts, knee socks, halter tops, and bikinis. Lisa had been sexually abused when she was 12 years old by her best friend's father. Since her mother would accuse Lisa of lying all the time, and would not believe anything she said, Lisa never told anyone about the abuse, not even Rich. I was the first person to hear about it.

Lisa idealized her father and finally went to live with him when she was 16. He had married a woman who was a religious fundamentalist. Lisa went from the frying pan into the fire of hell and damnation. Forced to read the Bible and pray twice a day, Lisa was also carefully monitored at her father's house by her stepmother. While she was not called the names her mother called her, it was implied that she had uncontrollable sexual urges that needed to be warded off. She could be protected from these urges by praying.

She had curfews and limits to where she could go and with whom she could socialize. School dances were heavily chaperoned. The school psychologist diagnosed her as "hyperactive" and also as having a learning disability. Her parents chalked up her problems at school to laziness. Threatening to run away at 17, she prevailed upon her father to let her live in another state with her paternal grandmother and finish high school there. They acquiesced and were relieved to see her go. After she finished high school, Lisa moved to California and married Rich, the first man to ask her. He was an Air Force pilot that Lisa met while waitressing at a bar near the base. Soon after they married, Rich went to sea on an aircraft carrier for a year. She continued to have sex with anyone who asked her.

Lisa told me that she finally had begun to realize she needed help and had accepted that she was a *sex addict*. True to character, she bought every book she could find on the subject, and they all seemed to be written about her. She was validated by her reading. She had a history of abuse, problems with alcohol, depression, and anxiety that all seem to go along with these types of sexual problems. She agreed she was always looking for a "high with a guy." Her obsession was to go into any public place, establish a "3-second" eye contact with a man, and then "move in." I have several married male clients who do the same thing. It is a fairly common phenomenon. Some do it occasionally; others, like Lisa, are caught up in it almost daily. The search, finding the eye contact, making the connection, and then having sex, make up a compelling quest. Some spend many hours of each day fantasizing and planning for these events.

Lisa's fantasy was that one of these men would be Prince Charming, sweep her off her feet, and provide her with a life of riches and adventure. She was searching for the *methadone man*. He would cure her *addiction*. He would stop her compelling need to run away from herself, to get love even if for one night. The fantasy was always that the next man would be the last man. He would make her feel better. Sometimes she lingered with a man she met, and it would become an ongoing affair. However, she had not been able to stop the game, the seeking, even when she had an affair that lasted for a few months. Her girlfriends were aware of what she was doing, and some even participated in the same game, but not to the extent Lisa did. This same group of women often went to resorts together, "just the girls," for a vacation. But for

Lisa it was always about the adventure of anonymous sex. Lisa says she invited Rich to go but he was never willing.

What finally shook Lisa and Rich out of denial was a man Lisa met from Italy. He was very sophisticated and suave, spoke English with an Italian accent (always a seduction), dressed well, and had his own plane. He was married, but he and his wife "had their own lives, went their separate ways," so he said. He came to the United States often for business. Lisa lost her ability to move on to the next man after she met Antonio. She had finally met her *methadone man*. Antonio was the ultimate drug. She could stop her wanderings, finally be faithful. He promised her things that no one ever had. He was so romantic, gave flowers, gifts, and told her he "wanted to look at her face the rest of his life." He took her away for the weekend to a luxurious inn when Rich was visiting his parents. She was ostensibly staying home to train for the next triathlon.

Lisa was in a highly limerent state, longing for some sign from Antonio that he would leave his wife and marry her. She lived from telephone call to telephone call and for clandestine meetings. "Impossibility ... a great big log thrown on the fires of love" (Kidd, 2001). She was really suffering from the anxiety and anticipation of being with Antonio. The ecstasy was exquisite, the pain unbearable. In a blinding limerent state, feeling that she had fallen in love, Lisa instead fell out of the blue sky of fantasy and crashed on the cement. Reality landed on her heavily. It is what generally happens when limerence reigns. Antonio told Lisa that his wife was about to have a baby. One wonders how Antonio and his wife accomplished that while "going their separate ways?" He ended the affair with Lisa abruptly. For a "remembrance," Antonio gave her a video of them having sex that he had clandestinely recorded. Rich found the tape when he turned on their video player. Oops! There is that unconscious wish to be discovered asserting itself.

So we rolled up our sleeves, Lisa and I, as she came roaring out of denial. Rich and Lisa went for couple work. Lisa went on medication for her depression and anxiety. It was amazing to see what medication and therapy did for Lisa. It was as if someone put her in a time machine, and she matured 10 year's worth in a year. But then she had been working up to it long before she actually invested in therapy. Her impulse control was significantly improved by medication, and she was able to contain her behaviors. She was not fond of keeping logs and resisted them for a long time. They are not for everyone, but we checked in every session to get the information that a log provides. Eventually Lisa read about the value of journaling in her endless search for the best "self help" program and learned not to equate this exercise with "school work," which she hated. Whatever works.

Lisa became very conscious of where her eyes and mind were going. Rich was learning not to enable her, to express his own feelings and needs, and to have them respected. She worked on understanding her childhood traumas, and said one day "I am beginning to feel inside what I always relied on my body for." I asked her to clarify that for me. She said that she figured if she looked sexy and desirable, she would attract men, and that would help her self-image. Now she felt good about herself without having to dress seductively and obsess about her looks and shape. She was interested in how she felt about herself and monitored her own feelings and thoughts rather than always looking outside for feedback.

The work that Rich and Lisa did together with the marital therapist was tough. On two occasions they separated for a short period of time, but they did have glue from their 15-year marriage. They had become great friends, and when they did things together they enjoyed each other's company and had a good time. In some ways they had many of the same values. They volunteered at a youth center and at a soup kitchen together. They loved their home and worked together to make it look nice. They both had the same sense of humor and laughed a lot. Rich's family was the big happy family Lisa had always fantasized about. They, in turn, loved her and expressed it often. They visited back and forth frequently, and Lisa always felt calm and happy on their farm. She and her mother-in-law were close. From Rich's mom, Lisa learned many skills she had never learned growing up such as how to bake and sew, to say nothing of how to be in a family.

Rich's family had been supportive of both Rich and Lisa during their separations, and Rich and Lisa honored a pledge that the family would not know the details of Lisa's sex life. Rich worked very hard at being more verbal and expressing his feelings in general, as well as his feelings of betrayal and his acute distress over Lisa's unfaithfulness. He learned to tell Lisa when he was worried about it. Lisa learned to hear his hurt and be supportive rather than defensive. They knew it would never "just go away," but both found a place to put it and to live with the past.

Eventually, Lisa asked Rich to marry her again as a symbol of how she felt about him. She wanted to make a commitment to him in an adult, mindful way, for the right reasons: She loved him. He was eager to do this because, for the first time in their lives, he felt he was finally married to a mature responsible woman rather than a little girl whom he had indulged for his own needs. She was happy to be choosing a husband who really was someone she wanted to be with and could feel great love and respect for, rather than marrying someone to take care of her.

It is a story with a truly happy ending, but it was hard-earned. Lisa and Rich will be working on it the rest of their lives; but then, they like it that way. And who do you know who is married for a long time that doesn't work at it? They were very grateful to have had the opportunity that this crisis afforded them to create a real marriage. They are engaged in an open and honest dialogue—no more denial, no more naiveté. Few couples survive this. I call them my "poster children."

Eileen and Susan

Eileen was an attractive, bouncy woman, who was so over-deter-minedly cheerful that she exhausted me. Talk about "putting on a good face"! She was 42 years old, beautifully groomed, and looked as if she took very good care of herself. She was a high-functioning executive, who, for 15 years, had been fast-tracked in her company. A few weeks before our first meeting, her manager discovered that Eileen had been in a chat room for sadomasochistic women while at work. The manager sent her home for the day, and said she would call her. She checked around town for therapists who could deal with Internet sex and gave Eileen my name.

During our first visit, Eileen volunteered: "I tried therapy once several years ago, when I began to feel out of control. It was not helpful." "What did not work for you?" I asked. She said: "The therapist kept blaming all my behavior on the fact that I am a lesbian woman. I was told to be abstinent and join a church for help and support." Eileen was skeptical about how helpful I might be. I told her that skepticism is healthy in many situations. "Once burned, twice cautious," my mother used to say.

I wondered how Eileen felt about the fact that I was not a les-bian woman. She ventured that the very fact that I had brought it up gave her hope that she might be able to trust me. She had also noticed a small sticker on the window of my office that indicated it was a "safe" place for homosexual people. We promised each other that if her sexual orientation became an issue for either one of us, we would talk about it. I encouraged her to call me on it if she felt I was not "getting it." I made sure to ask how she felt about our working relationship from time to time, and she appreciated being able to be open about how she felt. We learned how to manage and acknowledge the difference in our experiences.

Many therapists are not sensitized to working with other cultures or various sexual orientations. While some may believe that the same techniques and skills can apply to any group of people, which may be true in some respects, there are many unique therapeutic issues and contexts that lesbian women encounter that are important for therapists to understand. Charlotte Kasl, a well-known advocate for understanding the unique issues of women with compelling sexual habits, sums up the numerous dynamics and concerns that should be addressed by therapists who treat lesbian women: "These include: understanding the patterns of sexual addiction in lesbian relationships; a basic knowledge of issues lesbian women face in their daily lives; internalized oppression (the absorption of cultural stereotypes [about lesbian women]), the lack of cultural support for lesbian relationships, homophobia, the oppression-avoidance syndrome, typical sexual difficulties in lesbian relationships, subculture dynamics, and the coming out process" (2002). Kasl's article cited here is a very useful resource for anyone who wants to be educated about the issues in more detail.

Eileen had never had a committed relationship, even with her own family. She longed to have a partner, to be with someone for a lifetime, and to create her own family. During the year before we met, Eileen met Susan, who was 35 years old. They had been together for about eight months, a record for Eileen. Susan was a nurse with an MA in nursing administration and was doing well in her career. She was being promoted through the system at the hospital. Her goal was to have a high-level administrative position at some point and perhaps move out of the area to a larger hospital after she proved herself.

In spite of Eileen's bouncy and cheerful demeanor, she was quite depressed and anxious. She felt vulnerable, exposed, and humiliated. She was very worried that her manager had found out she was a lesbian woman. It was a very real possibility that her computer use for personal purposes during work would be an easy excuse to fire her. She was sure that it would be a "cover" for the company's homophobia. It is a realistic fear that lesbian women live with daily. She also told me that she was in the habit of keeping her feelings buried and "refused" to give into them. Her personal life was always a private matter, and she had been very careful not to reveal any of it at work.

Eileen had a well-deserved reputation for being powerful, competent, and successful. She was a perfectionist who could not understand how she had let herself be caught online at work. How, indeed. Sometimes our unconscious mind does us a favor, and we "slip" just at the right time. Eileen definitely needed help with the burdens she had been carrying around for many years, so it seemed logical to me that her being careless was a maybe-not-so-unconscious wish for some help.

It was also fortuitous that Susan, her partner, had been in therapy for three years, and that it had been very helpful. Susan encouraged Eileen to talk about many things in their lives, and it was the first time Eileen had really opened up to anyone. The conversations with Susan had made it easier for Eileen to be open with me. While getting therapy had been "strongly advised" by her manager, the dialogues with Susan also made it easier for Eileen to summon the courage to seek help again. Susan had many strengths and was very much in love with Eileen. Eileen, on the other hand, had very little training in what love was. She knew a great deal about sexual arousal and erotic feelings; however, love, intimacy, and honesty were new territories for her. Keeping feelings hidden was a well-entrenched habit. There was a very large gap between her public expression and her private persona.

Eileen met Susan on the Internet. She felt she had finally met the "perfect woman." When Eileen was caught online at work, she was "just looking, revisiting the old cyber neighborhood," but not actually seeking someone with whom to arrange a meeting. She was soothing her anxiety about her relationship with Susan, and had vowed to be monogamous—to try to make the relationship work. Eileen felt that going online was not breaking her commitment to Susan, although Susan was afraid Eileen might break her promise and actually arrange a meeting with someone. Eileen's sexual life until this time had become a well-rehearsed ritual to "medicate" her stress. It would take a while for Eileen to be in charge of her stress in more functional ways. She wanted to be certain that Susan was here to stay—that Eileen would not inadvertently send her away. For her part, Susan wanted to trust Eileen but her last partner had cheated on her and Susan could not allow herself to be in another co-dependent relationship.

Eileen's childhood memories were bleak. Her mother had worked as a housekeeper while Eileen and her sister, Josie, 3 years older, were left at home to fend for themselves. Her mother came home from work and drank all night, falling into bed in a stupor. Sometimes there were male visitors. Mom would hit the girls if they left their beds when the male visitors were there, even if they had to use the bathroom. Sometimes, the visitors would come in the girls' room after mom fell asleep and fondle one or both of them.

Eileen's mother died from alcoholism when Eileen was 12 years old, and she never knew her father. No one knew who he was. She and Josie had been brought up in the South and came to New York City when her mother's sister had agreed to take the girls after their mother died. Aunty Del was single and had no children of her own. She was educated, had a good job, was a loving person, and a good role model. Eileen remembered having a very difficult time adjusting to the urban setting of New York and missed the freedom she had in the low country of Georgia. She still dreamed of going back to the South and hoped her company would send her to work at a branch office there at some point in her career.

School had been a refuge for Eileen from the very beginning. She was very bright. Her teachers encouraged her and helped her succeed. Fortunately, there were also neighbors who helped the two girls—cooking meals, having them over, or just giving them a hug sometimes. When the girls came to New York, Aunty Del sent them to a parochial school. This turned out to be a great opportunity for Eileen. She was awarded a scholarship to a private high school and then went to college and graduate school, earning a master's degree in business administration.

During her high school and college years, Eileen realized that she was a lesbian. She had never had any interest in boys, but she sure noticed the girls in school. She was very shy, and when they moved to New York, she became even more withdrawn. But like so many young women, the thought of being a lesbian was something that rang terror in her soul. Who could she talk to? Would she be punished, burn in hell? It was better to work hard and keep to herself. Maybe it would go away.

While Eileen had been aware that she had crushes on girls and women teachers, she was afraid of the desire that she felt for women and suppressed it. She tried to rationalize that it was just because of the men her mother brought home, but she knew that was not really the "cause" of her fear. Finally, in the liberal atmosphere of college, she found she might have some support from the lesbian activist groups on campus. It was not until her junior year in college that Eileen allowed herself to become involved in some of the lesbian activities on campus. She met a woman who helped her come out. It turned out that the relationship was a bad one, and Eileen was devastated by it.

Looking for some of the things she had been missing in life, Eileen had idealized her lover, Sandy. Sandy was an alcoholic and wanted to experiment with sadomasochism. This frightened Eileen, but, at the same time, it excited her. She had her first orgasm with Sandy, who introduced Eileen to a world she had never even dreamt of: a dark, sensuous, secret, erotic, and frightening world. Sandy could not stay faithful for long, so the relationship ended very quickly. But Sandy had taken Eileen places, literally and figuratively, that introduced her to many sensations and to many people. She was in demand as a sexual partner and for the first time in her life had a feeling of belonging and being part of something. She began to become more aggressive in her search for sexual partners. She thought the way to find them was to have sex first and think (or avoid thinking) about who they were later.

Eileen had wondered why she, too, did not become an alcoholic like her Mother or Josie. She knew it ran in families. She drank on occasion to be sociable but she really did not like the taste of alcoholic beverages. More important, she did not want to run the risk that she would slip into unconsciousness with people she did not know very well, particularly when she was acting out some sadomasochistic scenario. Her self-control with alcohol amazed her because she often felt so out of control sexually. We began to look at other "addictions" or obsessions that did not serve her well: her work, her perfectionism, her multiple partners, and obsessions with sex to the exclusion of personal connections. Eileen began to understand that alcohol is not the only way to avoid unwanted feelings. Eileen had been abused and neglected. Therefore, her need to be in control also served the function of keeping her emotionally safe. We explored other ways to be emotionally safe that would serve her better.

Eileen settled into her job about 10 years before she consulted me. When traveling for business she began cruising gay bars for anonymous sadomasochistic encounters with women. For six or seven years she also occasionally exposed herself in the window of her apartment. For about three years prior to meeting Susan in a chat room, Eileen had begun using the Internet for sexual encounters. Eventually a pattern emerged over the years. Eileen had been seeking more and more sexual excitement that included sadomasochistic and anonymous encounters, exhibiting herself, and cruising the Internet. She was flirting with danger, and she liked it. She liked to be aroused. It made her feel alive to be in control and feeling erotic. She did not like to be the passive recipient of sexual advances, it was too similar to her childhood encounters with mom's male visitors.

Involvement in all these activities made Eileen feel as if she had a social life and was valued by others. But at the same time, she was lonely and felt empty when she went home alone. There was always the world outside her window or someone on the Internet to chat with and seduce: substitutes for a real relationship. This caricature of love and parody of an emotional connection was an empty feeling. The psychic dilemma Eileen had to struggle with was that if she really risked a close relationship, she might set her self up for another loss.

It took a few sessions to gather information about Eileen's past and determine what she wanted from therapy—where she wanted to go with her life. Susan had been the only person she had ever been truthful with before me. She expressed how good it felt to be "real" with someone and still feel accepted rather than judged. After all, she had been feeling judged by others and had been ashamed of herself for many years. When she and Susan met, Susan had made it clear that she wanted to develop a friendship with Eileen before becoming sexually involved. This was new for Eileen, and the anxiety it provoked led to her going back online and touching base with her old habits. Her goals were to give up cruising for relationships, make a commitment to Susan, and have a "normal" life. She wanted to feel good about herself and her personal life instead of just about her work. She was tired of guarding her sexual orientation and leading a secret life. These were healthy goals, but we both knew it would be easier said than done.

Diagnostic impressions, and thus treatment goals, often change throughout therapy. At this point I took stock of what Eileen's issues were and how I might proceed. Her childhood provided neglect, sexual abuse, and attachment issues. She had obsessive traits, impulse control issues involving multiple sexual partners, sado-masochistic behaviors, exhibitionist tendencies, depression and anxiety. She had relationship and emotional intimacy issues as well. Depression is an umbrella term with many symptoms, a large component of which is anxiety. Many clients will say to me: "I'm not depressed; I don't sit and look out the window and feel sad all the time." I explain that there are many symptoms that are lumped under the diagnostic term "depression." Treating depression might also help a person feel more in control, allowing a person to pause between the thought and the deed. Treatment also may improve self-esteem and patience and reduce anger. It seemed to me that Eileen would benefit from psychodynamic psychotherapy for the trauma and attachment issues; medication for depression, anxiety, obsessive traits and impulse control; and cognitive behavioral work for Internet use and sexual behaviors. At some point I would make a referral for relationship therapy, focusing on communication with Susan and their sexual relationship.

We had our work cut out for us. Eileen and I talked about the approach I thought would be useful, and she agreed with the plan, asking good questions about what was involved. Carnes, (1991) reports that 81% of a sample of 200 recovering "sex-addicted" people had been sexually abused as children, and that a large percentage of women who have compelling sexual habits have experienced neglect and abuse as children. Many women who have compelling sexual habits are likely to stay attached to the trauma they have suffered, acting it out repeatedly in relationships. Thus, it is important to recognize and understand these traumas and begin addressing and containing the sexual habits as soon as possible (Southern, 2002).

Working through trauma, however, does not mean it will go away. I tell my clients that I do not have a magic eraser that will make tragic and painful events disappear. It doesn't mean that I don't keep hoping I will find one someday. In the popular movie *The Eternal Sunshine of the Spotless Mind,* bad memories of failed relationships were erased from the mind by a machine that reprogrammed the brain. I can understand this movie's appeal. Perhaps someday we will be able to do that, but in the meantime traumas, in any form, can leave deep, ugly scars behind. Psychodynamic-oriented therapy can be fruitful for understanding and working with trauma and attachment disorders.

Eileen and I worked toward recognizing her emotional reactions to events or people for what they were. Some of her reactions stemmed from traumas she had undergone as a child: abandonment, anxiety, fear, sexual abuse, and neglect. This was the fallout from an alcoholic mom who could not nurture her children or control her boyfriends. Traumas are like land mines: They get hidden in the ground and we can step them on unwittingly at any time. We can find ourselves deep in the midst of these old events again because of an experience that may not seem, on the surface, to be the same at all.

For example, the day that her mother died, Eileen was at a neighbor's house. Her mother had been in the hospital for a few days, and a neighbor said she would take Eileen and her sister to see their mother. Each day the neighbor promised she would be able to see her mother, but they were not taken to the hospital. On the day her mother died, the neighbor once again put Eileen off when she asked to see her mother. Eileen became very anxious. She was not sure why the neighbor kept changing the subject and would not talk to her directly about it. Her anxiety built until finally the telephone rang, and the neighbor told her that her mother had died. Eileen was traumatized, and sobbed so hard for so long that the doctor was called. She was silenced with a large hypodermic needle filled with a sedative. It was still a vivid and painful memory.

The day Eileen's boss found her on the computer searching for sexual contacts, she sent Eileen home. She said she would call to let her know how things would be handled. Eileen went home, and felt a sudden burst of anxiety and began to sob uncontrollably. She found herself back at the neighbor's kitchen table, an untouched cookie and milk in front of her. The telephone was ringing. She could not pick it up. She did not want to hear what might be said if she did. It was a paralyzing experience for Eileen, who found herself in the past having the same painful feelings that had been evoked when her mother died. Anxiety caused her heart to pound so hard Eileen thought she might be having a heart attack. Eventually, she was able to connect the two events and understand how the present reality of perhaps losing her job conspired with the resonance of past events and touched her so deeply.

When Eileen finally was able to talk with her boss, she found out that her boss was supportive. This would not go on her record if she were to get help and if it never happened again. Employers are usually not so forgiving; most fire the errant employer on the spot. When Eileen talked to me about this, she also remembered some other experiences from the past that had the potential for "exploding" in the here and now. She realized that for many years she had been braced for punishment because she was a lesbian. She also learned that she could stop and talk about scary feelings during sex with Susan, and they became less upsetting. Scars are not the same as open wounds.

During these first few months of therapy, I found it difficult to get Eileen to look inside at her own feelings and to express them. She seemed more invested in "putting on a happy face," entertaining me, flirting with me, and impressing me. When she began to keep her logs, they were more like business reports and did not contain much affect. Hiding from her feelings had brought Eileen to my door. Relying on her intellect had also helped Eileen become a success at school and at work. She was a "linear thinker," someone who was not used to thinking abstractly or going inside and mucking around in her feelings. So I "began to watch for the face behind the face; and to listen for the words hiding behind the talk" (Morrison, 2005).

I prompted Eileen to "look inside" on many occasions. I was getting a little frustrated, when one day I pointed out a photograph hanging in my office. The photographer had captured a beautiful sunset that lit up a mountain top. The inscription under the photograph said, "All the wonders you seek are within yourself." Eileen was not so sure about the message. I suggested that maybe she would find some "wonders" if she dug around. She was skeptical. When things got off track, I would say "look inside," and she would pause and try to attach feelings to her deeds. It was tough going to learn this, but we kept at it, and eventually Eileen became much better at capturing and expressing her feelings.

Not too long into our relationship, Eileen began to express how wonderful I was. She imbued me with powers that were almost magical. She said I made her feel so wonderful, that she was so happy I was her therapist, that all she needed to do between sessions was to think about what I said and she felt happy and secure. I listened to these compliments for a few weeks and unsuccessfully tried to get behind them to what she was really feeling. Exasperated, I finally suggested that her compliments made me feel uncomfortable. She quickly, and with some alarm said, "I didn't mean to make you uncomfortable!" I replied that what was discomfiting to me was how these compliments negated *her* part in our relationship. After all, she was here only for one or two hours a week. What did she do the rest of the week to keep herself going besides think of me?

What about *her* thoughts and feelings? Was she worried I would reject her if I knew how she really felt?

Eileen sat silent and her eyes filled with tears. She tried to control herself, and I said, "Talk to me." She was very confused. She felt so badly about herself that she could only think that others thought the same about her. She confessed that she was always braced for rejection and abandonment not only by me but by others as well. A good offense is a good defense: Ward off rejection with compliments. She looked away, thinking for a few moments. I sat and waited for her to go on. Finally she said I had poked at her scars. I apologized if it hurt, but thought maybe we could have a more mutual and useful relationship if she did not endow me with powers I did not have. I wondered if she followed the same pattern with other people in her life. She shrugged noncommittally.

Then Eileen started to bring me little gifts, starting with one flower, some mints like the ones I had on the table next to my chair, and later a bouquet. At the same time she began to sit in the chair nearer to me instead of on the couch across from me and wore shorter and shorter skirts, crossing her legs and draping herself on the chair on a seductive way. Uh-oh, I thought, she was "falling in love" with me. This feeling of "love" was Eileen's habitual way of attempting to connect with others. It worked well for her; she "scored" that way all the time. She was being seductive with me; making flirtatious remarks, saying she liked my sweater, and asking to touch it. So when she brought in an exquisite bouquet of flowers, I knew my attempts to clarify the meaning of the gifts were failing. I suggested to her that we were stuck in acting out what I imagined was the script for all her relationships. I also understood Eileen's attempt at seduction as a protective defense against the intimacy of the therapeutic relationship.

I admired the bouquet, and said I would make a deal with her about it. I would put them in a vase in my office and keep them there for the 3 days between visits that we had planned for the week. While I kept them in my office and took care of them, I wanted her to think about each flower representing a feeling she had while she was trying to have a relationship with me. We would talk about these feelings during the next visit, and then she would take the flowers home to share them with Susan. She did not like the idea, and said she would refuse to take the flowers home with her next time. But she did agree to think about the feelings she had for me and try to put them in her log.

Eileen was experiencing a transference reaction with me. Every therapist has experiences like this: A client idealizes them, loves them, brings them gifts, wants to seduce them, or go out to lunch with them, and longs to break out of the confines of the therapeutic boundaries and feel 'special.' It is the therapist's job to discuss these gifts, these desires, and to maintain the boundaries. However, the very nature of the therapeutic situation encourages some of these feelings. The office provides a private, safe space and is designed to feel comforting and safe to a client. The dialogue is an intimate one, discussing emotional scenarios, feelings, and sexual behaviors. The client is the center of attention and I listen to every word, notice every nuance. I do not judge the client. I may offer a tissue for the tears, a cough drop, or a cup of tea. I nurture, listen, sympathize, and patch up broken egos. Who wouldn't want that kind of relationship with everyone, all the time? So I have to be very careful that I do not fall in love with the power I have, or the compliments, or the flowers. I make sure we stay well within the boundaries, while trying to understand the impulse of the client to go beyond them. The very act of keeping within the boundaries and the struggle it represents can be the essence of therapy.

Eileen learned what the compliments, the gifts, and seduction meant in our relationship and how it translated into her other relationships. I told her that when she gave me "magical" healing powers and put me on a pedestal, I felt distant from her. For her it may have been a safe place to keep me, especially in the beginning of our relationship. But it made me feel as if I could not access how she really felt and, therefore, was being kept out of a relationship with her. Her unconscious goal was to keep people away, to keep herself safe from the pain of loss she anticipated. For many years sex was her way of being close to someone. She had become so anxious when Susan wanted to develop a friendship with her that she went right back to her sadomasochistic chat room for comfort and safety. What a psychic dilemma, longing for closeness but being afraid of intimacy at the same time. She learned it was a pattern in a quilt that would never keep her warm.

What feelings in her life were being transferred to the relationship with me? How could we translate these feelings into another language? As it turned out, the flowers became very useful in my effort to help Eileen move closer to her goal of an authentic and committed relationship with Susan. In the days between sessions, she thought about the flowers in my office. Other clients were enjoying them, too. She told me she did not like that her gift to me was shared with other clients. I asked her to tell me more, to explain what she meant by having to share the flowers with other clients. Then, in tears, she said she wanted me to take the flowers home. Now we were getting somewhere. "Home?" I asked, leaving it ambiguous whether I meant her or the flowers. "Well, not really, but I want to be closer to you," she said. She wanted to feel special to me, not share me with others. If she gave me compliments and brought me gifts, it would make her better than other clients. We would be closer; I would like her more and she would become special to me. She was also afraid I would not like her if she cried because her mother used to slap her if she cried.

Eileen then began to talk about what it was like to share her mother with the men she brought home. She had never been able to get her mother's attention or love. Mom was always working, drunk, and in bed with men. Eileen was afraid to talk to Aunty Del about her mother or her longing for the other life that she had been removed from, even though she had been so deprived and neglected. She was afraid her aunt would think she was ungrateful, and then abandon her like her mother had. Finally Eileen was talking about her mother, not just giving me facts about her mother but telling me how she felt in relationship to her mother. It was the beginning of a fruitful dialogue. After this session of revelations, she refused to take home the flowers. I kept them and thanked her for them. I knew she needed to give her mother flowers, and I needed to accept them. It was a transferential moment. It was the beginning of the work that would eventually help her sort out her relationship with her mother, and thus with others.

Most of the next several months were spent working on Eileen's all too brief relationship with her mother. We would sift through those 12 brief years. She would share what she experienced emotionally while they lived together. She revisited her mom's death, and her feelings of abandonment. She found a place to put her grief and unhappiness, as well as a few happy memories. She was able to express how much she missed her mother, and all the regrets and anger she had with the events of her childhood. After all, her mother did not want her around and had not protected her from the men she brought to the house. Mom did not even allow the girls to go to the bathroom while the men were there, letting out what was inside. She had learned to hold back what might be "bad" inside—smelly, unpleasant, and painful. What she had taken from the way mom treated her was that she was not wanted or worth much.

Eventually, Eileen realized that the script she attempted to play out with me was one she had played out in almost all of her relationships. It was the only script she had. She would be cheerful and happy, show her good side, give little gifts so people would connect and attach to her, all the while compartmentalizing and hiding her difficult and complex feelings. She had always suppressed those feelings because she did not want to appear disloyal or unappreciative. She did that to survive her early years with her mother and continued in the same vein when she came to live with her Aunty Del.

The first few years of a child's life are important to their long-term ability to have a loving and intimate relationship as an adult. If a child is held, nurtured, "smoochied-up," talked to, played with, etc., it will have a positive impact on brain development, physical development, emotional and intellectual development. A secure relationship with Mom, creates a secure base from which the child can explore the world, learn that people can be trusted to be loving and kind and can respond to his or her needs. If this early secure attachment is missing, the child will often become anxious and hypervigilant, self-involved, and likely to attempt to control his or her environment in order to survive. Not knowing when or if anyone will provide his or her needs, the child becomes anxious and unable to trust or get close to others. That was what Eileen was left with when her mom died. It was not much to pack in her suitcase for her travels up North or for her journey through life. Like Ryan, who spent his adolescence frightened, obsessed, and sexualized, how had Eileen's sad childhood impacted on the "wellspring of her mind, heart and voice" (Giligan, 2003).

The script Eileen relied upon was to get attention and caring through sex. Mom had sex with many men. Sex became a substitute for emotional intimacy. It is common for many women to rely on this script. The pain Eileen parodied when having sadomasochistic relationships seemed to be a repetition of the pain mom caused her, as well as the trauma she suffered at the hands of her mom's lovers. It was a tragic parody, repeated again and again, of the relationship she really yearned for. Eileen preferred being dominant and in control of sexual situations. She had spent a good deal of her 42 years attempting to get what she had always longed for from her mom—attachment and nurturing. Now she attempted to get love by seducing women.

If the pain went away, what would replace it? Sometimes when people are traumatized, deprived, neglected, and abused in childhood, as Eileen certainly had been, they unconsciously repeat the trauma as a way to keep connected with what was at least familiar, even if it was bad. We all cling to the familiar, the known quantity. We resist change even if the status quo does not serve us well. My brother put it another way: "The devil you know is better than the devil you don't know."

The unfulfilling relationships Eileen had developed in adult life repeated some elements of her relationship to her mother. It was all she had of her childhood and her mother. How could she give them up? By being dominant in her sexual relationships, Eileen felt she could control what would happen. It was all designed to keep herself emotionally safe, to avoid getting close and risk being abandoned. In reality it felt really empty and out of control. She longed for more from relationships but could not make them feel safe.

While working on Eileen's early childhood traumas, we were able to achieve a more stable context within which we could explore Eileen's sexual behavior. We explored what needed to be contained, ended, improved upon, and/or developed. From the initial assessment and her log, I could see she was not in any physical danger with the current expression of her sexual needs. The exhibitionism was monitored, but it had stopped a few years ago. What did Eileen want from sex? Her pursuit of anonymous sexual encounters had been escalating when she first sought help. It was possible that if this cruising escalated, she could potentially place herself in harm's way. Her Internet use had to be under control. These issues troubled and humiliated her.

As therapy progressed, many of Eileen's sexual habits had changed or departed. While she had also become less depressed by this time, she was still very anxious, and therefore agreed to try some medication. It helped quiet her obsessional thinking, as well as her general anxiety. She had been assiduous about keeping a log of her daily thoughts, behaviors, and moods. It had helped her a great deal in terms of understanding how connected her sexual behaviors were to negative unexpressed feelings. "Looking inside" and talking with me and with Susan became easier. She had lost her desire to be on the computer for anything but work. Susan and Eileen decided to share the same email address at home so the computer felt like a safer, more "normal" place for both of them. She had finally become comfortable with the idea that neither Susan nor I would leave or reject her. She understood that relationships are not one-sided.

It was a wonderful experience to be able to see Eileen become real to herself. She was also able to learn that by controlling her own thoughts and monitoring her own feelings, she did not need to spend so much time and energy controlling others and events around her. Overall, she was much happier and felt that many of the ghosts from the past had much less power in her life. But she and Susan had been talking about their sexual relationship, which needed some work.

Eileen looked back on the act of exhibiting herself in the window and wondered how she had ever done something like that. She no longer felt lonely and empty. She and Susan had begun to see a therapist together. Eileen did not want to talk about the exhibitionism in couple therapy, but they had been able to discuss it at home. One of the things they learned in couple therapy was to have a supportive, comforting sexual dialogue rather than a polarizing one. Early in their relationship they made a commitment to monogamy. They also decided not to masturbate without the other being present in a loving way. They realized that while their sex lives might change as time went on, they must continue to have an open and honest dialogue about their sex lives. They joked about "lesbian bed death" but felt they could deal with problems as they presented themselves.

Susan had some experience with sadomasochistic relationships. She preferred to be passive. On occasion she enjoyed being loosely tied up by the wrists, which she could get out of if she wanted to. Eileen liked it when Susan gave her verbal directions. They both liked some biting, scratching, spanking during orgasm, and the use of sex toys from time to time. Susan could take it or leave it, but was open to variety and creativity. Most of all, they loved the mutuality and connectedness they began to experience as Eileen became less anxious. Eileen was also able to consider her own pleasure for the first time and to discover what felt good and what did not.

As is common with people who have been sexually abused as children, Eileen had been dissociating during sex for many years. Like everything else in their lives—cooking together, going to the movies, biking, shopping, and working; sex became one of the things they did together that felt good. They seemed to have it in perspective. The option to have a functional dialogue about their sexual relationship whenever there was an issue became a priority for both of them, and they had worked hard to put it in place. Eileen agreed that if she had a flashback from the abuse she had as a child, she would say so. They would stop, sit up, put a blanket or sheet around themselves, and talk about these images when Eileen wanted to or could. They would then hug and continue or discontinue their lovemaking. Sex is not an easy thing to learn to talk about.

Once things had stabilized for Eileen, she had a request from her manager to talk about the progress in therapy. Since there was still a pending issue at work about her computer use, Eileen was concerned about it. She asked me if I would talk with her manager. I explored this request with Eileen. After all, she is the expert on herself. I told Eileen I certainly would not feel comfortable talking about her without her being present. She admitted the impulse she had to be taken care of by the "good mother" but she was also afraid that her manager would reject her efforts. I could be her "security blanket." I understood the impulse, but I told Eileen that I had confidence she could represent herself well. Her manager would respect her for it.

As it turned out, her manager did compliment Eileen for the way she presented herself. The manager asked that I send her a summary about the therapy that would go in her folder and would be confidential. I told Eileen that I would be glad to send a brief summary, but that I would send it only after she had an opportunity to read it and comment upon it. I sent it to her manager. It said that I felt Eileen had fulfilled her goals in therapy. Eileen was not only more confident and less anxious she also had a clear idea of the tools she now had available if needed in the future. Therapy had been a long hard journey and Eileen and I both felt its rewards.

Chapter 8

Stabilizing the family system

Even now, all possible feelings do not yet exist. There are still those that lie beyond our capacity and our imagination. From time to time when ... something impossible to predict, fathom, or yet describe takes place, a new feeling enters the world. And then, for the millionth time in the history of feeling, the heart surges, and absorbs the impact.

Nichole Krauss

The ripples and waves from disclosure of secret sexual behaviors always threaten to capsize or sink both the dyad and the family boat. The ripples spread far and touch everyone in their way: children, immediate family, extended family, friends, corporations, communities, and governments. They can even spill onto the airwaves and into headlines, where everyone is exposed to them.

When a spouse or other person discovers a sexual infidelity, it often feels as if a bomb has exploded. Everyone gets mobilized. Something must be done about the situation; "it must stop immediately". Feelings are high. Anger, shame, guilt boil up and foul the atmosphere. Family, friends and even employers may feel that something has been amiss for some time and have not been able to identify what is wrong. It is not unusual for spouses or family members to have been in denial for a long time and "engaged in normalizing the addicts' problematic behaviors and denying their intuition" (Milrad, 1999). On the other hand, it is equally true that many people have hidden their secrets so well that their spouses do not have any idea about the secret life. I had a client who once said to me, "If she asks me if I have had an affair I always deny, deny, deny, and she believes me."

For those whose minds are constantly flooded and preoccupied with sexual thoughts, being intimately or sexually connected to a partner or spouse is very difficult. Often the spouse has felt lonely and rejected for some time before the secrets were discovered. A flooded and anxious mind may also be unable to focus on work or finish tasks efficiently. Depressed and anxious most of the time, these clients have little left over to bring to everyday life, work, and family relationships. Significant others, friends, and family often complain about the client's self-involvement, preoccupation, and lack of connectedness to those who love them. In addition, partners may have been blamed for being sexually inadequate as a way to cover up the secret sexual habits. Those with hypersexuality may have been obsessively demanding sex, which has been damaging and distressing to the relationship. It is likely that both partners have invested a lot of emotional effort in appearing to be happy and keeping up a façade of normalcy in hopes that "it" will all go away someday. Together and in their own ways, a couple will suffer from the illusions.

In addition to feeling angry and betrayed, members of the family, parents, boss, partner, or spouse are likely to be dealing with high levels of trauma from the discovery, depending on their own emotional terrain. Their illusions have been stripped away too. At the same time, it is likely that spouses or partners may be unconsciously participating in the problem. For reasons uniquely their own, they, too, may prefer emotional and sexual distance that creates a "safety zone," a comfortable but lonely and dysfunctional space between them. Perhaps they have a history of rape, sexual abuse, or neglect and this event resonates with their past in a powerful way. They will need tending to as well. Their questions and demands hang in the air: "Can I fix him? You need to make him stop! Should I get a divorce? I am leaving; I'm out of here! Shouldn't he be in a hospital or jail?"

CROSSING THE LINE

Unfaithfulness plays out in each relationship in unique and unpredictable ways. Most of us maintain expectations of fidelity in a committed relationship and typically draw a line in the sand beyond which we expect our partner will not go when it come to sexual behavior. Stephen Levine, M.D. (2007), a psychiatrist who has written much about infidelity, thinks about it this way: "Fidelity is a conventional rule for relationships and infidelity is a boundary violation." When someone in a committed relationship steps beyond that convention, it is a devastating and life-changing event. This chapter focuses on stabilizing the family unit when a sexual event has been disclosed or discovered. Stabilizing the crisis is not an end point; it is just the beginning.

Many couples disagree on the definitions of monogamy, infidelity, or an affair. On the other hand, some couples agree to swinging or have polyamorous relationships—a consensual agreement to have more than one loving and intimate relationship that generally includes sex and is sometimes referred to as responsible non-monogamy. At the other end of the spectrum, there are those who may feel betrayed if a partner looks at or even talks with another person. Still others may feel their husband has committed adultery if he looks at *Playboy Magazine* or sexually explicit material online or shares confidences with a woman friend on the telephone. Research on cybersex has revealed that "the majority did see this [cybersex] as not only real infidelity but also as having as serious an impact on the couple as a traditional offline affair. The most important finding here was that emotional infidelity was given as much attention as sexual infidelity was" (Whitty, 2005). It is also possible that some people may experience many of these behaviors as natural and inconsequential: It's just pictures on the 'net; boys will be boys; she's just a flirt; it's no big deal, we're just friends.

It is ubiquitous to the human condition that during a lifetime we must give up some treasured illusions about how life could or should be. Intense grieving for a treasured illusion about fidelity occurs when a spouse or partner is discovered to be unfaithful. It is typical that in the initial stages of the discovery of infidelity and/or other sexual secrets, the hurt party, prevalently the woman, is often paralyzed by grief, anger, and pain. She may be so traumatized that she can barely function and is unable to go to work or take care of her children. My clinical observations are that if a man is the hurt party, his experience will typically represent a deep narcissistic wound with great damage to the self and the ego. A man might experience this event in a different way than women, and be more internal with unexpressed grief and with difficult long-range consequences that seem to interfere with the healing process and future relationships.

In addition to having an affair with another woman, for example, the unfaithful spouse may have been caught exhibiting himself in the library or looking at men online at sexually explicit sites. For both men and women, the disclosure of martial infidelity in any form is a highly traumatic event with devastating and far-ranging consequences that deserve the attention of mental health providers. The typical stance of the person who has been unfaithful is that their infidelities were separate from the relationship and not intended to harm or interfere with it. The husband's usual mindset is that if their wife does not nag, demand answers about the affair, or "get into the middle of things," it will go away. "It's not your problem; it has nothing to do with our marriage or the family!" Nevertheless, not only is the hurt party in need of treatment and support, but it is also important to recognize the role that partners may play in the recovery of the hypersexual partner or spouse (McCarthy, 2002).

IT TAKES TWO TO UNTANGLE

It is essential for the clinician to consider that not only are both parties in the dyad destabilized when secrets are uncovered, but so are the children and perhaps the extended family, co-workers, or even the neighborhood. ("Don't go to Kara's house; her father is a womanizer—or worse!") During the early phase of the crisis, each person in the dyad has a different agenda. The unfaithful person will generally want to keep the sexual secrets and give up as little as possible. Or, paradoxically, he or she may strategize that spilling all the secrets might preempt a divorce and, temporarily at least, assuage their guilt. For example, Senator John Edwards confessed all. It was a blatant attempt, to ward off his feelings of guilt and anxiety about being discovered. "I'll tell all, and I promise to never do any of this again."

However, dumping all the sexual secrets may create a worse situation than was intended. It is like throwing oneself on the mercy of the court, hoping to be believed and convince everyone that "I'll never do anything bad again!" This strategy often backfires, like when Senator Edwards revealed that he had waited until his wife's cancer was in remission. This strategy also implies a promise that is unrealistic and often cannot be kept, particularly if the sexual habits are well-ingrained and the marriage is a long one. Research confirms that the longer the marriage before disclosure, the worse the trauma to the spouse (Steffens & Rennie, 2006). I would add that the stage of a client's personal development, their inherent mental health, and how many compelling sexual behaviors are being acted out will also have an effect on the course of this crisis.

It is useful to get the details of how the infidelity was uncovered by the hurt spouse or partner. It reveals a great deal of information about the tone and context of the relationship from the hurt person's point of view. Has it been a marriage filled with distrust for many years? Does the partner perceive the marriage to be close and intimate? Has it been difficult for a long time for one or the other parties? First I listen to the client's story as she or he would like to tell it and fill in the blanks by talking to the hurt partner. What, if anything, had he suspected? How long has he lived with the suspicion? What specifically did she find out: i.e., what are the details of the sexual behaviors in so far as she can describe them? Were any of the behaviors illegal? Will there be legal proceedings? Are the involved parties the same gender or different genders? How long has this been going on? Once again, these various issues point to the need for the clinician to be flexible and able to follow the client down the path to his or her own reality. Do you recall Lisa from Chapter 5 and the tape of her and Antonio making love?

It is necessary for the therapist to distinguish between individuals who have "just" an affair and individuals who have compelling sexual behaviors. Typically, men who are hypersexual have been found to have an average of three compelling sexual behaviors (Carnes, 1991; Schneider & Schneider, 1996). There are differences in the situation when someone has had an affair with one person over a long period of time or one brief affair in a lifetime. The prognosis for long-term control is better when there are fewer secrets and the marriage is young (Goodman, 1999).

In general, the motivation for extra-relational sexual contact is also different for each gender. Women who have compelling sexual behaviors do not seem to engage in as many multiple sexual behaviors as men do and are generally looking for emotional attachments. Men are typically seeking "easy sex," no responsibility or emotional context. When there are multiple sexual behaviors, they may be both legal and illegal: pressuring a spouse or partner for frequent sexual encounters, using prostitution, masturbating frequently instead of seeking partnered sex, having sex with someone of the same gender, using telephone sex, using the Internet for various sexual experiences such as viewing sexually explicit material, arranging multiple anonymous sexual encounters, voyeurism and exhibitionism. Treatment for both the unfaithful person and the hurt individual must be contextualized and tailored for their particular situation.

There are many common themes to the experience of disclosure of sexual secrets that emerge when a spouse has been unfaithful. It is a time of high emotions: grief, anger, depression, anxiety, and disbelief. There is a sense of "I am living in a nightmare and life is surreal." A lifetime of illusions about the spouse or partner as the "faithful, devoted family man" or "sweet devoted wife" have died. Many people express the sense that they no longer know who their spouse is and feel as if they are living with a stranger. They are frightened.

Most of the hurt people in this situation will compare themselves negatively to the phantom man or woman with whom their partner or spouse is having sex. He or she is likely to feel sexually inadequate, have a poor body image and poor self-esteem. Some may be physically abusive to their spouses or become suicidal, perhaps in need of hospitalization. Both the hurt person and the unfaithful person will be emotionally labile. It will most assuredly be an emotional roller coaster ride; fasten your seat belts. Questions about the infidelities are hurled at the spouse obsessively. The hurt person is consumed with "getting the whole truth and nothing but the truth." It is common and almost intuitive for the hurt client to badger his or her partner with questions because the perception is that information will lead to more control of the situation. But it is an illusion that the answers will keep a person in control and thus safe. It is also highly unlikely that all the answers will be given.

Confusion and ambivalence reign. Much time is given over to trying to decide if the marriage should end or if it is worth saving. I recommend that important decisions be put off for a while until things stabilize. Some of my clients have had brief affairs to "pay back" their spouse. Some women will initiate frequent sex with their spouse that is calculated to emulate the kind of sexual activity the wife thinks her husband is missing, for example, oral sex, acting out S & M fantasies, or wearing seductive clothing. It is a temporary strategy that will be quickly abandoned because it is usually ego-dystonic and not in her value system, for the wife to have sex that way. It objectifies sex in ways that undermine the emotional connection she has most likely been missing and has the potential for repeating past traumas.

If family members and friends are told about the infidelity, they are apt to give much unsolicited advice that is generally not helpful, timely, or unbiased and can make matters worse. "Throw the bum out" is not useful; although the family member may think it is a supportive thing to say, it is poorly timed and badly delivered. While I will discuss the impact these crises have on the children further on, it is important for therapists to note that a deceived, depressed, and needy parent may confide in a child. Using a child of any age as a confidant is inappropriate and likely to be harmful. It is indicative of family dysfunction that the mother or father is emotionally dependent on the child for support. It is also inappropriate for either parent to solicit a child for confidences about the other parent. Couples should be encouraged to make ground rules about who should know about the events and who should not, and how to deal with the children. I advise that the client pick one or two people he or she can feel safe confiding in and who will be discreet and unconditionally supportive without condemnation of the unfaithful partner. Well-meaning extended family members and friends can be put off sometimes or told politely, "I really don't want to talk about this now."

It is essential to keep in mind that both parties will experience shame, guilt, humiliation, and exposure. Each is likely to feel sexually inadequate and believe that everyone will know this is the reason they could not keep their spouse "at home." It is also common that many women have been living with a husband who has had sexual secrets for years, which also means they have been deceived and lied to for a long time. When a spouse finds out about the sexual behaviors and is given a promise that they will end, she still is likely to spend many years being hypervigilant about the behaviors of her husband. This may take the form of constant monitoring of the spouse's behavior and whereabouts, checking emails and cell phones. The levels of paranoia and fear about what they will find diminishes self-esteem and emotional resources. The face of Silda, New York Governor Spitzer's wife, as she stood next to the governor during his very public announcement about his relationships with prostitutes, was indeed telling of the humiliation and pain she felt. The grief and anguish was palpable.

TREATING THE BROKEN HEARTS

Examining effective treatment models for those traumatized and hurt by sexual lies and infidelities, Steffens and Rennie (2006) reviewed three models for individual treatment: the Addiction Model, the Trauma Model, and the Attachment Model. This research also highlights the continuing struggle to reconcile the addictive model with other models for framing these sexual behaviors. "Addiction therapy views the WSA [wife of sex addict] as carrying an illness into a relationship from which she must recover, while trauma theory views her as someone who had a bad thing happen to her. Trauma theory also posits that the survivor can find healthy ways to cope and adapt to the trauma exposure." Regardless of the situation, a traumatized person "seeks what she cannot find: safety in an unsafe situation" (Steffens & Rennie, 2006).

Both the Trauma Model and Addictive Model have similar goals, which include promoting growth and developing coping skills. The Trauma Model clearly validates the wife's "significant distress or impairment in social, occupational, or other important areas of functioning" (American Psychiatric Association, 2000) as being normal reactions to abnormal, unexpected, and devastating situations. Referring to the Trauma Model, Steffens & Rennis (2006) stated: "Rather than addicted and pathological, the WSAs' most disruptive behaviors are framed as attempts to adapt to a serious threat and more likely to result in empowerment and a sense of safety."

The Attachment Model describes the trauma as a significant injury to the dyadic bond, which in turn evokes behaviors of clinging, pursuit of the partner, and policing behaviors. This rupture in attachment is often experienced as a sudden death of the marriage with attendant emotions that the sudden death of a loved one would also induce. "Something impossible to predict, fathom, or yet describe takes place, a new feeling enters the world" (Krauss, 2005).

The goals of treatment for the hurt parties are to:

- Stabilize the deceived person and help him or her feel safe.
- Help them "fire themselves" from the job of policing their spouse or partner.
- Help them understand that they cannot stop their spouse; the spouse has to stop him/herself.
- Clarify that the injured party is not inadequate, flawed in some way, or ugly.
- Focus on ameliorating the grief about lost illusions.
- Help him or her regain self-esteem and independence.

In sum, while working with hurt clients on personal needs and issues, I encourage disengaging from focusing on controlling their spouse, pointing out that it has halted their own growth and prevented their own individuation. I offer my perspective that when some of these tasks have been accomplished, the need for answers will diminish. This strategy of empowering the hurt person to take charge of his or her own life also allows the unfaithful person some space within which to begin learning self-monitoring skills. This will preclude the perceived need to be in a defensive mode all the time because their partner is trying to control them. It is important for the couple to recognize this self-defeating cycle so that they both can take the responsibility to stop it.

AND WHAT ABOUT THE CHILDREN?

Talking with children of any age about sex for any reason takes some thoughtfulness, be it for healthy sex education or because there have been negative consequences from sexual behavior. Therapists must take into account the strengths and weaknesses of the family system, including the developmental stage of the children and their mental status. It follows that the increasing stability of adults will resonate with and be helpful for the child. This is not always possible. For example, in the case study that follows, it was not possible to get the parents stabilized enough so that the children could get help with what was already out of control.

In truth, many of these issues for children and families have been around for a long time and are pervasive. When marriage became the custom, one did not have to be monogamous for much longer than 15 to 20 years because people died very young. Currently, marriages have only a 50/50 chance of surviving, and more than half the divorces (68%) are caused by infidelity that results from meeting a new partner on the Internet (Manning, 2006). The impact of divorce—let alone exposure to Internet pornography, public revelations about a parent's visit to prostitutes, or headlines about illegal behaviors of a family member such as exhibitionism or child abuse—is damaging to children. No matter what the root cause, children who are exposed to family disruption and dysfunction are much more vulnerable to mental health issues that will need treatment and management over a lifetime. Therapists have a unique role in cases when children are involved in their parent's struggle with compelling sexual behaviors. It is often an opportunity to help parents interrupt the generational cycle of unhealthy sexual habits by guiding them toward age-appropriate sex education materials and having appropriate conversations about sexual health and behavior with their children.

It is essential to assess the needs of the entire family system when sexual secrets are revealed. But what is appropriate to tell children about their parent's or parents' sexual behaviors? Black et al., (2003) suggest that mid-adolescence is the minimum age at which these discussions should take place. When family chaos breaks out, young children really need reassurance more than information. It is essential that parents refrain from fighting, swearing, and hurting each other in front of their children. At any age, dependent children need to know, if possible, that both parents will still be accessible, that they will be able to live in the same house, have the same school, be near their friends, and continue with familiar routines. I have adapted five "pertinent" reasons for disclosure to mid-adolescent children from Black et al. (2003):

1. *Validation*: "I am not crazy." Giving the child validation that what they have suspected is true and the anger in the air is not about them.
2. *Exposure*: Preempting the trauma of the child finding out from the media or other people in their environment.
3. *Safety*: The child may be at risk for physical, emotional, or sexual abuse.
4. *Reassurance*: Helping the child identify a safe place or person they can call upon for help if parents seem out of control.
5. *Breaking the generational cycle*: Helping the child process and discuss the risk for repeating abusive or compelling sexual behaviors.

Children's exposure to the Internet: Playing with fire

Children are often exposed to the sexual secrets of their family and become the keeper of secrets as well (Cottle, 1980). They also have their own sexual secrets, many of which involve the Internet. In the past 10 or 15 years, the Internet has drawn children into its web. Feeling isolated or lonely, looking for friends and connections, children can be seduced into the online sex-for-sale industry and become perpetrators as well as victims of crime. In a brilliant piece of journalistic sleuthing, Kurt Eichenwald, a reporter for *The New York Times*, researched and reported on the sexual exploitation of minors on the Internet (2005). Eichenwald met an 18-year-old boy, Justin Berry, who allowed the journalist into his secret life, which began on the Internet when Justin was 13.

> Beginning on an afternoon in 2000, [Justin] was lured into selling images of his body on the Internet over the course of five years. From the seduction that began that day, this soccer-playing honor-roll student was drawn into performing in front of the Webcam—undressing, showering, masturbating, and even having sex—for an audience of 1,500 people who paid him, over the years, hundreds of thousands of dollars. (Eichenwald, 2005)

Justin's life on the Internet was secret for five years. It escalated into a larger habit than he ever thought possible. What began as a way to meet friends escalated into a full-scale relationship with adults who purchased Webcam images of him performing various sexual acts. He learned from the men who "chatted" with him that all he had to do was post a "wish list" on Amazon.com and he would be given whatever he wanted. Thousands of dollars would be deposited into his bank account. He told his mother that he was starting his own website-design business. He began to do poorly in school. His activities were interfering with his relationship with his family.

Eventually, his pictures were also found by classmates, who distributed them around school. He withdrew from school and asked to be home-schooled. His parents did not seem to be very interested in getting answers about why Justin was withdrawing and doing poorly. What happened that a family was so disengaged and detached from Justin's reality? He was being sexually exploited and abused by the adults who groomed and manipulated him. Eichenwald, during his six-month investigation, found that this enormous and dangerous industry involving thousands of minors had been largely outside the scrutiny of law enforcement agencies. Ernest E. Allen, chief executive of the National Center for Missing and Exploited Children, a private group, was quoted by Eichenwald (2005) as saying, "We've been aware of the use of Webcam and its potential use by exploiters, but this is a variation on a theme that we haven't seen. It's unbelievable."

While society is quick to blame children for going online and selling themselves, it is an egregious error to think that these children "asked for it." Parents must be vigilant. Adults are authority figures for children and often are good at manipulating children to do their bidding. In this cogent investigation done by *The New York Times*, information was garnered about the 1,500 people who had paid Justin to perform for them on his Webcam. Of these 1,500 people, 300 were investigated. It was found that the majority were doctors, lawyers, businessmen, and teachers: all in a position of power to groom and exploit children.

When Eichenwald found Justin and talked with him, Justin finally realized he needed help, as did the other children who were also being exploited and abused. The men who bought Justin's photographs had also seduced Justin and other children to meet them off line. Justin gave the information he had saved on his computer for five years to a lawyer. The lawyer extracted immunity for the now 18-year-old Justin in return for his help in trapping the adults who manipulated children into real-time encounters. Jason was threatened by three men when he tried to shut down his web contacts and is now protected by the FBI. He is in treatment and has started a new life.

TONI'S CRISIS: PREGNANT AND DECEIVED

Toni was a tiny woman with a bulging stomach. I heard her breath catch with a sough as she sat down. It was the sound of despair. She huddled in the corner of the couch as if she wanted to disappear in the cushions. Her feet barely touched the floor. She had black curly hair that framed her pretty face and grey circles under her eyes. Toni was a bright, capable 25-year-old who had just begun the seventh month of her first pregnancy. Everything about her spelled fragility and vulnerability. "I have been betrayed," she whispered, her eyes filling with tears. *Betrayal*. There is a dark, desperate edge to the word. She was in a state of shock. I felt the defeat, the loneliness, the fear, the damage that went with her words. Toni learned that Jay, her husband of three years, had been having an affair with a married woman he met online. He also had been looking at men online. Questions tumbled out of her: "I never thought this would happen to us! What did I do wrong? Can I ever get over it? Will these feelings go away? How can I forgive and forget? How will this affect our children? I'm afraid my mental state will hurt my baby; pregnant mothers need to be calm."

Toni needed a reality check. How *could* he? Seven months pregnant and her husband was unfaithful to her! I was not neutral on the issue either, but I kept it to myself. She loved and trusted him and had counted on him to protect her while she was pregnant. Trying to gain control in a chaotic situation, Toni had put herself in a double-bind, as many do in this situation. She felt that she had to get as much information as possible about her husband's affair, believing it would help her gain control over the situation. She did not want to be blindsided again by any new information. She was completely traumatized. At the same time, she was ambivalent about limning the depths of his behaviors. Did she really want to know all about his affair? And yet she felt compelled to ask Jay again and again what he had been doing. She was so hurt she did not know the right thing to do.

Toni tried to reason that information would help her heal and understand what went wrong, perhaps letting her gain some control over her emotions. Some of the questions that roiled were: Should she have had more sex with Jay to make things better? Was the pregnancy too much for him to handle? Should she color her hair blonde? Dress sexier? Clean the house better? Cook his favorite foods more often? It would take a long time before Toni realized that what happened was *not* because she was inadequate. She was also very worried that Jay's affair might have exposed her to sexually transmitted infections, or blackmail, financial ruin, or endanger her child in some way. Toni was desperate for answers. But right now Toni also needed a safe place to ground her, allow her to find her way, and offer some reassurance, validation, and support.

Toni told me what led her to be suspicious about Jay. He had been somewhat distant in the past few months and seemed preoccupied much of the time. At first she thought he was overworked and worried about the pregnancy and dismissed it. Recently, Jay had begun receiving many telephone calls from the woman he was having an affair with, whom he told Toni was a "supplier." Toni thought this was unusual; Jay was seldom called at home for work issues. When questioned about it, Jay lied and insisted it was not unusual that the supplier had to check the prices of the materials that had been ordered.

Toni's fears and suspicions about Jay's behavior led her to see what was on their computer. She was not very technologically knowledgeable but she did find some pictures of two men having sex that shocked her. She had heard that some men who are really homosexuals marry women to cover up their preference for men. Jay had not been having sex with her very often, even though she had tried to initiate it. Was Jay homosexual? Toni reasoned that he must be if he looked at those pictures and he did not desire her very much. He *must* be homosexual. She confronted him, and he spilled all his secrets.

After listening to Toni's questions, I asked her to put them down on paper and bring them in to me so we would talk about them the next time we met. I also promised that we would go over some of them when she and Jay came in together. She agreed to give it a try. I have used this cognitive–behavioral technique for years in many situations. A lot of issues get clarified this way. It helps to put things down on paper and read them back to yourself. It is also useful when the concerns are edited many times.

I reassured Toni that she was not crazy to be asking these questions. I supported her need to know and to keep herself and her child safe. I also assured her that one of the important goals in treatment would be to foster openness and honesty between them and injected some hope and reassurance that in a few months things were likely to look different than they did now. I encouraged her to write things down when she felt obsessed with questions and try to let them stay on the page rather than pursue Jay for answers when he came home from work. I also strongly suggested that the "discussions" they were likely to have at home should be structured rather than open-ended. I promised, too, that when the three of us met, I would give them some skills for how to accomplish this.

We agreed that at some point I would meet with Jay and that we would have a few conjoint sessions while we were getting organized. Toni was relieved. During her pregnancy, I saw her as often as she wanted, sometimes two or three times a week. Toni was very depressed and told me she had had some depressive episodes in the past and had taken medication to recover. Her mother had been hospitalized with bipolar disorder, and Toni was very worried about her own mental health. I suggested she talk with her obstetrician about the use of medication and about the risk of post-partum depression. I also suggested that she contact a psychiatrist who could coordinate with her obstetrician if need be. She took me up on this suggestion, and we had a consult with the psychiatrist who then consulted with the obstetrician. Toni also told me that she had insisted Jay see a doctor to test for other possible infections. He agreed to this and was given a clean bill of health. Everyone was relieved, and Toni felt safer.

Our first order of business was, of course, to see Toni through the pregnancy with as much support from Jay as she could get. She also had a community of friends that she depended on. Both Jay and Toni's immediate family lived in the Midwest, and the couple worked on sorting out what, if anything, they wanted to tell them.

Jay's assessment

Jay was a nice looking 27-year-old man, of medium height, well groomed, with brown hair and intense, anxious brown eyes. He looked embarrassed and ashamed, but he was able to look me in the eye when he talked. As he was sitting down, he spilled out, "How could Toni even imagine I am a homosexual? I am so ashamed. I've done a stupid and cruel thing. I love Toni and feel terrible that I hurt her." He was intelligent and honest. He knew this was a crisis and he needed to "show up."

Jay had moved to Vermont from the Midwest and took a two-year course in construction management. He had been hired quickly when he finished his courses and after five years was moved up to management level in the firm he worked for. He had never been in trouble with the law, did not use alcohol or drugs, and had never been unfaithful to Toni or anyone else until six months ago. Before he met Toni, Jay had two girlfriends with whom he had been sexually active. These two women seemed indifferent to him and the sex, so he did not pursue them.

I was relieved when I learned that Jay was not involved in multiple sexual behaviors or obsessed with the Internet. He had met the woman he had an affair with while he was looking for suppliers on line at work. She was married and lived in Vermont, and he talked with her a lot on the telephone for work. One day she came to a work site with a delivery and met Jay in person. She made the first moves, and he followed along. He knew it was wrong but he did it anyway.

When I questioned Jay about the pictures of men that Toni had discovered on line, he told me that he had always been somewhat turned on by the thought of anal sex. He had been introduced to it when he and a friend played doctor when he was six or seven. Toni did not want to experiment with anal sex and neither did the woman with whom he was having an affair. He turned beet red and had trouble discussing this with me. He told me that he had never had sex with a man and was afraid to pursue it because he thought it was too risky. "You can get diseases." He had never had any interest in having a relationship with a man. His Internet search for pictures of men had been a one-time event driven by curiosity. He was not aroused by what he saw. He also did not masturbate to that fantasy. He also admitted, with much embarrassment, that he seldom masturbated and when he did it was to fantasies about the woman he had an affair with. He had been raised in a religious household and thought it was shameful, especially since he had a wife. He admitted that he knew very little about sex and probably could benefit from some basic education. I recommended Bernie Zilbergeld's *Male Sexuality* (1992) and McCarthy & Metz's *Men's Sexual Health* (2008), which were very helpful to him.

Jay was quite worried that he would somehow never be able to make this right. He apologized to Toni all the time at home and promised the affair was over. When I asked him about it directly, he said he had told the woman it was over, and it seemed to him that they both were relieved to call it quits. They had been having sex every few weeks for about five or six months (maybe seven or eight times altogether). He said he was glad to get rid of the anxiety these trysts caused him. Anxiety was a chronic thing for Jay. He had always worried about doing things right: Was he a good enough worker, husband, and father? Based on his sexual experiences prior to Toni, Jay was also not sure that he was even sexually adequate with Toni, who was more sexually experienced than he was.

When I asked Jay how he felt about becoming a father, he said he was very anxious about the pregnancy. Even though they had medical assurances that the baby was fine, he had a younger sister who was born with multiple congenital defects, and he had always been anxious about having his own children. He felt he should not talk about these worries with Toni because he did not want her to worry, too. He admitted he was keeping some distance from her and had infrequent sex with her because he was concerned that he would hurt the baby. When he wasn't anxious about it, he anticipated this baby with much excitement. He even looked forward to the sleep deprivation, he said with a sudden smile. The smile won me over. I thought, "Well, maybe Jay isn't such a cad after all." I suggested a referral to a male colleague who I knew would be a good match. Jay was relieved to have a place to explore what had happened to him. I also told him that I would see him with Toni for a few visits until things stabilized. Eventually I would recommend couple therapy.

Jay also asked me how to handle all the questions Toni was throwing at him. He wanted to be honest but she was so obsessed with the details that he was not sure he ought to share everything with her. Good instincts. As I have pointed out that while honesty is the best policy it is not always appropriate. In this instance, generalities rather than the "gory details" would be better. For example, it would be best if Toni did not have a real description of everything Jay and his lover did at the local motel, which was pretty standard fare as Jay described it. It would serve everyone better not to know the name of the woman Jay had been meeting or how she looked or where they met. It is possible that if Toni had some of these details she might have flashbacks every time she heard the woman's name or went by the motel. It would be a setback. If she and Jay resumed their sex life she also might have flashes of what Jay and the "other woman" did if she knew the details. She might have her own fantasies about it and that would also be disturbing. Toni was already feeling in competition with Jay's secret lover, feeling ashamed that she was not good enough or thin enough, or pretty enough. The details would likely make this worse. Frank Pittman, M.D. (1991), a psychiatrist who has written many books and articles on the subject of infidelity observes: "Couples need not tell each other every detail of their activity … but they do have to talk about the bad news … those things that are unsettling, guilt-producing or controversial." In time, openness is a goal.

A team approach: Jay and Toni

When we had our conjoint meeting to summarize the problems and discuss a treatment strategy, we acknowledged that we only had three months, more or less, before the baby was due. Since it was the main focus of Toni's anxiety, I started with the subject of Jay's curiosity about homosexuality and encouraged Jay to be open about the development of his interest in anal sex. He was very embarrassed, but he bit the bullet and talked to Toni about it. He was able to reassure Toni that he was not a homosexual and convinced her that he did not expect her to fulfill his desire for anal sex and would not go elsewhere for it. He had gone online to view a few pictures because he was curious. Toni apologized for being so quick to jump to conclusions and judge him without enough information. I emphasized that fantasy is not behavior.

We also talked about this new stage of life that they were about to embark on and their individual visions of parenthood. They were candid about their expectations and anxieties about the baby. We sorted out how we would work together over the next few months. Jay had his own therapist, and I would occasionally see them together until they were ready to see a couple therapist. There were no other secrets, and each was committed to making the marriage work. They both had felt very positive about each other and their marriage before the discovery of the affair, which also boded well for the future.

We would have to work quickly to put in place a way in which Toni and Jay could work as a team. I gave them some structured exercises to do at home. They needed to be able to talk with one another and co-parent. Even without sexual secrets, having a new baby is stressful enough! The exercises I suggested were designed to eliminate arguing about what happened and structure the conversations in a way that would maximize the possibility that they would actually listen to one another express feelings without blaming and defensiveness. I knew this was a tall order this early in the game, but we needed to move toward stabilization quickly. Jay had begun individual therapy with a colleague, and we all agreed a team approach was a good idea at this point.

The most difficult part of these exercises is to make time to do them. It is helpful to work on resistance to treatment and avoidance of intimacy when an individual or couple keeps coming back saying they could not organize the time. I asked Jay and Toni to pick two or three occasions each week when they knew they would be emotionally available and free to meet with each other for at least half an hour, but no more than three-quarters of an hour. It was an agreed-upon priority and nothing short of an emergency should derail it. They each made a commitment to show up and be present at these meetings. The agreed that these meetings should be put on a calendar posted in a place where they would both be able to keep track of them (on the refrigerator is a good place), so they would not have to wait for the other to initiate the meeting. At the appointed time they would sit at the kitchen table across from each other so they could look at each other in the eye.

I asked them to look at their own copies of *After the Affair* (Spring, 1996) and *Becoming Parents : How to strengthen your marriage as your family grows* (Jordan, Stanley and Markman, 1999) at their own pace, picking out what seemed relevant or interesting to them at this time. There are many such books I recommend to couples, and while it was maybe a little soon, this seemed to fit the situation and the couple. I asked them to underline anything that had some meaning to them. It could be something good, uncomfortable, or something they always wanted to say but were afraid to. Using someone else's words offered a quick, non-threatening way to give them some distance from the emotions and a clearer perspective, as well as a sense that they were working together. At the agreed upon time, one of them would read out a sentence or two of his or her own choice and ask the other person to comment on it. They took turns to read and to respond. When the time was up, they were to agree to stop and do something pleasant like have a cup of tea and talk about other issues that were not emotionally charged. Maybe, if it felt right, they could give each other a hug or some touch that connected them and felt acceptable. I encouraged them to take notes during these sessions so that between times they might reflect on what was said and how it felt.

We had occasional conjoint sessions during this time and would go over how their structured meetings went in both individual and conjoint sessions. I encouraged them not to talk about the affair between their exercise sessions but to write thoughts down if they began to obsess about some issue. It was important to attempt to "normalize" their interactions as best they could. No shouting and fighting. The computer was in a nook in the kitchen where Toni could see it when Jay used it. They valued their structured talks, although the books were merely jumping-off points for other topics. They both agreed their marriage could use some important changes and that Toni should pursue some of her needs more aggressively. In the meantime, Toni and I worked on marshalling her strengths to get her through the birth of her child.

We worked on Toni's personal issues with depression and how it was to grow up in a house with a bipolar, needy, and dependent mother. Toni's self-esteem took a big hit with the affair, and we worked at that as well. It would need watching. Eventually she was able to understand that the affair was Jay's issue and stopped comparing herself to the other women. Jay was able to learn about his anxiety and poor-self esteem, an important factor in his development and in the affair he had. Both had come from religious homes and acknowledged that they both were very naïve about sexual matters. Jay offered that he was learning a lot from the book I had suggested on men's sexuality. At some point that would get sorted out, too. Toni was able to understand why Jay had distanced himself from her and appeared not to be interested in sex with her. It was not because Jay was homosexual. Toni knew about Jay's sister and her baby who had birth defects. They had consulted a genetic counselor and been reassured, but Toni was still frightened about their baby. However, she had kept her worries to herself. Now they both tried to be openly supportive and optimistic.

The crisis stage quieted down, and both Toni and Jay were fully engaged in their own therapy and in fruitful dialogues with one another. Both of them were very invested in making many changes in their young marriage. They also knew that individually they needed to understand their own issues and work on them as well. It would take a long time and a lot of work, but because they were young and Jay's sexual habits were contained, I was optimistic that this would turn into the opportunity that crisis presumably invites. As I have mentioned, research has identified that the earlier the sexual secrets have been revealed and the younger the marriage, the trauma for the hurt person will be considerably lessened. A young marriage is also resilient (Steffens & Rennie, 2006).

Tony and Jay had a healthy baby boy and named him Jonas. Lest you have any illusions about Toni and Jay's "happy ending," let me remind you that 68% of divorces happen because of the Internet (Manning, 2006). Some couples cannot, or perhaps should not, try to make a new marriage. If the marriage has been bad for many years, a complete make-over may not be possible. It may have "fatal flaws" (McCarthy, 1999). Ending of the marriage may be a relief-—no more dealing with alcoholism, cross dressing, masturbating for hours to online videos. Do you remember what happened when Rose told her husband Larry that I called him a "sex addict?" Because he berated her constantly for her struggle with sobriety from alcohol, she was happy to finally have something to reprimand him with. Rose was Larry's third wife. Larry was in his sixties and had never been faithful to any one in his whole life. It did not appear that he would ever be able to "get it right." Rose divorced him.

A THERAPIST'S DILEMMA

Building a new relationship, or gluing together the cracks, takes a lot of commitment and work. The hurt partner has to dig deep inside to restore even a measure of trust. The sexual behaviors that have been discovered may just be the tip of the iceberg. In these treatment situations, I am likely to hear secrets that have not yet been disclosed to a spouse or partner. For individuals that have had compelling sexual behaviors for many years, the letting go process may take a long time. Just as the habits themselves have escalated over time, so does the letting go of them take time. When spouses get more impatient to hear the secrets, the secrets get more tightly held. It is difficult to convince a husband that when his wife wants honesty and openness she really means it. Many women believe, and try to convince their husbands, that the dishonesty is actually worse than the unfaithful act. Pittman (1991) observes that maintaining the secret sexual behaviors ends more marriages than being honest about their existence. For those with the secret sexual habits, this may seem counterintuitive and downright impossible. It is difficult to manage the anxiety that surrounds full disclosure. Sometimes—with prompting, support and time—the whole story comes out. Sometimes it does not. If honesty fails to materialize and promises made are not kept, or if the partners finds out about behaviors that have not been completely revealed, the repercussions will be far worse.

When the therapist is privy to secrets that should be told but are not, it is an ethical dilemma that takes pondering. One day I had a call to help a couple with their languishing sex life. Lila, the caller, said it was her fault because she had no sexual desire whatsoever. I asked if her husband also could come to the telephone, and I talked with them both at the same time. I gave the pitch that "two people own the same sex life" and thus it would be useful if he were part of the evaluation. During my typical evaluation routine, in which I meet separately with each person in the dyad, Lila told me she had been raped when she was 16 years old. She was 40 years old now. She and Doug had been married about 15 years and had two sons, 13 and 11. She had never told anyone, including her husband, but knew that holding that secret was not getting her anywhere. When I asked Doug about sex outside the marriage, he did not hesitate to tell me he had sex with married women when he traveled. He also had never told anyone. Doug rationalized that his behavior was because his wife was not interested in sex at all. "What's a man to do?"

Having gone over the ground rules with each of them about confidentiality and other logistical considerations, I found myself in a bind. I was not willing to keep secrets, and I knew that supporting the family myth that their sex life was unsatisfying because of Lila's "problem" would sabotage the treatment. Lila volunteered she was ready to discuss the rape with Doug and wanted professional help with telling him. She knew she could enjoy sex more and be a better sex partner. Doug, on the other hand, was adamant that his infidelities not be brought up. How does a therapist handle this? I had been clear about my boundaries on confidentiality with Doug. While I would have to honor his confidences, I told him that for ethical and technical reasons, it was not possible for me to do couple therapy while colluding with his secret. Lila had identified herself as the "dysfunctional wife." She cried through her whole session. Doug and I agreed to think about this until the conjoint session, when I promised to give them some feedback and make some recommendations.

I tossed and turned for a few nights as I usually do when I am put in these situations. Fortunately it is a rare occurrence. I had to think over the rationale for my recommendation that they each have individual therapists before they signed up for "sex therapy." In the conjoint session, Lila revealed to Doug the details of her rape. Doug was shocked, genuinely upset, and very supportive. He had no idea what she had gone through and was horrified that she kept it a secret for so long. He felt terrible that he had not been there to protect her. Much to my surprise, Doug spontaneously asked me if he could see me for a few sessions to work out his feelings about Lila's disclosure. Cynically, I thought, "A good offense is a good defense." Lila seemed delighted that he wanted to understand her better and agreed it was a great idea. She was relieved to have someone else try to get him to understand what she seemed unable to. Fair enough. I was also relieved that I would be able to work with Doug on his sexual adventures while traveling. My plan had been to refer each of them to individual therapists before they did couple work. I was glad to be off the hook but I was somewhat suspicious about Doug's preemptive strike.

When Doug came back for an individual meeting, he told me he had done a lot of thinking about the boundaries I had laid out, and they made a lot of sense to him. He made a conscious decision to end his traveling escapades and work on his and Lila's relationship. Doug realized that he had as much to gain from being open as Lila did. "That's what a man needs to do!" Doug had made a commitment to therapy and to end his assignations. It was a good start. We'll see. Whew!

Consultation with colleagues and a good handle on your own ethical standards are helpful in these types of situations that are bound to surface in most practices from time to time (Corley & Schneider, 2002). It is also a good idea to know the legal standards for confidentiality in your state. Clinicians need to keep in mind that "The determination of whether a counselor's behavior is ethical is independent of whether it is either legally acceptable or therapeutically effective" (Herring, 2001). I remember a professor in graduate school telling us many times that "boundaries are everything in life!" Well, maybe not everything, but they are very important and useful.

As time went on, I met with Lila and Doug several times and consulted occasionally with Lila's's therapist. It became clear that Lila's history of rape and her role in her family of origin had implications for her marriage. She was conflicted about sex with Doug. She was happy Doug traveled since she did not have to face the pressure for sex when he was away, even though she suspected he might have sex with others while he was traveling. She became aware that Doug's pressuring her was partly a function of her own guilt for not having sex with him. She would view any overtures for closeness such as holding hands, a request for a hug, even taking a walk or going out for the evening as pressure for sex. Lila had been raised in a family where she was the caretaker of three younger siblings and ran the household. Her father was an alcoholic and could not hold a job. Her mother had to work long hours as a nurse to keep them fed and clothed. When Doug returned from trips, she would not allow him to help out. She kept Doug at a distance. It was it too difficult to relinquish the power and control she needed to keep herself safe and feel she was contributing to the work of the household and "earning her keep."

When Lila had been in therapy for a while and felt much better about herself, she asked Doug about his traveling. He admitted that he sometimes had sex with other women and took full responsibility for his behavior. She was relieved to know the truth and understood what might have been enabling behavior on her part. The marriage got to a much better place than it had been before. Both acknowledged their role in what had happened and were committed to a healthier relationship.

Caught in the crossfire

Sometimes I get caught in the crossfire during the crisis of discovery. It is not unusual that each person in the dyad will want the therapist to side with them. While I tenaciously hang on to my neutrality, I still run the risk of being condemned by the spouse who has been hurt if I do not come right out and condemn the "guilty" party. I am, by default, seen as choosing sides if I do not plant the "fault" squarely on the unfaithful's shoulders. Actually, no matter what I do, I may still be "damned if I do, damned if I don't." For instance, Greta called me one weekend saying she had been referred to me by a lawyer. She said she was in crisis and needed to see me as soon as possible. She insisted that she and her husband come in together for the first visit. Greta was in her late 40s, and worked as a paralegal in a successful prosecuting attorney's office. She had discovered some pictures of naked men on the family computer and confronted her husband of 15 years, convinced that he was a "closet homosexual." He had denied it, but she believed it to be true and nothing was going to change her mind. In attempting to offer a little hope and be helpful until we met, I said to her on the telephone that "people do not always act on their fantasies."

Following her wishes, I saw them together as soon as I could. During our meeting, Greta barked questions at me. She kept pulling papers out of her briefcase about homosexuality and quizzed me: Did I know the research and the author? I was clearly "on the stand." I noticed that Greta's foot was bandaged and she limped in. I asked what had happened. She said she fell on the ice. Patrick, in an attempt to get a word in, blurted out that during a very angry quarrel; Greta kicked the wall, breaking some of her toes.

If looks could kill, Patrick would have been dead. Greta was furious that Patrick had leveled with me and contradicted her. Noting the level of anger, I asked about their children. There were three children, a 10-year-old girl, a 12-year-old boy, and a 14-year-old girl. They had all been home at the time of the argument. I did not beat around the bush about how important it was that the children be protected from such anger, and that perhaps they would benefit from a safe place to talk about what was happening at home. Instead of acknowledging that the children needed help in coping with this crisis, Greta began to shriek at Patrick about his lies: "Why didn't you think about the children when you hid your homosexuality?" Patrick sat there passively. I tried to ask Patrick a few questions, but Greta interrupted me each time and would not let him answer.

Patrick huddled on the couch and tried to make himself invisible. He managed to tell me that he was not a homosexual, but he did say that he had fantasies about men from time to time. I tried to support and validate them both but Greta interrupted me at every turn, unable to express her grief and anger in any other way. It was better to sit quietly and just listen. Finally, Greta blurted out angrily that when I told her on the telephone that people do not always act on their fantasies, it trivialized her feelings. As I began to speak, she picked up her briefcase, signaled to Patrick to stand up and announced they would not be working with me. "I know you will not be able to get Patrick to tell the truth." He timidly walked behind her and they left. I reaped the whirlwind. Someone had to.

Chapter 9

Rapprochement and relapse prevention
"There is still a future"

> It is like being saved. From shipwreck, from obsession, from evil spirits. An exorcist has been here and left, taking with him all the mess. I breathe freely. There is still a future.
>
> Per Petterson

This therapeutic journey started with transparency imposed and has moved slowly toward transparency willed. A change of earth-moving proportions has been made in order to let go of secret sexual behaviors and change the relationships and the lifestyles that developed around them. It is like moving to a strange country and having to learn a new set of social skills, develop a new identity, and acquire a new language with which to express your needs. It is a very difficult thing to maintain. Some get very homesick for the "old country."

Rapprochement is a French word that is defined as an "establishment of or state of having cordial relations." To some it may seem strange to place the discussion of relapse prevention in the same chapter with the "establishment of cordial relations." But they are dependent on one another. Relapse Prevention Therapy (RPT) and rapprochement are both goals we have aimed for from the beginning of therapy. After the relationship stabilizes and has weathered the necessary changes, the couple may be together, cordial, and engaged. The person in the dyad who was "in the grip" manages her or his urges and lapses well enough to avoid a relapse. Like stabilizing the family, relapse management and rapprochement are not end points. Letting go of compelling sexual behaviors often takes a lifelong commitment and is a "challenge that entails continuing ... efforts to maintain and strengthen interpersonal relationships, and avoidance of triggers —all directed at preventing any kind of lapse or relapse" (Earle & Earle, 1995). Throughout life, we are all a work in progress and so are our relationships.

URGES, SLIPS, AND LAPSES

Learning the skills to contain compelling sexual behaviors is the first order of business when someone comes into therapy. These containment skills develop over the course of therapy and contribute to the growth and health of the client. This growth and its attendant changes also create ripples—healthy ones that reach into the family unit and contribute to the maintenance of the dyad.

RPT was originally developed as a maintenance program for use in the treatment of addictive-type behaviors (Marlatt & Gordon, 1985; Parks & Marlatt, 1999). RPT, combined with social learning and cognitive-behavioral techniques, is also routinely used in sex offender programs (Marques et al., 1994). Today, RPT skills are integrated into therapy for containing unwanted and legal sexual behaviors. In a meta analysis, Irvin et al. (1999) found that relapse prevention training is effective "across various classes of addictive behaviors." In addition, Goodman (1998) observed, "Relapse prevention [for sexual behaviors used addictively] consists of three components: risk-recognition, urge-coping, and slip-handling," all of which should be introduced from the beginning of therapy.

Integrated into therapy from the very beginning, with the help of the log, is the development of a deliberate and conscious understanding of triggers, cycles, risk factors, seemingly unimportant decisions, and coping strategies. The log that the client uses throughout therapy encourages the daily habit of mindfulness and also serves to keep people on track with their stated goals. We are exchanging a lifestyle built around secrets and lies for a lifetime of transparency and accountability. At the same time, the partner or spouse (if there is one) is trying to give up controlling or policing the sexual behaviors and being vigilant about the activities and whereabouts of the person with the compelling sexual habits. Spouses and partners must learn to take charge of their own lives. This results in putting the responsibility for the sexual acting out squarely where it belongs: on the person who has the problem. Both members of the dyad have difficult tasks laid out for them. It is frightening to stop blaming someone else for your behaviors, and it is equally unsettling to stop controlling someone else's behaviors to keep yourself safe.

Learning to recognize the slide

An *urge* is a feeling state ("I want" or "I need"). It is generally accompanied by a *lapse* (a fantasy or a thought about returning to the unwanted behavior) or a *relapse* (a return to unwanted behaviors). For example, after a nice dinner, a person who has given up smoking announces to the other dinner guests: "I'd love a cigarette right now;" or a recovering alcoholic expresses a desire for a glass of wine with the dinner. Some guests may react with anxiety and admonitions not to return to smoking or drinking, and some may understand that is it better said than done. A person is standing in line at the supermarket, sees an attractive woman, thinks about following her, and feels an erotic buzz (fantasy and urge). The person waiting in line recognizes the feeling of boredom (trigger), does not act on the fantasy, and the urge goes away.

It is important to prepare clients and their partners that sexual fantasies and urges for past sexual behaviors of many years' duration are likely to occur. This is a natural part of the process of giving up the behaviors. These thoughts and fantasies are a common occurrence for most people. Fantasies do not necessarily presage sexual acting out. An important part of therapy is to give the client confidence that the tools they have accumulated during therapy can be counted on to work when they feel at risk for a relapse. Those who feel sexual urges and have fantasies about people they see may be frightened and worried that they will act on these urges and fantasies. Most eventually learn not to be afraid of these thoughts and to trust that they indeed have "executive control" of their behavior. Feeling aroused, "horny," or turned on is not a demand. But it does require introspection.

When a lapse or a relapse actually occurs, it is usually the result of stressors. For instance, the same week that Dylan's father died unexpectedly, his cellar flooded, and he did not get the promotion he thought he was in line for at work. Dylan, whose case follows, called this combination of events "a perfect storm." In a study of people with a variety of "addictive behaviors," Parks and Marlatt (2000) identified "three high-risk situations that were associated with almost 75% of the relapses reported: negative emotional states, interpersonal conflict and social pressures." For Dylan, these events boiled down to a sudden, traumatic loss of his father, an important and close attachment (negative emotional state), financial anxiety about the necessary repairs to the cellar (financial pressure), and a narcissistic wound—being passed over for a job (interpersonal conflict). He was emotionally overwhelmed. After about three years of not visiting a massage parlor, Dylan went to have a massage with a "happy ending" to escape his overwhelming feelings. This had been a behavior he counted on as an escape from bad feelings.

Dylan and his wife, Kelly, had been in therapy with me for about two years with fairly good results. I had not seen them for approximately a year when he called me for a "booster shot." We went over the plan for risk-managing and coping when emotional stressors built up. We reviewed and rehearsed some techniques such as visualizing aversive consequences—for example Kelly leaving him, getting AIDS, or being arrested. We reviewed keeping a log for self-monitoring ("where's my head at?"), which he had eventually given up after he ended therapy. He also promised himself that he would work harder at talking with his wife about his feelings and fears *before* he relapsed. The dramatic events of Dylan's life also had an effect on Kelly. Not only was she grieving for her father-in-law, whom she had loved, she worried about Dylan's lost promotion and how they would pay for the leak in the cellar. She also feared that he would have a relapse. It was up to both of them to be accountable and communicate their feelings.

They came in for a few sessions together for a refresher course on talking with each other. These tasks require constant tending. Their situation was a setback but not a tragedy because both of them learned from it. They learned that they cannot let days and weeks go by without checking in with one another about their feelings and thoughts and tending to their relationship. Communicating is not only for the person who has compelling sexual behaviors but also for the partner or spouse. Communication is central to both maintaining the relationship and preventing a relapse. Both parties have feelings that must be examined and discussed with each other.

The strategies of keeping logs and being aware of seemingly unimportant decisions are the foundation for teaching clients coping skills and recognizing the signs of lapses and potential relapses. A major component of relapse prevention is communicating the prospect of relapsing. If I had my way, "competency in effective communication" would be a requisite for a high school diploma. Everyone seems to endorse the idea that it is important to have good communication skills, but actually doing it is entirely another matter. Most people find it almost impossible to have an open conversation about the "I and the Thou" state of their relationship or intimate sexual matters. Even in the 21st century, bombarded as we are with sexual information, the average couple is daunted by the task and can't even think where to start. Communicating thoughts and feelings is a task fraught with high anxiety about becoming vulnerable with each other. Most of the couples I work with project or anticipate that open communication will create a conflagration of epic proportions. But we persevere. Some learn to be open and accountable and others can't.

Remember Ed who blamed a missed appointment on his wife? From that moment on, he was learning to become personally accountable. Clients must first learn to be accountable to themselves and take responsibility for their own behaviors. This accountability is an important paradigm shift for someone with compelling sexual habits. Typically the list of "reasons" that become excuses for sexual acting out is quite long. Sometimes, I ask clients to make a list of behaviors for which he or she must take responsibility. For each behavior, I invite the client to put the "rationale" used to justify the behavior. For instance, Lisa's list included taking responsibility for hurting her husband when she flirted with his best friend and for having affairs. The "rationale" she used was that he was a bad dancer and wouldn't go out and party with her. Gil's list included taking responsibility for his visits to prostitutes and how they hurt his wife. His "rationale" was that she was pregnant and couldn't have sex. Sometimes we get to laugh about the excuses. You have to keep a sense of humor.

Parks and Marlatt (2000) suggest the following strategies for coping skills to prevent relapse, and I have added a few that seem to work, as well:

- Understand relapse as a process.
- Identify and cope effectively with high-risk situations.
- Cope with urges and cravings.
- Implement damage control procedures during a lapse to minimize its negative consequences.
- Stay engaged in treatment even after a relapse.

- Learn how to create a more balanced lifestyle.
- Pay attention to daily mood states.
- Be in communication daily with a spouse about how it's going, and if you aren't in a relationship find a friend or sponsor when triggers appear.

These techniques build on one another to create a solid set of skills for coping with stressors in a healthy way. There are many things that can contribute to the overall goal of relapse prevention. For example, some people may need social skills training, which might help with being able to have a relationship. People in a good relationship improve their chances for controlling their unwanted sexual habits (Kafka, 2007). Assertiveness training, relaxation techniques, and exercise training to reduce stress or cope with anger management are all healthy components of managing moods and affect in a healthy way. Irvin et al. (1999) also found that RP was most effective when "combined with the adjunctive use of medication."

A GROUP EFFORT

It is useful to segue from the end of individual therapy into group therapy if there is a good resource available in the community. Group therapy can be very effective in maintaining healthy coping strategies (Yalom, 1975). Groups run by professional leaders would be my preference, but resources offering 12-step approaches are also available in many communities worldwide. They are free and can be accessed easily for one-time meetings or for ongoing connections. It is common that many people use business travel as an opportunity for sexual liaisons; these include having a sexual massage, engaging in sex with a prostitute, and meeting sex partners at conferences, business meetings, or in hotel bars. Knowing where to find a group for Sex Addicts Anonymous (SAA); Sexual Compulsives Anonymous (SCA), Sex and Love Addicts Anonymous (SLAA), and Sexaholics (SA) anywhere in the world might be a useful tool in preventing lapses. SAA has a good website in English and Spanish listing worldwide resources. In general, groups offer opportunities to get validation, feedback, and support; in addition, they offer a sense of belonging when a person may feel isolated in a foreign country or distant city.

RAPPROCHEMENT: MOVING
FROM CORDIAL TO SEXUAL

After individual therapy or couple therapy, or perhaps a combination of the two, has stabilized the situation for both parties, the couple may decide to stay together and improve the relationship emotionally, affectionately, and sexually. If a couple should decide to divorce, the therapist can also have an important role in helping the couple work together toward a divorce that provides potential for growth rather than the destruction that could occur if the dyad is left to its own devices. It is a sad but not uncommon event that a very nasty divorce can often include a false accusation of child abuse and revenge by an angry and out-of-control spouse. Remember Ryan and Martha? Fortunately, their children were able to speak for themselves and the situation abated, but Ryan will live with the suspicion of his neighbors for many years.

I consider the establishment of cordial relations a basic requirement for a couple who wants to move beyond the secret sexual behaviors to a better place … like bed! Before a sexual relationship is resumed it is essential that the couple has productive communication skills, accountability, restructuring negative cognitions about each other, changing sexual attitudes, and learn basic information about healthy sexuality and sexual behaviors. During the early phase of disclosure or discovery, many women will engage in "revenge sex," designed to pay back their husband for hurting them, or smother their husband with "honeymoon sex" motivated by a desire to compete with the "phantom lover." This response generally wears off, and the sexual relationship will falter. I have learned that trying to retread a dysfunctional sex life is about as effective as buying a retread tire for a cross-country trip! A blow-out is bound to occur. Better start from scratch with a brand new tire.

As we have discussed, many partners of people with sexual secrets also have histories of neglect and abuse, rape, substance abuse, and other mental health problems. These issues must be acknowledged and integrated into the couple work. It is essential to work on the relationship and improve communication skills before taking baby steps toward a sexual relationship. "Talking is foreplay" becomes the ground rule for intimate sex. We have seen that many compelling sexual behaviors are ways to avoid the interpersonal. Thus, communication skills for discussing potentially conflictual issues must also be built into a relapse prevention/rapprochement program. Trying to leave their anonymous or impersonal sexual liaisons behind, persons with sexual secrets face the daunting task of creating an intimate connection with their partners. Remember how Larry sabotaged Rose every time she wanted to have an intimate conversation with him about their relationship?

Intimate moments: Creating and expanding the sexual repertoire

Continuing to build on acquired skills, my clients and I move toward an altogether new sexual paradigm. After we have fully explored distorted cognitions, sexual myths, information about female and male anatomy, and appropriate developmental changes depending upon the couple's age, many couples still resist shifting the sexual paradigm. It is not possible to explain adequately how difficult it is to learn new patterns of sexuality, particularly if there has been past deception and trauma. Who wants to have sex with someone they are angry with? To aid in this delicate and difficult couple work, there are a few books that I find useful. I suggest that each partner buy and read his or her own book then set up the structure within which the books can aid the conversation about difficult sexual issues. There are many good books about sexual relationships. I try to match the book to the couple and situation and I find the following particularly helpful: McCarthy and McCarthy's (2003) *Rekindling Desire: A step-by-step program to help low-sex and no-sex marriages*; Goodwin and Agronin's (1998) *A woman's guide to overcoming sexual fear and pain*; Butler and Lewis's (2002) *The new love and sex after sixty*. In addition, Barbach's books: (1976) *For Yourself: The Fulfillment of Female Sexuality*; (1982) *For each other: Sharing sexual intimacy and Zilbergeld*; (1992) *The New Male Sexuality*; and Milsten and Slowinski's (1999) *The Sexual Male: Problems and Solutions*.

Assuming there is real rapprochement, and everyone is communicating well, we begin to work on affectional behaviors before anyone takes their clothes off. Many of the couples with whom I work have avoided even casual touching for a few years. I advise them to begin with non-genital touching. It is best to start with sharing affection such as giving a hug, holding hands, and maybe kissing. The first initiative toward this effort is to counsel the couple that if a flashback of a traumatic event occurs during any physical contact, the individual who is experiencing the flashback must stop the activity, cover themselves with a blanket or sheet if they are naked or in bed, and talk about the flashback. It must be supported and validated by both parties. The couple might continue with whatever they were doing or move to another activity. But at least the pain has not been ignored; it has been acknowledged and can be soothed. The person is no longer alone with the trauma. Even if the hurt party feels ready for physical contact, in reality he or she may not be able to manage it. Many times this brings up the issue of ending the marriage.

As we attempt to shift the sexual paradigm from a disconnected sex life to an intimate and connected one, each person will need to:

- Learn to discuss and take responsibility for his or her own feelings and sexual attitudes.
- Take responsibility in sexual situations.
- Understand his or her negative cognitions about sex. For instance, "(S)he always wants sex more than I do. My body is ugly. I am always worried about how he will like my sexual performance. I am inadequate in bed (e.g., no orgasms or no erections, ejaculate too soon, not adventuresome enough). Sex will never be as exciting as it was with prostitutes. I will never be able to satisfy her(him)."
- Take responsibility for knowing and expressing sexual needs and preferences—e.g., "I'm too embarrassed to ask for what I need, and I want to change that. How do I tell him he needs to shower?"
- Understands the other's boundaries and respect them at all times.

As several of the cases have illustrated, books and structured exercises are a non-threatening way to generate communication and facilitate education and attitude shifts about sexual issues. Using my variation on the theme of Masters and Johnson's (1974) sensate focus exercise requires a slow desensitization to partnered sexual activity that demands a great deal of creativity, patience, and support. But sometimes one or the other in the dyad simply cannot return to partnered sex.

Cindy and Rod

Cindy and Rod, both in their late 50s, were married 37 years when they came to see me. Cindy's therapist had recommended me when Cindy, who had been in therapy for two years, felt less depressed, had more self-esteem and self-confidence and believed she was ready to try to be more sexual with Rod. Rod had been obsessed with the sexual need for Cindy and pressured her for sex their whole married life. She had been chronically depressed and not terribly interested in sex. They had two children, who were both grown. Rod had become involved in group sex and swinging six years previous, which Cindy found out about when she saw Rod's car parked in front of an unfamiliar house while she was out antiquing with a friend. She confronted him when he came home that night. Rod blurted it all out and told Cindy he had been having a relationship for several years with another couple in the neighborhood that he located online. "After all," he said, "You won't have sex with me, and I need to get it somewhere!"

Cindy asked Rod to leave, which he did for a while. His children would not talk with him, and he was not allowed to see his new grandchild. After a year of separation and therapy, Cindy felt ready to ask Rod to come back home, which he was glad to do. Neither of them had ever wanted a divorce. Their son found it easier to forgive Rod than their daughter, who was very angry that Cindy had allowed Rod to move back in. Cindy made it clear to Helen, their daughter, that she had to work out *her* feelings about her father and not interfere with their marriage. Rod was available and eager to do this, but Helen retreated.

Rod assured Cindy that in spite of everything he loved her more than anyone else. The group sex was about sex, not love. They lived with a peaceful "détente" but with no sexual contact for another year. Cindy still worked with her therapist and was on a good regimen of medication. She felt ready to work with Rod on their sexual relations because she felt she was missing something by repressing her own sexuality. During the year, much to Cindy's surprise, Rod also saw a therapist. He was a "man's man" and did not believe in all that "crunchy granola" stuff called therapy. On the other hand, he knew he had to stay away from the couple he had met, which was difficult. The therapist and some medication helped him, too. He showed me the workbook (Sbraga & O'Donohue, 2003) that he and his therapist used and he also shared it with Cindy. We were both impressed at his attitude shift about sex and women.

Rod and Cindy were also dealing with some medical problems that neither one had anticipated. Cindy fell down the icy garage stairs a few months after beginning couple therapy and broke her hip. Rod had a heart attack and underwent a quadruple bypass. These events happened about a month apart. Both needed a lot of care and support when they returned from the hospital. Their children and neighbors pitched in, and Cindy and Rod recovered well. During this period, with lots of time on their hands, they began to talk to each other more and went from détente to real conversations about where they were in life and what they wanted their future to look like. During her recovery, Cindy realized how much she missed being touched and held as the physical therapist held her up and helped her walk, supporting her emotionally. Rod found he was frightened of dying and realized how much his family meant to him. Helen, their recalcitrant daughter, began to bring their grandson to the house for brief visits. While she had not forgiven her father for hurting her mother, she did not deprive them of their grandson.

After deciding to stay together, most couples like Cindy and Rod are committed to working on a new monogamous relationship with each other. This is easier said than done. It is important to keep in mind that most people with compelling sexual habits have objectified their sex partners and have discovered a way to have sex without any emotional or intimate context or commitment. Rod would think for days about meeting with the couple and feel aroused. He had to leave behind the quick high he felt when sneaking off to the couple's house, and he worked hard at letting it go. He also admitted that the erotic fantasies that he had developed around his secret life were also filled with guilt and anxiety and he wanted his "innocence" back. "Interesting use of words," I thought. Cindy and Rod needed to build a new relationship with each other—almost as if they were meeting for the first time. Beginning a new relationship does resonate with innocence; his reference made good sense.

Over the next two years Cindy and Rod worked at moving closer to each other emotionally and sexually. Their sexual issues were somewhat complicated by the usual issues of aging and the medical problems they had experienced. For the first time they thought consciously about their sexual relationship. Rod confessed that he had been seeking stimulation because he thought he was sexually inadequate. He thought Cindy did not like sex with him because he "did it wrong." He wanted to see what happened when the situation was exotic and new and, while it turned him on, he was still worried he was not good enough in bed. Cindy had never had an orgasm and had been lying to Rod about how satisfying sex was. She read Barbach's *For Yourself* and ran out to buy a vibrator.

Rod read Spring's *After the Affair* and realized that no affair could compare with a long-term committed marriage. Together they read Butler and Lewis's *The New Love and Sex over Sixty*. Both of them were satisfied with the new skills they had and how far they had come on their long and difficult journey.

Dale and Joan: Rapprochement and relapse

The dust had begun to settle on Dale and Joan's crisis. After about two years of couple therapy, Dale had learned to take charge and contain his own sexual behaviors, which included Internet sex and visiting massage parlors. Joan had built her own life; she got a part-time job that she loved, and was learning to trust Dale, no longer monitoring him all the time. Joan's trust was built on Dale's commitment to talk with her. They learned through therapy to be open and honest with each other. At first it was with great ambivalence and resistance that they honored their commitment to check in with each other every day after supper for a few minutes: "When you did not call at lunchtime, I had a flashback of you meeting with that woman you chatted up online. I was feeling angry or bored at work, and I felt like going online and masturbating in the men's room." As time went by these meetings became less frequent, and they needed to get back on track, like Dylan and Kelly.

Communicating well with each other builds emotional intimacy and is the first step to a renewed sex life no matter what the marital foibles are. Joan had built her own model for sexuality on what I call "the fairy princess role," which many women have been socialized to believe even today. She would wait for the prince (in this case Dale) to initiate sex. She could then pretend she was a "good girl" and not be seen as sexually aggressive, i.e., the "bad girl." Joan worked hard to develop her sexual self. She read a few books on female sexuality that were enlightening and helpful (Barbach's *For Yourself* and Levine and Barbach's (1980) *Shared Intimacies*). She began to assert her need for Dale and not always wait for him to initiate a sexual encounter. They started with non-intercourse behaviors and developed a repertoire of foreplay strategies that gave them more choices for expressing their affectional/pleasuring needs. Eventually they integrated a variety of genital/intercourse behaviors that made for a better, more mutually connected sex life. Dale still had sexual fantasies, but he was happier without his guilt when he spent hours on the Internet.

Even though things had been good for a few years and their sex life was better, Dale had a relapse while he was traveling. He had several drinks at dinner, went online in his hotel room for a few hours and masturbated. They came back to see me. Joan was not traumatized to the point she had been when I first met them a few years before. It was easier because Dale told her about it. He felt guilty, and it was no fun. If the stakes are high enough for the marriage to continue, couples adapt to a sex life that is mutually "good enough." He also agreed to go to Alcoholics Anonymous meetings.

A "NORMAL" LIFE

"Normalizing" a lifestyle or "creating a balanced lifestyle," as Parks and Marlatt (2000) suggested, would seem to be a natural consequence of therapy. Of course, everyone has his or her own definition of what normal means. And not all therapy really ends that way. The goal I aim for is that therapy will leave people in a better place than they were when they initially came to see me. It works in many instances, but it is never the end of the story. The work continues (or should) long after therapy is over. A relationship needs to be tended to so it will grow and nurture both parties. When therapy ends, for one reason or another—hopefully because the goals that were set out in the beginning have been met—people are embarking on a new life. The hope is that family life will be less stressful, more connected, as well as more authentic and fun: Alcohol or drugs are in remission; family life feels more like a team effort; people talk to one another, share activities together, eat meals at the same time (well, most of the time) and are more authentic in expressing feelings about themselves and others. Or, at least, that's the goal.

It takes a very long time to heal from the trauma of disclosure and discovery and to create a new life. Martin Kafka, M.D. (2007) cautions that "The healing and recovery period that is necessary when PRDS [compelling sexual behaviors] disrupt the pair bond should be measured in years, not months." Many of my colleagues and I sometimes use a medical analogy when talking with a client about the rigors of a life lived with sexual secrets. I liken it to what it must be like to live with diabetes or a kidney transplant, high blood pressure, or high cholesterol. People with these conditions must spend their lives tending to their medical problems, taking medication and getting regular checkups and live fulfilling rich lives. When it comes to sexual secrets, life must also include keeping a watchful eye for return of symptoms and tending to a relationship or marriage that was once seriously damaged.

While it is true that the magnetism of sexual secrets may fade and some people are able to forgive the deceit that accompanied it, both relapse and rapprochement are a never-ending process. Some couples can make these adaptations and build a new life. We should not underestimate the capacity for some people to forgive. Others continue to live together without a real solution, but get what they need from each other: financial security, social compatibility, and an antidote for loneliness. "Love is a deal" (Levine, 2007). And still, there is a future.

"Cradlers of secrets"

"We are cradlers of secrets. Every day patients grace us with their secrets, often never before shared. Receiving such secrets is a privilege given to very few. The secrets provide a backstage view of the human condition."

Irvin D. Yalom

When all has been said and done, I listen for the tonic chord, but there is no dénouement, no grand finale. There are no endings to the stories I have written. I have gone on these journeys with people who are searching for answers they may never get and seeking places they will never reach. It is the journey that I value, and I accept that nothing will ever be completely finished or perfect. Our lives are always a work in progress. Sometimes I make mistakes along the way, sometimes I struggle to make the therapeutic relationship work, and sometimes it is as magic as Zingara's predictions.

I have tried to put a human face on these very real and pervasive sexual behaviors. I have attempted to model understanding for people who are in the grip of sexual secrets and struggle to integrate their sexual desires into a more modulated, connected sexual life. I am careful not to judge but I am clearly not unopinionated. I am acutely aware that some may not be happy with my nonjudgmental stance. I try to understand and offer empathy. I offer some roads maps for a way out of the secret garden my clients have created. It is not a garden filled with sunshine and joy; its dark corners are filled with shame and guilt. We laugh and sometimes cry together and try to find a way to make life easier to bear. Life will always be filled with mysteries and challenges. People love and still betray trust; people long for what they cannot have; people die too soon. And yet, our collective resilience never ceases to amaze me, and I am in awe of how many of my clients can rise to the occasion, adapt, and forgive.

Over the years I have shared many intense emotions, both joy and sadness. I have had my own foibles mirrored back at me. My clients and I have been changed forever because we have taken the risk to trust one another. I have entered a life and stay close to the client, sharing and holding the pain and shame. In doing so, I can see the grip loosen on the impulse to stay hidden and on the fear of being transparent. I watch as despair turns into hope, and I experience the restorative power of our relationship.

Since I began this book, there have been a great many changes in the world. Some of what I have written about may be deemed out of date by the time it goes to press. Nevertheless, human nature, being what it is, seeks change and new horizons so I also expect that some of the answers to compelling sexual problems might eventually be revealed and fine tuned. Perhaps the next generation will find the answers when we are long gone. However, there is one thing I know to be constant: Sex remains illusive, mysterious, and powerful. It is at the center of the life force.

In this book, I have attempted to share the experience of letting people into my life as a therapist— maybe to lighten my load or soothe some of my anxiety. But, try as I might, I cannot describe what writing this book has been like for me. It was compelling; I was obsessed with it, and in a way have joined with all my clients who were and remain similarly compelled and obsessed with their sexual habits. My empathy for obsession has certainly deepened.

So I send this book off, as I do my clients, never knowing how or where it will all end but with a deep appreciation for the remarkable journey. After all these years, I never fail to feel privileged and in awe of the work I signed on for.

References

American Psychiatric Association. (2000). *Diagnostic and statistical manual of mental disorders* (4th ed.). Washington, DC: Author.

Bancroft, J. (2003). Foreword. In T. P. Sbraga & W. T. O'Donohue, *Sex Addiction: Proven strategies to help you regain control of your life.* Oakland, CA: New Harbinger Publications.

Bancroft, J. (2002). Foreword. In A. Cooper (Ed.), *Sex and the Internet: A guidebook for clinicians.* New York: Brunner Routledge.

Bancroft, J., & Vukadinovic, Z. (2004). Sexual addiction, sexual compulsivity, sexual impulsivity, or what? Toward a theoretical model. *The Journal of Sex Research, 41.*

Bandura, A. (1969). *Principles of behavior modification.* New York: Holt, Rhinehart and Winston.

Barbach, L. (1982). *For each other: Sharing sexual intimacy.* Garden City, NY: Doubleday.

Barbach, L. (1976). *For yourself: The fulfillment of female sexuality.* Garden City, NY: Doubleday.

Barlow, D. H., & Durand, M. V. (1998). *Abnormal psychology: An integrative approach* (2nd ed.). Boston: Brooks/Cole.

Beck, A. T. (1967). *Depression: Clinical, experimental and theoretical aspects.* New York: Harper and Row.

Berger, D., *Don't lock child offenders up for life.* Burlington Free Press, November 23, 2005.

Berman, B. (Executive Producer), & Ramis, H. (Director). (1999). *Analyze this* [Motion picture]. Hollywood, CA: Warner Brothers.

Binik, Y., & Meana, M. (2007, March). *The future of sex therapy.* Paper presented at the 31st Annual Meeting of the Society for Sex Therapy and Research, Atlanta, GA.

Black, C., Dillon, D., & Carnes, S. (2003). Disclosure to children: Hearing the child's experience. *Sexual Addiction & Compulsivity, 10,* 67–78.

Blanchard, R. (2003, March). *Self reported head injuries in pedophiles.* Paper presented at the 28th Annual Meeting of The Society for Sex Therapy and Research, Miami Beach, Florida.

Blanchard, R., Christensen, B. K., Strong, S. M., Cantor, J. M., Kuban, M. E., Klassen, P., Dickey, R., & Blak, T. (2003). Retrospective self-reports of childhood accidents causing unconsciousness in phallometrically diagnosed pedophiles. *Archives of Sexual Behavior, 31*(6), 511–526.

Bok, S. (1983). *Secrets: On the ethics of concealment and revelation.* New York: Vintage Books.

Boyle, T. C. (2004). *The inner circle.* New York: Viking Books.

Bregman, A. (Producer), & Gondry, M. (Director). (2004). *Eternal sunshine of the spotless mind* [Motion picture]. Universal City, CA: Focus Features.

Brogan, M. M., Prochaska, J. O., & Prochaska, J. M. (1999). Predicting termination and continuation status in psychotherapy using the transtheoretical model. *Psychotherapy, 36*(2).

Butler, R. N., & Lewis, M. I. (2002). *The new love and sex over sixty.* Toronto, Ontario, Canada: Ballantine Books.

Campbell, R. J. (2004). *Psychiatry dictionary* (8th ed.). New York: Oxford University Press.

Camus, A., (1957). *The Fall.* New York: Vintage International.

Carey, B. (2004, November 9). Long after Kinsey, only the brave study sex. *The New York Times.*

Carnes, P. (2001/1991/1983). *Out of the shadows: Understanding sexual addictions* (3rd ed.). Center City, MN: Hazelden.

Carnes, P. (1991). *Don't call it love: Recovery from sexual addiction.* New York: Bantam Books.

Carnes, P. (1989). *Contrary to love: Helping the sexual addict.* Minneapolis: CompCare.

Carnes, P. J., Delmonico, D. L., & Griffin, E. J. (2001). *In the shadow of the net: Breaking free from compulsive online sexual behavior.* Center City, MN: Hazelden Foundation Press.

Carroll, R. (2007). Gender dysphoria and transgendered experiences. In S. Leiblum (Ed.), *Principles and practice of sex therapy* (4th ed.). New York: Guilford Press.

Chase, D. (Writer/Producer). (1999). *Sopranos* [Television series]. New York: HBO Time Warner.

Coleman, E. (1995). Treatment of compulsive sexual behaviors. In R. Rosen & S. Leiblum (Eds.), *Case studies in sex therapy.* New York: Guilford Press.

Coleman, E. (1992). Is your patient suffering from compulsive sexual behaviors? *Psychiatric Annals, 22,* 320–325.

Coleman, E. (1986). *Sexual compulsion vs. sexual addiction: The debate continues.* New York: SIECUS Report.

Cooper, A. (1997). The Internet and sexuality: Into the new millennium. *Journal of Sex Education and Therapy, 22.*

Cooper, A., Delmonico, D. D., & Burg, R. (2000). Cybersex users, abusers, and compulsives. *Sexual Addiction & Compulsivity, 7,* 5–29.

Cooper, A., Golden, G. H., & Marshall, W. L. (2006). Online sexuality and online sexual problems: skating on thin ice. In W. L. Marshall, Y. M. Fernandez, L. E. Marshall, & G. A. Serran (Eds.), *Sexual offender treatment: Controversial issues.* West Sussex, England: John Wiley and Sons, Ltd.

Cooper, A., & Marcus, I. D. (2003). Men who are not in control of their sexual behavior. In S. B. Levine, C. B. Risen, & S. E. Althof (Eds.), *Handbook of clinical sexuality for mental health professionals.* New York: Brunner Routledge.

Cooper, A., Putnam, D. E., Planchon, L., & Boies, S. C. (1999). Online sexual compulsivity: Getting tangled in the net. *Sexual Addiction & Compulsivity, 6,* 79–104.

Coppolla, F. (Executive Producer), & Condon, B. (Writer/Director). (2004). *Kinsey: Let's talk about sex* [Motion Picture]. Los Angeles, CA: Fox Searchlight Pictures.

Corley, M. D., & Schneider, J. P. (2002). Disclosing secrets: Guidelines for therapists working with sex addicts and co-addicts. *Sexual Addiction & Compulsivity, 9,* 43–67.

Cornog, M. (2003). *The big book of masturbation: From angst to zeal.* San Francisco: Down There Press.

Cottle, T. J. (1980). *Children's secrets.* New York: Anchor Press/Doubleday.

Davies, R. (1975). *The world of wonders.* New York: Viking Press.

Davin, P. A., Hislop, C. R., & Dunbar, T. (1999). *Female sexual abusers.* Brandon, VT: Safer Society Press.

Davis, J. (2003). Voyeurism: A criminal precursor and diagnostic indicator to a much larger sexual predatory problem in our community. In C. Hensley & R. Tewksbury (Eds.), *Sexual deviance: A reader.* London: Lynne Rienner.

Delmonico, D. L., Griffin, E. J., & Carnes, P. (2002). Treating online compulsive sexual behavior: When cybersex is the drug of choice. In A. Cooper (Ed.), *Sex and the Internet: A guidebook for clinicians.* New York: Brunner Routledge.

Denov, M. (2003). The myth of innocence: Sexual scripts and the recognition of child sexual abuse by female perpetrators. *Journal of Sex Research, 40,* 303–314.

Doidge, N. (2007). *The brain that changes itself.* New York: Viking Press.

Dollard, J., & Miller, N. E. (1950). *Personality and psychotherapy: An analysis in terms of learning, thinking, and culture.* New York: McGraw Hill.

Dorland's Illustrated Medical Dictionary (1994). Philadelphia: W.W.Saunders.

Dorland's Illustrated Medical Dictionary (2003). Philadelphia: W.W, Saunders.

Earle, R. H., & Earle, M. R. (1995). *Sex addiction: Case studies and management*. New York: Brunner/Mazel Publishers.

Edwards, M. (2003). SEICUS Reports. 31 (4).

Eichenwald, K. (2005, December 19). Through his webcam, a boy joins a sordid online world. *The New York Times*, p. A1.

Elkin, M. (1984). *Under the influence*. New York: Norton.

Ellis, A. (1958). *Sex without guilt*. New York: Lyle Stuart.

Ellis, A. (1957). Rational psychotherapy and individual psychology. *Journal of Individual Psychology, 13*, 38–44.

Ellis, H. (1905). *Studies in the psychology of sex*, (Vols. 1-2). New York: Random House.

Ellis, H. (1900). *Studies in the psychology of sex*. Philadelphia: Davis.

Erian, A. (2005, March 27). Eternal sunshine of an addicted mind. *The New York Times Magazine*.

Erickson, E. (1963). *Childhood and society*. New York: W. W. Norton.

Fackler, M. (2007, November 18) In Korea, a boot camp cure for web obsession. *The New York Times*.

Fedoroff, J. P. (2003). The paraphilic world. In S. B. Levine, C. B. Risen, & S. E. Althof (Eds.), *Handbook of clinical sexuality for mental health professionals*. New York: Brunner Routledge.

Fedoroff, J. P., Fishell, A., & Federoff, B. (1999). A case series of women evaluated for paraphilic sexual disorders. *The Canadian Journal of Human Sexuality, 5*, 127–140.

Fernandez, Y. M., & Serran, G. (2002). Characteristics of an effective sex offender therapist. In B. K. Schwartz (Ed.), *The sex offender: Current treatment modalities and systems issues* (Vol. IV). Kingston, NJ: Civic Research Institute.

Finklehor, D. (1994). Current information on the scope and nature of child sexual abuse. *The Future of Children, 4* (2) 31-53.

Finkelhor, D., Mitchell, K.J., Wolak, J. (2000) Online Victimization: A Report on the Nation's Youth. Durham, New Hampshire. National Center for Missing and Exploited Children: Crimes against Children Research Center.

Fox, R. (Producer), & Eyre, R. (Director). (2006). *Notes on a scandal* [Motion picture]. Los Angeles, CA: Fox Searchlight Films.

Freeman-Longo, R. E., & Blanchard, G. T. (1998). *Sexual abuse in America: Epidemic of the 21st century*. Brandon, Vt.: Safer Society Press.

Freud, A. (1966). *The ego and the mechanisms of defense*. Madison, CT: International Universities Press.

Freud, S. (1963/1905). *Three essays on the theory of sexuality*. (J. Strachey, Trans.). New York: Basic Books.

Freud, S. (1958). *The standard edition of the complete psychological works of Sigmund Freud*. (J. Strachey, Trans.). London: Hogarth Press.

Freund, K. (1990). Courtship disorders. In W. Marshall, D. Laws, & H. Barbaree (Eds.), *Handbook of sexual assault: Issues theories and treatment of the offender.* New York: Norton.

Gathorne-Hardy, J. (2000). *Sex and the measure of all things: A life of Alfred Kinsey.* Bloomington, IN: Indiana University Press.

Gilligan, C. (2003). *The birth of pleasure: A new map of love.* New York: Vintage Books.

Goldstein, R. L., & Laskin, A. M. (2002). De Clérambault Syndrome (erotomania) and claims of psychiatric malpractice. *Journal of Forensic Science, 47*(4), 852–856.

Goodman, A. (1998). *Sexual addiction: An integrated approach.* Madison, CT: International Universities Press.

Goodman, B. (Writer/Producer/Director), & Maggio, J. (Producer/Director). (2005). *American experience: Kinsey* [Television broadcast.]. Boston: Public Broadcasting System/WGBH.

Goodwin, A., & Agronin, M.,(1998). *A woman's guide to overcoming sexual fear and pain.* Oakland, CA: New Harbinger.

Gotwald, W., & Golden, G. (1981). *Sexuality: The human experience.* New York: MacMillan & Co.

Greenfield, D., & Orzack, M. (2002). The electronic bedroom: Clinical assessment of online sexual problems and Internet-enabled sexual behavior. In A. Cooper (Ed.), *Sex and the Internet: A guidebook for clinicians.* New York: Brunner Routledge.

Groneman, C. (2000). *Nymphomania: A history.* New York: W.W. Norton.

Guidry, L. (2002). Addressing the victim/perpetrator dialectic—Treatment for the effects of sexual victimization on sex offenders. In B. K. Schwartz (Ed.), *The sex offender: Current treatment modalities and systems issues.* Kingston, NJ, Civic Research Institute.

Hall, C. S., & Nordby, V. J. (1973). *A primer of Jungian psychology.* New York: New American Library.

Hall, E.R., Howard, J.A. & Boezio, S. (1986) Tolerance of rape: A sexist or antisocial attitude. *Psychology of Women Quarterly, 10,* 101-118

Herring, B. (2001). Ethical guidelines in the treatment of compulsive sexual behavior. *Sexual Addiction & Compulsivity, 8,* 13–22.

Hollender, M.H., & Callahan III, A.S. (1975). Erotomania or de Clérambault Syndrome. *Archives of General Psychiatry, 32,* 1574–1576.

Irvin, J. P., Bowers, C. A., Dunn, M. E., & Wang, M. C. (1999). Efficacy of relapse prevention: A meta-analysis. *Journal of Consulting and Clinical Psychology, 67*(4), 563–570.

Jamison, K.R. (2000). *Night falls fast: Understanding suicide.* New York: Vintage Books.

Jamison, K. R. (1996). *An unquiet mind: A memoir of moods and madness.* New York: Vintage Books.

Jewison, N. (Producer & Director). (1987). *Moonstruck* [Motion picture]. Los Angeles, CA: Metro-Goldwyn-Mayer.

Johnson, C. (2000). Been there done that: The use of clinicians with personal recovery in the treatment of eating disorders. *The Renfrew Center Foundation Perspective, 5*(2), 1–4.

Jones, J. H. (1997). *Alfred C. Kinsey: A public/private life.* Collingwood, PA: Diane Publishing Company.

Jordan, P. L., Stanley, S. M., & Markman, H. L. (1999). *Becoming Parents: How to strengthen your marriage as your family grows.* San Francisco: Jossey-Bass.

Jung, C. (1964). *Man and his symbols.* New York: Windfall Books, Doubleday.

Kafka, M. P. (2007). Paraphilia-related disorders: The evaluation and treatment of nonparaphilic hypersexuality. In S. Leiblum (Ed.), *Principles and practice of sex therapy* (4th ed.). New York: Guilford Press.

Kafka, M. P. (2000). The paraphilia-related disorders: Non-paraphilic hypersexuality and sexual compulsivity/addiction. In S. Leiblum & R. Rosen (Eds.), *Principles and practice of sex therapy* (3rd ed.). New York: Guilford Press.

Kafka, M. P. (1991). Successful antidepressant treatment of nonparaphilic sexual addictions and paraphilias in men. *Journal of Clinical Psychiatry, 52,* 6–65.

Kafka, M. P., & Hennen, J. (2003). Hypersexual desire in males: Are males with paraphilias different from males with paraphilia-related disorders. *Sexual Abuse, 15,* 307–321.

Kafka, M. P., & Hennen, J. (1999). The paraphilia-related disorders: An empirical investigation of nonparaphilic hypersexuality disorders in 206 outpatient males. *Journal of Sex and Marital Therapy, 25,* 305–319.

Kafka, M. P., & Prentky, R. A. (1998). Attention deficit hyperactivity disorders in males with paraphilias and paraphilia-related disorders: A comorbidity study. *Journal of Clinical Psychiatry, 59,* 388–396.

Kafka, M. P., & Prentky, R. A. (1994). Preliminary observation of DSM-III-R Axis I comorbidity in men with paraphilia-related disorders: A comorbidity study. *Journal of Clinical Psychiatry, 55,* 481–487.

Kafka, M. P., & Prentky, R. (1992). Fluoxetine treatment of nonparaphilic sexual addiction and paraphilias in men. *Journal of Clinical Psychiatry, 6,* 189–195.

Kalichman, S. C., & Rompa, D. (1995). Sexual sensation seeking and compulsivity scales: Reliability, validity, and predicting HIV risk behavior. *Journal of Personality Assessment, 76,* 379–395.

Kasl, C. S. (2002). Special issues counseling lesbian women for sexual addiction, compulsivity, and sexual codependency. *Sexual Addiction & Compulsivity, 9*(4), 191–208.

Kasl, C. S. (1989). Women, sex, and addiction: A search for love and power. New York: Ticknor and Fields.

Kidd, S. M. (2002). *The secret lives of bees.* New York: Penguin Books.

Kinsey, A. C., Pomeroy, W. B., & Martin, C. E. (1948). *Sexual behavior in the human male*. Philadelphia: Saunders.

Kinsey, A. C., Pomeroy, W. B., Martin, C. E., & Gebhard, P. H. (1953). *Sexual behavior in the female*. Philadelphia: Saunders.

Knapp, C. (1997). *Drinking. A love story*. U.K.: Delta.

Kohut, H. (1997). *The restoration of self*. Madison, CT: International Universities Press.

Kovacs, M. G. (Trans.). (1990). *The epic of Gilgamesh*. Stanford: Stanford University Press.

Krafft-Ebing, R. von. (1965/1886). *Psychopathia sexualis* (Trans.). New York: Routledge.

Kramer, P. (1993). *Listening to prozac*. New York: Penguin Books.

Krauss, N. (2005). *The history of love*. New York: W. W. Norton.

Kubler-Ross, E. (1997). *On death and dying*. New York: Scribner Publishing Co.

Ladinsky, D. (Trans.). (2003). *The subject tonight is love: 60 wild and sweet poems of Hafiz*. New York: Penguin Compass.

Lane, F. (2001). *Obscene profits: The entrepreneurs of pornography in the cyber age*. New York: Routledge.

Langstrom, N., & Zucker, K. (2005). Transvestic fetishism in the general population: Prevalence and correlates. *Journal of Sex and Marital Therapy, 31*, 87–95.

Lasser, M. R. (1996). Recovery for couples. *Sexual Addiction & Compulsivity 3*(2), 97–109.

Lauman, E., Gagnon, J., Michael, R., & Michaels, S. (1994). *The social organization of sexuality*. Chicago: University of Chicago Press.

Leiblum, S., & Rosen, R. (Eds.). (2000). *Principles and practice of sex therapy* (3rd ed.). New York: Guilford Press.

Lethum, J. (2003). *The fortress of solitude*. New York, Doubleday.

Levi, H. (Creator), Whalberg, M. (Executive Producer), & Garcia, R. (Writer/Director). (2008). *In Treatment* [Television series]. New York: HBO Time Warner.

Levine, L., & Barbach, L. (1980). *Shared intimacies*. New York: Anchor Press/Doubleday.

Levine, S. (2007). *Demystifying love: Plain talk for mental health professionals*. New York: Brunner Routledge.

Levinson, R., & Link, W. (Producers). (1971). *Columbo* [Television series]. New York: National Broadcasting Company.

Lief, H. (1976). Introduction to sexuality. In B. J. Sadock, H. S. Kaplan, & A. M. Freedman (Eds.), *The sexual experience*. Baltimore: Williams and Wilkins.

LoPiccolo, J., Heiman, J. R., Hogan, D. R., & Roberts, C. W. (1985). Effectiveness of single therapists versus cotherapy teams in sex therapy. *Journal of Consulting and Clinical Psychology, 53(3)*, 287–294.

Maas, L. C., Lukas, S. E., Kaufman, M. J., Weiss, R. D., Daniels, S. L., Rogers, V. W., Kukes, T. J., & Renshaw, P. F. (1998). Functional magnetic resonance imaging of human brain activation during cue-induced cocaine craving. *American Journal of Psychiatry, 155*(1), 124–126.

Manning, J. C. (2006). The impact of Internet pornography on marriage and the family: A review of the research. *Sexual Addiction & Compulsivity, 13,* 131–165.

Marlatt, G. A., & Gordon, J. R. (Eds.). (1985). *Relapse prevention: Maintenance strategies in the treatment of addictive behaviors.* New York: Guilford Press.

Marques, J. K., Day, D. M., Nelson, C., & West, M. (1994). Effects of cognitive-behavioral treatment on sex offender recidivism: Preliminary results of a longitudinal study. *Criminal Justice and Behavior, 21,* 28–54.

Marquez, G. G. (2006). *Memories of my melancholy whores.* New York: Vintage International.

Marshall W. L., Laws, D.R. & Barbaree, H. E. (Eds.) (1990). *Handbook of sexual assault, issues theories and treatment of the offender.* New York: Plenum Press.

Marshall, W. L., Fernandez, Y. M., Marshall, L. E., & Serran, G. A. (Eds.). (2006). *Sexual offender treatment: Controversial issues.* West Sussex, England: John Wiley and Sons, Ltd.

Marshall, W. L., Jones, R., Ward, T., Johnson, P., & Barabee, H. E. (1991). Treatment outcome with sexual offenders. *Clinical Psychology Review, 11,* 465–485.

Masters, W. H., & Johnson, V. E. (1996). *Human sexual response.* Boston: Little, Brown.

Masters, W. H., & Johnson, V. E. (1974). *The pleasure bond.* Boston: Little, Brown.

Masters, W. H., & Johnson, V. E. (1970). *Human sexual inadequacy.* Boston: Little, Brown.

Mayo Clinic. (2008). Mental health: Attention-deficit/hyperactivity disorder (ADHD). Retrieved 2008 from www.mayoclinic.com.

McCarthy, B. (2002). The wife's role in facilitating recovery from male compulsive sexual behavior. *Sexual Addiction & Compulsivity, 9,* 285–292.

McCarthy, B. (1999). Relapse prevention strategies and techniques for inhibited sexual desire. *Journal of Sex and Marital Therapy, 25,* 297–303.

McCarthy, B., & McCarthy, E. (2003). *Rekindling desire: A step-by-step program to help low-sex and no-sex marriages.* New York : Brunner Routledge.

McCarthy, B.W., & Metz, M.E. (2008). *Men's Sexual Health.* New York: Brunner Routledge.

McEwan, I. (2007). *On Chesil Beach.* New York: Doubleday.

Merryman, M. (1999). Removing sex from sex: Mainstream feminism's incomplete dialogue. In J. Elias, V. Elias, V. Bullough, G. Brewer, J. Douglas, & W. Jarvis (Eds.). *Porn 101: Eroticism, pornography, and the First Amendment.* Amherst, NY: Prometheus Books.

Metz, M. E., & McCarthy, B. W. (2004). *Coping with erectile dysfunction.* Oakland, CA: New Harbinger Publications.

Milosz, C. (1991). *At the end of the century.* Chapel Hill, NC: University of North Carolina Press.

Milrad, R. (1999). Coaddictive recovery: Early recovery issues for spouses of sex addicts. *Sexual Addiction & Compulsivity, 6,* 125–136.

Milsten, R., & Slowinski, J. (1999). *The sexual male: Problems and solutions.* New York: W. W. Norton & Co.

Missildine, W., Feldstein, G., Punzalan, J. C., & Parsons, J. T. (2005). S/he loves me, s/he loves me not: Questioning heterosexist assumptions of gender differences for romantic and sexually motivated behaviors. *Sexual Addiction & Compulsivity, 12,* 65–74.

Money, J., & Lamacz, M. (1989). *Vandalized love maps.* Buffalo, NY: Prometheus Books.

Morrison, J. (2008). *The first interview* (3rd ed.). New York: Guilford Press.

Morrison, T. (2005). *Love.* New York: Vintage International Edition.

Moser, C., & Kleinplatz, P. (2003, May 5). Paper delivered at American Psychiatric Association Meeting, San Francisco, CA.

Moser, C., Kleinplatz, P., Zuccarini, D., & Reiner, W. (2004). Situating unusual child and adolescent behavior in context. *Child and Adolescent Psychiatric Clinics of North America* 13(3): 569–589.

Moyers, T. B., & Rollnick, S. (2002). A motivational interviewing perspective on resistance to psychotherapy. *Psychotherapy in Practice, 58*(2), 185–193.

Muench, F., Morgenstern, J., Hollander, E., Thomas, I., O'Leary, A., & Parsons, J. (2007). The consequences of compulsive sexual behavior: The preliminary reliability and validity of the comprehensive sexual behavior consequences scale. *Sexual Addiction & Compulsivity, 14*(3), 207–220.

Nathan, S. (1995). Sexual addiction: A sex therapist struggles with an unfamiliar clinical entity. In R. Rosen & S. Leiblum (Eds.), *Case studies in sex therapy.* New York: Guilford Press.

Offit, A.K. (1981). *Night thoughts: Reflections of a sex therapist.* New York: Congdon and Lattes.

O'Neil, S. E., Cather, C., Fishel, A. K., & Kafka, M. (2005). "Not knowing if I was a pedophile…"—Diagnostic questions and treatment strategies in a case of OCD. *Harvard Review of Psychiatry, 13*(3), 186–96.

Oz, A. (2003). *A tale of love and darkness: A memoir.* United States: Harcourt Books.

Parks, G. A., & Marlatt, G. A. (2000). Relapse prevention therapy: A cognitive-behavioral approach. *The National Psychologist, 9*(5). Retrieved 2008 from The National Psychologist website: http://nationalpsychologist.com/articles/art_v9n5_3.htm.

Parks, G. A., & Marlatt, G. A. (1999). Relapse prevention therapy for substance abusing offenders: A cognitive-behavioral approach in what works. In L. E. Lanham (Ed.), *Strategic solutions: The international community corrections association examines substance abuse* (pp. 161–233). Alexandria, VA: American Correctional Association.

Patterson, R. (2008, March 3). Students of virginity. *The New York Times Magazine.*

Peterson, M. R. (1992). At personal risk: Boundary violations in professional relationships. New York: W. W. Norton & Co.

Petterson, P. (2005). *Out stealing horses.* St. Paul, MN: Greywolf Press.

Pittman, F. (1991). Private lies: Infidelity and the betrayal of intimacy. New York: W. W. Norton.

Plaut, S. M. (2008). Sexual and nonsexual boundaries in professional relationships: Principles and teaching guidelines. *Sexual and Relationship Therapy, 23*(1), 85–94.

Plaut, S. M. (2003). Understanding and managing professional-client boundaries. In S. B. Levine, C. B. Risen, & S. E. Althof (Eds.), *Handbook of clinical sexuality for mental health professionals.* New York: Brunner Routledge.

Posner, R.A., & Silbaugh, K.B. (1996). *A guide to America's sex laws.* Chicago: Chicago University Press.

Protter, B., & Travin, S. (1985). Sexual fantasies in the treatment of paraphilic disorders: A bimodal approach. *Psychiatry Quarterly, 58*, 270–297.

Public Broadcasting System. (2007, November 27). Retrieved 2008 from www.pbs.org.

Quadland, M. C. (1985). Compulsive sexual behavior: Definition of a problem and an approach to treatment. *Journal of Sex and Marital Therapy, 11*, 121–132.

Rabinowitz, I. (Ed.). (1998). *Inside therapy: Illuminating writings about therapists, patients, and psychotherapy.* New York: St. Martin's Press.

Ray, F., Marks, C., & Bray-Garretson, H. (2004). Challenges to treating adolescents with Asperger's Syndrome who are sexually abusive. *Sexual Addiction & Compulsivity, 11*, 265–284.

Reid, R. C. (2007). Assessing readiness to change among clients seeking help for hypersexual behavior. *Sexual Addiction & Compulsivity, 14*, 167–186.

Reid, R. C., & Wooley, S. R. (2006). Using emotionally based therapy for couples to resolve attachment ruptures created by hypersexual behaviors. *Sexual Addiction & Compulsivity, 13*(2), 219–239.

Rogers, C. (1957). The necessary and sufficient conditions for therapeutic personality change. *Journal of Consulting Psychology, 21,* 95–103.

Sbraga, T. P., & O'Donohue, W. T. (2003). *The sex addiction workbook.* Oakland, CA: New Harbinger Publications.

Scheer, R. (1976, November). Interview with Jimmy Carter. *Playboy Magazine.*

Schmidt, G. A. (1998). Sexuality and late modernity. *Annual Review of Sex Research, 9,* 224–241.

Schneider, J.P. (1994). Sex addiction: Controversy within mainstream addiction medicine, diagnosis based on the DSM- III-R, and physician case histories. *Sexual Addiction and Compulsivity,* 1(1), 19-44.

Schneider, J. P., & Schneider, B. H. (1996). Couple recovery from sexual addiction/coaddiction: Results of a survey of 88 marriages. *Sexual Addiction & Compulsivity, 3*(20), 111–126.

Schneider, J. P., & Schneider, B.H. (1991). *Sex, lies, and forgiveness: Couples speak out on healing from sex addiction.* Minneapolis: Hazelden Educational Materials.

Schwartz, B. (Ed.). (2002). *The sex offender: Current treatment modalities and systems issues.* Kingston, NJ: Civic Research Institute.

Schwartz, J. (2001, April 9). New economy: The steamy side of the Internet, pervasive resilient to recession, is the underpinning of a new online cash venture. *The New York Times.*

Schwartz, M. F., & Brasted, W. S. (1985). Sexual addiction. *Medical Aspect of Human Sexuality, 19,* 103–107.

Setterfield, D. (2006). *The thirteenth tale.* New York: Washington Square Press.

Singer, I. B. (1979). *A little boy in search of God.* Garden City, NY: Doubleday.

Skinner, B. F. (1938). *The behavior of organisms.* New York: Appleton-Century-Crofts.

Spring, J. A. (1996). *After the affair.* New York: Perennial.

Steffens, B. A., & Rennie, R. L. (2006). The traumatic nature of disclosure for wives of sexual addicts. *Sexual Addiction & Compulsivity, 13,* 247–267.

Stein, D. J., Hollander, E., Anthony, D. T., Schneier, F. R., Fallon, B. A., Liebowitz, M. R., & Klein, D. F. (1992). Serotonergic medications for sexual obsessions, sexual addictions, and paraphilias. *Journal of Clinical Psychiatry, 53,* 267–271.

Stone, B. (2008, May 5). An e-commerce empire: From porn to puppies. *The New York Times.*

Sunderwirth, S., Milkman, H., & Jenks, N. (1996). Neurochemistry and sexual addiction. *Sexual Addiction & Compulsivity, 3*(1), 22–32.

Swisher, S. H. (1995).Therapeutic interventions recommended for treatment of sexual addiction/compulsivity. *Sexual Addiction & Compulsivity,* 2(1), 31–39.

Tavris, C., *The Mismeasure of women.* (1994). New York. Simon Schuster.

Tennov, D. (1979). *Love and limerence: The experience of being in love.* New York: Stein and Day Publishers.

Tennov, D. (2001). Conceptions of limerence. Everaerd, W., Laan, E., & Both, S. (Eds). *Sexual appetite, desire and motivation: Energetics of the sexual system.* Amsterdam, Netherlands: Knaw Edita, 111-116.

Travin, S., & Protter, B. (1993). *Sexual perversion: Integrative treatment approaches for the clinician.* New York: Plenum Press.

Viorst, J. (2003). *Grown-up marriage.* New York: The Free Press.

Warwick, H. M. C., & Salkovskis, P. M. (1990). Unwanted erections in obsessive-compulsive disorders. *British Journal of Psychiatry, 157,* 919–921.

Wasserman, I. M., & Richmond-Abbott, M. (2005). Gender and the Internet: Causes of variation in access, level and scope of use. *Social Science Quarterly, 86,* 1252–69.

Watson, L. (1993). *Montana, 1948.* New York: Washington Square Press Pocket Books.

Weiser, B. (2004). A Judge's Struggle to Avoid a Penalty he Hated. *New York Times.*

Weinberg, G. (1998). The taboo scarf. In I. Rabinowitz (Ed.), *Inside therapy: Illuminating writings about therapists, patients, and psychotherapy.* New York: St. Martin's Press.

Weiner, M. (Producer & Creator). (2007). *Mad Men* [Television series]. Jericho, NY: American Movie Classics.

Weldon, J. (1999). Topping from below: Does female dominant pornography endorse the rape of women? In James Elias (Ed.), *Porn 101: Eroticism, pornography, and the First Amendment.* Amherst, New York: Prometheus Books.

Wertheimer, A. (2003). *Consent to sexual relations.* Cambridge University Press, Cambridge, England.

Whitman, W. (1983/1855). *Leaves of grass.* New York: Bantam Books.

Whitty, M. T. (2005). The realness of cybercheating: Men's and women's representations of unfaithful internet relationships. *Social Science Computer Review, 23*(1), 57–67.

Wilcox, B. & Wyat, H. (1997) Adolescent Abstinenece Education Programs: A Meta Analysis. Paper Presented at SSSS Meeting. Arlington, Virgina.

Wincze, J. P. (2000). Assessment and treatment of atypical sexual behavior. In S. Leiblum & R. Rosen (Eds.), *Principles and practice of sex therapy* (3rd ed.). New York: Guilford Press.

Winnicott, D. W. (1975). *Through pediatrics to psychoanalysis.* London: Hogarth Press.

Winnicott, D. W. (1969). The use of an object. *International Journal of Psychoanalysis, 50,* 711–716.

Wurtzel, E. (1995). *Prozac nation: Young and depressed in America.* New York: Riverhead Books.

Yalom, I. D. (2002). *The gift of therapy.* New York: Harper Collins.

Yalom, I. D. (1993). *When Nietzsche wept.* New York: Penguin Books.

Yalom, I. D. (1989). *Love's executioner & other tales of psychotherapy.* New York: Perennial Classics.

Yalom, I. D. (1975). *The theory and practice of group psychotherapy* (2nd ed.). New York: Basic Books.

Zernike, K. (2005, December 11). The siren song of sex with boys. *The New York Times.*

Zilbergeld, B. (1992). *Male sexuality.* Boston: Little Brown.

Zucker, K. L., & Spitzer, R. L. (2005). Was gender identity disorder of childhood diagnosis introduced into DSM-III as a backdoor maneuver to replace homosexuality? A historical note. *Journal of Sex and Marital Therapy, 31,* 31–42.

Index